The Best of PANTRY

From June

Christmas 1998.

D0572067

Camden House · Bookmakers Press

The Best of

PANTRY

From the Editors of Harrowsmith Country Life

© Copyright 1995 Camden House Publishing
(a division of Telemedia Communications Inc.)

All rights reserved. The use of any part of this publication, reproduced, transmitted in any form or by
any means, electronic, mechanical, photocopying,
recording or otherwise, or stored in a retrieval sys-
tem, without the prior consent of the publisher—or,
in case of photocopying or other reprographic copy-
ing, a license from Canadian Reprography Collec-
tive—is an infringement of the copyright law and
is forbidden.

Canadian Cataloguing in Publication Data

Main entry under title:
  The best of Pantry

Includes index.
ISBN 0-921820-96-8

1. Cookery.

TX714.B47 1995   641.5   C95-931-119-X

Published by Camden House Publishing
(a division of Telemedia Communications Inc.)

Camden House Publishing
Suite 100, 25 Sheppard Avenue West
North York, Ontario M2N 6S7

Camden House Publishing
Box 766
Buffalo, New York 14240-0766

Printed and distributed under exclusive license from
Telemedia Communications Inc. by
Firefly Books
250 Sparks Avenue
Willowdale, Ontario
Canada M2H 2S4

Firefly Books (U.S.) Inc.
P.O. Box 1338, Ellicott Station
Buffalo, New York 14205

Produced by
Bookmakers Press
12 Pine Street
Kingston, Ontario
K7K 1W1

Edited by
Laurel Aziz

Design by
Linda J. Menyes
Q Kumquat Designs

Color separations by
Mutual/Hadwen Imaging Technologies Inc.
Ottawa, Ontario

Printed and bound in Canada by
Metropole Litho Inc.
St. Bruno de Montarville, Quebec

Front Cover: Chicken Fricot, Corn Bread, Fruited
Yogurt, Multigrain and Maple Walnut Muffins and
Spaghetti Salad With Tuna. Photograph by Ernie
Sparks. Concept and styling by Linda Menyes and
Laurel Aziz.

Back Cover: Apple-Carrot-Raisin Muffins, Oat Bran
Bread, Oat Bran Brownies and Oat Bran Raisin
Cookies. Photograph by Ernie Sparks. Concept and
styling by Linda Menyes and J. Manson.

Contents

Contents

Contents

Contents

Contents

INTRODUCTION

here are few more joyous social experiences than preparing and sharing a meal with friends. Our appreciation of the allure of fine food has meant that cooking has always enjoyed a central place in the editorial tradition of *Harrowsmith Country Life*, and with every issue, we celebrate our esteem for that tradition in "Pantry," our much-loved food department. For the editors at *Harrowsmith Country Life*, both past and present, it is now time to pause and pay a simple tribute to our culinary history.

In the almost 20 years since the founding of *Harrowsmith* magazine, North Americans have faithfully maintained a tumultuous love affair with food. In that time, food fads have predictably come and gone, sometimes lingering, sometimes enjoying no more than their fabled 15 minutes of celebrity. We have witnessed the reinvention of pasta in the '70s,

the broccoli and bran brouhahas of the '80s and, more recently, the popularization of low-fat cooking and cultural exotica. One might expect that in a culture which gobbles up facts on food so voraciously, food writing would also swing dramatically with the times.

In reviewing the history of "Pantry," however, it is apparent that the flavor of the day has rarely influenced the food editors at *Harrowsmith Country Life*. Nothing could be more antithetical to food hype than "Pantry," and the explanation for that is simple: Good food has not really changed all that much. The basic tenets for successful cooking in *Harrowsmith Country Life* are bound by the common thread that links our devotion to quality of life with the richness of country living. Our recipes draw on the abundance of backyard and market gardens because our taste for

Introduction

good food is simply an extension of the principles that guide us in designing our gardens and our shelters. In our view, the pleasure of preparing and eating a dish is only enhanced when the cook can walk out the kitchen door into a garden to select, for instance, a few vine-ripened tomatoes and trim some hot peppers and coriander to make a dish of fresh salsa.

If it is our belief at *Harrowsmith Country Life* that good food brings people together, we have also learned how strong an agent it is in *keeping* them together. Even a cursory glimpse at our contributors' list shows that successive members of our family of food editors have each shaped the character of "Pantry" over the years. The strength and originality we have gained from the diversity of voices provided by staff writers Pamela Cross, Rux Martin and JoAnne Cats-Baril and such regular contributors as Winston Collins, Andrea Chesman and more than 20 others defy the adage that "too many cooks spoil the broth." Each has made a lasting contribution to the well-stocked *Harrowsmith* larder, and each has earned the gratitude of thousands of readers who have left their dining tables more satisfied for having tried their culinary offerings.

More than 300 "Pantry" recipes are gathered together in this volume. Originally presented in thematic tributes to such subjects as seasonal harvests or international styles of cuisine, the recipes are now organized into nine somewhat more conventional chapters. We have taken this liberty to create a more accessible countertop volume for cooks. Appearing throughout the book are tips for preparation, some of which have been adapted from the original magazine articles.

It is a truism that people who love to cook as well as people who want to learn how spend a great deal of time thinking about food. They patronize diverse kinds of restaurants, they travel to places where they can experience unique regional cuisine, they read food books and magazines and tirelessly experiment with their own cooking in a constant search for inspiration. Describing this quest some 35 years ago, the beloved American food writer M.F.K. Fisher wrote in *An Alphabet for Gourmets*: "There is no better antidote for me, when I have read perforce too many modern recipes, quasi-practical or purely fluffy, than a quiet look backward." In *The Best of Pantry*, we, too, wish to take a quiet, albeit celebratory, look backward.

We welcome both our longtime readers, who have grown up with us, and readers meeting us for the first time, who wish to partake of the reliable pleasures of a 20-year cooking tradition. Please join us as we throw open the "Pantry" doors and tip our hats to the best of the best recipes put up by a generation of fine *Harrowsmith Country Life* cooks.

—From the Editors
Fall 1995

Chapter 1

BRUNCHES & LIGHT LUNCHES

"Eating is an art worthy to rank with the other methods by which men choose to escape from reality," noted an understandably obscure French viscount. Pity the poor cook who faced the task of amusing this disgruntled aristocrat with breakfast.

While palates around the modern breakfast table may not be able to compete with the nobleman's pedigree, peevish appetites and bearish attitudes that come with the new day are timeless. Still, the morning meal is an important one and remains a cook's most challenging undertaking. Given school-bus schedules and car-pool commutes, today's workday breakfasts sometimes look more like a track meet than a family gathering; at times, it's hard to locate even a hint of *joie de vivre* floating around the bottom of a bowl of cold cereal. When time is at a premium, however, an ample supply of homemade muffins or warm biscuits and fresh fruit will help take the edge off even the most harried tablemates.

With five days a week ruled by the perfunctory, however, we urge you, on occasion, to rise and shine to a more civilized celebration of the first, and most important, meal of the day. A weekend morning, a holiday or a snowy day when closed schools and banks keep everyone lounging in pyjamas and slippers are all opportunities to enjoy a leisurely family feast. Instead of succumbing to the cardiac-care menu of bacon and eggs, consider preparing something different: fresh-squeezed orange juice, croissants, Orange Crumb-Coated French Toast or Fruit-Filled Crêpes. For a snack later in the day, anti-breakfast types may prefer one of our delicious sandwiches. Your family will appreciate these easy-to-make and nourishing alternatives, which are, undoubtedly, breakfasts fit for a king.

Brunch

FRUIT COMPOTE

Combine cooked dried fruit with oranges and pineapple for a tangy, fresh-tasting source of fiber that is ideal for quick breakfasts during the week. It stores well in the refrigerator, so save some for a weekend brunch, served with a topping of yogurt.

1 cup	dried apricots	250 mL
1¼ cups	pear juice or nectar	300 mL
2 Tbsp.	honey	25 mL
1	piece fresh gingerroot (2 inches/5 cm long), peeled & quartered lengthwise Zest of 1 lime	1
1 cup	large pitted prunes	250 mL
8	dried figs, cut in half (preferably unsulphured)	8
1	large seedless orange	1
1 cup	fresh pineapple, diced	250 mL
½ cup	orange juice	125 mL
2 Tbsp.	lime juice	25 mL

In a small bowl, cover apricots with boiling water. Let stand for 5 minutes, then drain. In a large saucepan, combine 1½ cups (375 mL) water, pear juice, honey, gingerroot and lime zest. Bring to a simmer, and reduce heat to low. Add drained apricots, prunes and figs. When the mixture returns to a simmer, cover, and cook gently for 20 to 30 minutes or until fruit is tender.

Transfer mixture to a bowl; remove gingerroot and lime zest, and let cool to lukewarm. With a sharp knife, remove rind and white pith from orange. Cut orange segments from their surrounding membranes, and add to fruit mixture. Add pineapple, orange juice and lime juice. Mix gently, cover, and chill.

Serves 6 to 8.

FRUITED YOGURT

When fresh fruit is not in season, you can use frozen. Allow it to thaw, then drain off most of the juice. Do not add the cranberry juice in this case. Nuts can also be folded into the basic recipe.

3 cups	plain yogurt	750 mL
1 cup	fruit (bananas, berries, peaches or a combination)	250 mL
½ cup	cranberry juice	125 mL
1 Tbsp.	honey	15 mL
1 tsp.	vanilla extract	5 mL

Blend all ingredients until well mixed. Chill thoroughly in the refrigerator.

Makes about 4 cups (1 L).

ICED CHERRIES

Simplicity itself, this hardly qualifies as a recipe, yet the results are unforgettable. As delicious as sun-warmed cherries are straight off the tree, chilling intensifies the flavor and improves the texture. Everybody likes them, so get more than you think you could possibly need. A great treat on a picnic.

2-4 lb.	cherries on the stem, washed	1-1.8 kg
1	bag ice, crushed or chipped	1

To serve, arrange the cherries in a shallow bowl nestled in crushed ice.

BERRY CRÈME BRÛLÉE

Incredibly rich, incredibly good. Theoretically, this recipe serves six, but three or four custard addicts could polish it off with no problem, especially if it were the star dish of a Sunday brunch.

2 cups	heavy cream	500 mL
5	eggs	5
3	egg yolks	3
1 qt.	fresh strawberries, raspberries or blueberries, or a mixture	1 L
1¼ cups	light brown sugar	300 mL

In a heavy pan, heat cream until bubbles form around the edges. While it heats, beat eggs and egg yolks together until foamy, then, beating constantly, pour hot cream into eggs.

Return mixture to pan, or transfer to a double boiler, and cook, stirring, over low heat or over vigorously simmering water until custard is *very* thick.

Transfer custard to a shallow bowl, and let cool to room temperature, stirring once or twice to prevent a skin from forming, then cover tightly, and chill thoroughly.

Just before serving, lightly butter a 1-quart (1 L) gratin pan or other flameproof nonreactive serving dish no more than 2 inches (5 cm) deep. Heat oven broiler.

Arrange a layer of fruit in the bottom of the dish, keeping it as level as possible, then spread the custard over it. Hold a strainer a few inches above the surface, and push brown sugar through to make an even topping about ⅜ inch (9 mm) thick.

Now, give the brûlée your undivided attention. Place the pan about 2 inches (5 cm) from the broiler, and cook just until sugar melts. Keep shifting the pan so that the sugar melts evenly, and watch out for scorch—sugar loves to burn.

Let the brûlée sit for 2 to 3 minutes or until the hot sugar cools to a crispy crust, then serve at once.

Serves 4 to 6.

CRÈME BRÛLÉE TRICK

Classic recipes for Crème Brûlée call for nestling the serving pan in a pan of cracked ice during the broiling process to prevent the custard from curdling.

ORANGE CRUMB-COATED FRENCH TOAST

Crusty outside, custardy inside and permeated with the taste of orange, this French toast is sumptuous. Because orange skins are often coated with waxes, use organically grown oranges whenever possible.

5	eggs	5
1⅔ cups	orange juice, plus ¼ cup (50 mL)	400 mL
½ tsp.	salt	2 mL
2½ tsp.	grated orange zest	12 mL
2½ tsp.	vanilla extract	12 mL
1¾-2 cups	white breadcrumbs	425-500 mL
8	slices good-quality white bread (thickly sliced)	8
1 cup	mild honey	250 mL

Combine eggs, 1⅔ cups (400 mL) juice, salt, orange zest and vanilla, beating well. Pour into a large flat pan. Place breadcrumbs in another flat pan. Soak each slice of bread in the egg mixture for about 5 minutes, turning once. Dredge in breadcrumbs, and brown on a hot, lightly oiled griddle, turning once or twice. Meanwhile, combine honey and remaining juice in a small saucepan, heat for a few minutes, and serve with French toast.

Serves 4.

CORNCAKES WITH MAPLE-YOGURT TOPPING

Slightly crunchy, these corncakes are so light, you'll think they were made with yeast.

2	large eggs, beaten	2
¾ cup	milk	175 mL
2 Tbsp.	vegetable oil	25 mL
¼ cup	yogurt	50 mL
¾ cup	stone-ground cornmeal	175 mL
½ cup	white flour	125 mL
½ cup	whole wheat flour	125 mL
½ tsp.	salt	2 mL
1 tsp.	baking powder	5 mL
2 Tbsp.	sugar	25 mL

Topping
8 oz.	yogurt	250 g
2 oz.	maple syrup	50 g

Stir together eggs, milk, oil and yogurt. In another bowl, combine dry ingredients. Gradually stir dry mixture into liquid, a third at a time. Fry corncakes in a lightly oiled pan.

Combine topping ingredients, and spoon over corncakes.

Makes 6 to 8 corncakes.

BUCKWHEAT BLINI
(Yeast-Risen Pancakes)

Pancakes that are light but stretchy enough to roll around a filling such as smoked salmon and sour cream, blini may also be served with maple syrup or with sautéed onions and sour cream.

3¾ cups	milk	925 mL
2 cups	buckwheat flour	500 mL
4 tsp.	active dry yeast	20 mL
4 tsp.	sugar	20 mL
5	large eggs, separated	5
4 Tbsp.	butter, melted, plus extra for browning	50 mL
1 tsp.	salt	5 mL
2 cups	white flour	500 mL
	Sour cream and smoked salmon for filling (opt.)	
	Chopped scallions or fresh dill for garnish (opt.)	

Scald 3 cups (750 mL) milk, and cool to lukewarm. Place buckwheat flour in a large bowl, and gradually stir in milk. Mix yeast and sugar together, and stir into buckwheat mixture. Cover with a cloth, and set in a warm place for 10 to 15 minutes or until mixture is frothy and almost doubled in volume.

Beat egg yolks together, and stir into flour mixture along with butter, salt and white flour. Beat at low speed with an electric mixer until well blended and smooth, then beat at medium speed for 2 minutes. If the batter is too thick, add the remaining ¾ cup (175 mL) milk (or as needed to make the batter thick but pourable), and beat for 1 minute.

Whip egg whites until stiff peaks form, then fold into batter. Cover, set in a warm place, and let rise for 40 to 45 minutes or until doubled in volume.

Grease a griddle with a small amount of butter, then heat. Ladle about 2 Tbsp. (25 mL) batter onto griddle for each blini. Cook over medium heat until the bottom is lightly browned and the surface is covered with bubbles—about 1 minute. Turn and lightly brown on the other side. Place blini on a plate, and keep warm in a 225°F (105°C) oven.

If desired, spread each blini with sour cream, add a slice of smoked salmon and a few minced scallion tops, then roll up.

Makes about 30 blini roughly 4 inches (10 cm) in diameter.

Brunch

BUCKWHEAT CRÊPES

Fill these crêpes with creamed spinach, asparagus or chicken, transforming leftovers into a fine, fast meal at any time of the day. For quick dessert crêpes, sauté, in a little butter, a few fresh pears that have been cored, peeled and sliced, then splash in some maple syrup and sprinkle with nutmeg.

½ cup	buckwheat flour	125 mL
¼ cup	white flour	50 mL
¾ tsp.	salt	4 mL
2 Tbsp.	sugar (if filling will be sweet)	25 mL
3	eggs	3
1¼ cups	milk	300 mL
2 Tbsp.	butter, melted, plus extra for browning	25 mL

Sift flours, salt and, if making dessert crêpes, sugar into a large bowl. Make a well in the center, and whisk in eggs and ¼ cup (50 mL) milk. Stir until smooth. Gradually whisk in remaining milk. Cover, and let stand at room temperature for 1 hour, or refrigerate for up to 1 day. Return to room temperature before continuing.

Whisk butter into batter. If batter is too thick, add a little more milk; it should be the consistency of heavy cream. Heat a skillet over medium-high heat. When it is hot, brush skillet with a little butter. When butter is melted, remove skillet from burner and pour ¼ cup (50 mL) batter onto the skillet, tilting it until the batter thinly covers the surface. Return the skillet to medium-high heat, and brown the crêpe first on one side, then on the other.

Makes 10 crêpes.

FRUIT-FILLED CRÊPES

Keep a batch of crêpes in the refrigerator or freezer to make a variety of easy and healthful breakfast treats. The simple fruit fillings featured on the facing page turn crêpes into an elegant, colorful breakfast that will appeal to both adults and children.

¾ cup	flour	175 mL
1 tsp.	sugar	5 mL
1 tsp.	finely grated lemon zest	5 mL
	Pinch salt	
1 cup	milk	250 mL
2	large eggs	2
2 Tbsp.	melted butter, slightly cooled	25 mL
	Vegetable oil for brushing pan	

In a medium bowl, stir together flour, sugar, lemon zest and salt. In a small bowl, whisk together milk, eggs and butter until blended. Add to dry ingredients, and whisk until smooth. Refrigerate, covered, for 1 hour.

Lightly brush the surface of an 8-inch (20 cm) crêpe pan or skillet with oil. Heat pan over medium heat until drops of water flicked from your fingers sizzle. Remove pan from heat, and hold at a slight angle. Pour in 2 Tbsp. (25 mL) batter, tilting the pan back and forth so that the batter forms a thin, even layer on the bottom of the pan. Return pan to burner, and cook until the surface looks set, 30 to 40 seconds. Loosen at one edge with a spatula, and turn the crêpe with your fingers. Cook for about 30 seconds, and slide the crêpe onto a plate. Repeat until the batter is used up. (If the crêpes begin to stick, lightly brush the pan with additional oil.)

To store: Seal the cooled crêpes in a plastic food bag. Refrigerate for up to 3 days, or freeze for up to 4 weeks.

To reheat: Stack up to 8 crêpes on a plate, and heat in the microwave on the high setting for 1 minute. Or stack crêpes on a baking sheet, cover loosely with foil, and warm in a 325°F (160°C) oven for 5 to 7 minutes.

Makes about 16 crêpes.

WARM BLUEBERRY & RASPBERRY FILLING

1½ cups	frozen unsweetened blueberries, thawed	375 mL
2 Tbsp.	sugar	25 mL
1 Tbsp.	cornstarch	15 mL
2 cups	frozen unsweetened raspberries, thawed	500 mL
8	crêpes, warmed	8
¼ cup	sour cream or yogurt (opt.)	50 mL

In a small saucepan, lightly crush ½ cup (125 mL) blueberries with a wooden spoon; stir in sugar and cornstarch. Cook over medium heat until mixture starts to thicken, about 1 minute. Add remaining blueberries, and cook, stirring gently, until heated through, about 2 minutes. Gently stir in raspberries, and cook for 1 minute longer.

Spoon 2 Tbsp. (25 mL) filling into center of each crêpe, and fold into quarters.

Place two filled crêpes on each serving plate, and top with 1 Tbsp. (15 mL) fruit filling and a dollop of sour cream, if desired.

Serves 4.

BANANA FILLING WITH WARM STRAWBERRY SAUCE

⅓ cup	strawberry preserves	75 mL
1 lb.	frozen whole strawberries, partially defrosted	500 g
4	bananas	4
8	crêpes, warmed	8
½ cup	sour cream or yogurt	125 mL

In a small saucepan, stir strawberry preserves over medium-low heat until hot, about 1 minute. Add whole strawberries, and stir gently over high heat until berries release their juices and sauce is bubbly and hot, about 1 minute.

Slice bananas diagonally, and lay a row of slices down the center of each crêpe. Spread with 1½ tsp. (7 mL) sour cream. Fold sides of crêpe over filling.

Place two filled crêpes on each serving plate. Spoon warm strawberry sauce on top, and add a dollop of sour cream.

Serves 4.

THE CLASSIC PANCAKE MIX

For quick batches of hassle-free breakfast pancakes or waffles, a large quantity of the dry ingredients can be mixed in advance and kept in the refrigerator for two months or in the freezer for six. Let it warm to room temperature before using.

10 cups	white flour	2.5 L
10 cups	whole wheat flour	2.5 L
1 cup	baking powder	250 mL
4 cups	instant milk powder	1 L
2 Tbsp.	salt	25 mL
½ cup	sugar	125 mL
4 cups	shortening	1 L

Combine dry ingredients, mix well, and cut in shortening until it is the consistency of cornmeal. Store, tightly covered, in the refrigerator. Makes 10 pounds (4.5 kg) of dry mix.

To prepare batter, beat together 1 cup (250 mL) milk and 1 egg. Stir in 1½ cups (375 mL) dry mix, ½ tsp. (2 mL) cinnamon and ¼ tsp.(1 mL) cloves. Make peach or blueberry pancakes by mixing the fruit right into the batter. Cook the pancakes in a greased frying pan.

For a lighter pancake or a waffle, separate the egg yolk from the egg white. Beat the egg yolk with the milk, but whip the egg white until it is stiff, and fold it into the batter just before cooking.

Serves 4.

PANCAKE HELPER

Laced with fresh blueberries or chopped peaches, dusted with confectioners' sugar or slathered with butter and pure maple syrup, hot pancakes are a satisfying breakfast treat.

For a light pancake, mix the liquid and dry ingredients together minimally, leaving any lumps that form. For a fluffy pancake, allow enough time to chill the batter for at least an hour before cooking so that the flour particles can expand.

While many pancake cooks find that a non-stick frying pan is unmatched for its convenience, others swear by the well-seasoned cast-iron skillet for its ability to conduct heat and distribute it evenly. Obtaining a golden brown color and a smooth surface on a pancake is simple if you possess the willpower to turn each pancake only once, letting the formation of holes on top of the raw side be your clue as to when to turn it over; the second side will cook in about half the time of the first.

SMOKED SALMON & GOAT CHEESE STRATA

This is a new twist on the strata, a layered dish that has been around for centuries. Baked in a springform pan and served in wedges, this lusty version is perfect for a weekend brunch.

$\frac{1}{4}$ cup	butter, softened, plus 1 tsp. (5 mL) for scrambling eggs	50 mL
13	slices firm white bread	13
5	large eggs	5
$\frac{1}{3}$ cup	plus 2 Tbsp. (25 mL) milk	75 mL
$\frac{1}{4}$ tsp.	salt	1 mL
$\frac{1}{4}$ tsp.	white pepper	1 mL
	Pinch each nutmeg & cayenne pepper	
	Pinch each salt & freshly ground pepper	
1 Tbsp.	fresh dill, chopped, or 1 tsp. (5 mL) dried dillweed	15 mL
1 tsp.	dried green peppercorns	5 mL
2 tsp.	drained capers	10 mL
1 cup	firm goat cheese, crumbled	250 mL
$\frac{1}{2}$ cup	sun-dried tomatoes, chopped (dry, not oil-packed)	125 mL
6 oz.	smoked salmon, cut into strips	175 g

Use 2 tsp. (10 mL) softened butter to grease a 9-inch (2.5 L) springform pan. Lightly spread the rest of the softened butter on both sides of the bread slices. Cut slices in half diagonally. Line the sides of the pan with about 9 bread triangles, with the long side down and overlapping slightly. Line the bottom of the pan with about 8 bread triangles, cutting to fit as necessary. Reserve remaining triangles.

In a small bowl, whisk together 3 eggs, 2 Tbsp. (25 mL) milk, salt, white pepper, nutmeg and cayenne. Drizzle about one-third of the mixture over the bread in the bottom of the pan. Set remaining mixture aside.

In a small bowl, whisk together 2 eggs, 2 Tbsp. (25 mL) milk and a pinch each of salt and pepper. Melt 1 tsp. (5 mL) butter in a small skillet over medium heat. Add the egg mixture, and stir with a wooden spoon until the eggs are softly scrambled.

Spread scrambled eggs over the bread slices. Sprinkle with dill, peppercorns and half of the capers. Top with half of the cheese, the tomatoes and the salmon, reserving a few strips of salmon for garnish. Cover the filling with remaining bread triangles, and drizzle remaining egg mixture evenly over the top. Sprinkle with the rest of the cheese. Cover overnight, along with remaining salmon and capers.

Preheat oven to 375°F (190°C). Place strata on a baking sheet, and bake for 35 to 40 minutes or until top is golden. Let stand for 5 minutes, then remove sides of springform pan, and transfer to a serving plate. Garnish with salmon and capers.

Serves 8.

TORTILLA ESPAÑOLA
(Spanish Omelet)

Of all the international egg-bound vegetable cakes, this simple potato, onion and egg mixture is perhaps the most beloved in its homeland. Served hot, cold or (best) just warm, it is a popular snack, a children's lunch and an hors d'oeuvre. There are as many different recipes as there are cooks; this one is a souvenir from a traditional Spanish household.

½ cup	olive oil	125 mL
2 lb.	baking potatoes, peeled & thinly sliced	1 kg
1	medium Spanish onion, halved & thinly sliced	1
6-8	eggs, beaten lightly with pinch of salt	6-8

Use a high-sided heavy iron pan, such as a chicken fryer. Pour in oil, and heat almost to smoking, then fry potatoes, uncrowded, in batches until thoroughly cooked and just starting to turn golden. Transfer potatoes to a mixing bowl using a slotted spoon.

Lower heat to medium, and fry onions in the same oil until limp and transparent but not at all colored. Use the slotted spoon to lift them out, and add to potatoes. Pour off and reserve most of remaining oil, leaving just enough to prevent eggs from sticking.

Combine eggs with potatoes and onions, and turn into the pan. Cook until the bottom is brown but the top is still damp. Run a spatula around the sides to loosen tortilla, then reverse it onto a flat plate or cookie sheet. Add a slick of reserved oil to the pan, if necessary, then slide the tortilla back in, and cook just long enough to brown the other side.

Serves 4 as a main dish or 6 to 8 as an appetizer.

TURKEY MUFFALETTAS

Leftover turkey and relish-tray fixings easily convert into this delicious version of New Orleans' famous muffaletta sandwich.

½ cup	stuffed green olives, drained	125 mL
½ cup	pitted black olives, drained	125 mL
½ cup	mixed pickled vegetables, drained	125 mL
½ cup	mixed pepper salad, drained	125 mL
1	celery stalk, sliced	1
¼ cup	red onion, chopped	50 mL
	Juice of ½ lemon	
1 Tbsp.	extra-virgin olive oil	15 mL
½ tsp.	oregano	2 mL
1	round loaf Italian or French country bread	1
¼ lb.	provolone cheese, thinly sliced	125 g
½ lb.	roasted turkey, sliced	250 g

Preheat oven to 300°F (150°C). Combine green and black olives, pickled vegetables, pepper salad, celery and onion in a food processor fitted with a steel blade. Pulse on and off about 10 times to chop finely. Do not overprocess. Transfer to a medium-sized bowl, and stir in lemon juice, oil and oregano.

Slice bread in half horizontally. Remove the soft insides of the bread, leaving the crust intact. Spread about half of the olive mixture over both halves of the bread. On the bottom crust, layer half of the cheese. Spread with some olive mixture. Arrange turkey over the top. Spread with remaining olive mixture, and top with remaining cheese. Add the top crust, and press together. Wrap tightly in aluminum foil, and bake for about 15 minutes. Remove from foil, cut into wedges, and serve at once.

Serves 6.

Sandwiches & Snacks

GRILLED CHICKEN & RED-PEPPER SANDWICHES

These quickly cooked morsels may be eaten right off the stick like kabobs, mixed into a rice salad or slathered with Herbed Yogurt Sauce and wrapped in warm flour tortillas or pitas. Almost any kind of citrus fruit makes a tangy marinade—try grapefruit or tangerines for a nice change.

⅔ cup	fresh orange or lemon juice	150 mL
⅓ cup	olive oil	75 mL
1 Tbsp.	grated orange or lemon zest	15 mL
4	cloves garlic, minced	4
2 tsp.	fresh thyme, chopped, or ½ tsp. (2 mL) dried	10 mL
2 tsp.	fresh sage, chopped, or ½ tsp. (2 mL) dried	10 mL
	Salt & freshly ground pepper	
6	boneless, skinless chicken breasts, cut into strips	6
3	red or green bell peppers, seeded & cut into strips	3
6	flour tortillas or pitas	6
	Herbed Yogurt Sauce (recipe follows)	

In a small bowl, whisk together juice, oil, zest, garlic, thyme and sage. Season with salt and pepper. Set aside ¼ cup (50 mL) for basting. Place chicken in a heavy-duty plastic bag. Pour remaining juice mixture over chicken. Seal bag tightly. Marinate for 30 minutes at room temperature or for up to 8 hours in the refrigerator, turning the bag occasionally.

Soak six bamboo skewers in water for 30 minutes. Prepare a charcoal fire, or preheat a gas grill. When the coals are ready, thread chicken and peppers onto separate skewers. Place chicken at the center of the grill and peppers at the outer edge. Cook for 3 to 4 minutes. Brush chicken with reserved marinade, then turn chicken and peppers. Cook for 3 to 4 minutes longer or until chicken is no longer pink inside and peppers are slightly charred. Remove from skewers, place inside tortillas, and serve with Herbed Yogurt Sauce.

Serves 6.

HERBED YOGURT SAUCE

Mild onions give this sauce a bit of bite, especially gentle red Bermudas, but any yellow onion will do. If you cannot find fresh mint or cilantro, try basil and oregano or chives and tarragon or simply add a squeeze of lemon juice, a bit of grated lemon zest and lashings of black pepper.

1 cup	yogurt	250 mL
½	onion, chopped	½
1	cucumber, peeled & diced	1
	Salt & freshly ground pepper	
1 Tbsp.	fresh cilantro, chopped	15 mL
1 Tbsp.	fresh mint, chopped	15 mL

In a small bowl, mix together all the ingredients. Serve immediately, or keep cool for up to 8 hours. Serve as a sauce, in sandwiches or as a dip.

Makes 2½ cups (625 mL).

Sandwiches & Snacks

CURRIED CHICKEN SALAD

Sweet and mildly spicy, this mixture can be stuffed into a lettuce- or sprout-lined pita for a tasty afternoon meal.

2 cups	chicken stock	500 mL
6	boneless, skinless chicken breasts	6
½ cup	mayonnaise	125 mL
½ cup	yogurt	125 mL
½ cup	mango chutney	125 mL
2 tsp.	curry powder	10 mL
1	tart apple, cored & chopped	1
¼ cup	currants or raisins	50 mL
3	pitas	3
	Lettuce leaves	

In a large, shallow pan with a lid, bring chicken stock and 2 cups (500 mL) water to a boil. Add chicken breasts, reduce heat to low, and simmer, partially covered, for 10 to 12 minutes or until chicken is no longer pink inside. Chill breasts and liquid in the refrigerator until cold—at least 1 hour. Remove chicken from the cooking liquid, and dice.

In a medium-sized bowl, stir together mayonnaise, yogurt, chutney and curry powder until well blended. Add chicken, apple and currants, tossing until completely coated.

To assemble, cut each pita in half and line with lettuce leaves, then spoon in the chicken salad.

Serves 6.

DEVILED TOFU SANDWICH FILLING

Even confirmed tofu haters will be hard-pressed to identify the main ingredient in this faux egg-salad sandwich filling. Chilling the mixture before serving is essential.

3	tofu cakes	3
2	celery stalks, finely chopped	2
3-4	green onions, finely chopped	3-4
1 cup	Garlic Mayonnaise or plain mayonnaise (page 140)	250 mL
3 Tbsp.	vinegar	45 mL
1 tsp.	celery seeds	5 mL
¾ tsp.	salt	4 mL
¾ tsp.	turmeric	4 mL

Slice tofu lengthwise, and press with toweling to remove excess water. Chop finely, and mix with celery and onions.

Combine remaining ingredients, then stir into tofu-vegetable mixture. Chill.

Makes 3 cups (750 mL).

SALMON SEVICHE

This seviche is a little out of the ordinary, as it uses oranges rather than the traditional limes. Serve on a bed of Boston lettuce with pickled cucumber for a wonderfully refreshing appetizer or light meal.

3	lemons	3
3	oranges	3
3	cloves garlic	3
3	green onions	3
2 Tbsp.	sugar	25 mL
½ tsp.	salt	2 mL
1 Tbsp.	red peppercorns (opt.)	15 mL
	Dash white pepper	
1½ lb.	fresh red salmon	750 g

Squeeze juice of lemons and oranges into medium-sized bowl. Slice garlic and onions, and add to juice. Add remaining ingredients, except fish, and stir to dissolve sugar. Thinly slice salmon, and add to marinade. Marinate for at least 4 hours before serving. The fish will be opaque and will look cooked when it is ready to eat.

Serves 6 to 8 as an appetizer.

TYROPITTAKIA
(Savory Cheese Triangles)

Great as appetizers or finger food, these tasty morsels can be made several days in advance, wrapped in aluminum foil and frozen. Thaw before baking.

1½ lb.	feta cheese, crumbled	750 g
½ lb.	farmer cheese	250 g
4-5	eggs	4-5
1 Tbsp.	(heaping) dried mint	15 mL
	Freshly ground pepper	
	Dash paprika	
	Dash nutmeg	
1 lb.	phyllo sheets	500 g
1 cup	unsalted butter, clarified	250 mL

Combine feta cheese, farmer cheese, 4 eggs, mint and spices in a large bowl. Mix and mash with a fork until all ingredients are well blended and soft. If feta cheese is hard, you may need another egg.

Lightly grease 4 cookie sheets. Unroll phyllo, and cut lengthwise into 4-inch (10 cm) strips. Stack and cover with a damp cloth to keep from drying out. Preheat oven to 350°F (180°C).

Brush one strip at a time with butter. Place 1 scant Tbsp. (15 mL) filling in the left bottom corner, and fold up a triangle of phyllo until the corner meets the far edge at 90 degrees. Continue folding to form a layered triangle, then place on the cookie sheets, and cover until ready for the oven. Bake until golden brown, about 25 minutes. Serve hot.

Makes about 50 triangles.

Sandwiches & Snacks

TEA-LEAF EGGS

It is hard to believe that anything so easy to make could look so elegant and taste so good. The pickling liquid marbleizes the eggs with random tracings of warm brown while imparting a rich smoky flavor to whites and yolks. For low-fat stuffed eggs, replace the yolks with a puree of grilled mushrooms.

24	small eggs	24
3 Tbsp.	Lapsang Souchong tea	45 mL
¾ cup	tamari or other aged soy sauce	175 mL
3	star anise	3

Cover eggs with cold water, slowly bring to a simmer, and cook for 25 minutes. Drain at once, and run cold water over eggs until all the heat has left.

While eggs are cooking, put tea in a big teapot or a nonreactive pan with a tight-fitting lid, and pour 4 cups (1 L) boiling water over it. Allow to steep for 8 minutes, then strain into a deep nonreactive pan. Add tamari and star anise, and set aside.

Gently tap the hard-cooked eggs all over with the back of a spoon so that they are covered with very tiny cracks. Put eggs in tea mixture, and add water if they are not all covered. Partially cover the pan, put over low heat, and simmer very gently for 2 hours.

Allow mixture to cool, then refrigerate for 18 to 48 hours before removing eggs from marinade. They will keep for several days. Shell just before using.

PORTABLE POWER LUNCH

When planning ahead for lunches, remember to incorporate leftovers from dinner the night before. If dinner on Monday is shish kebabs, cook two or three extras. Then base Tuesday's lunch on sliced pita bread, lettuce, Garlic Mayonnaise (page 140) and shish kebab meat —an assemble-yourself sandwich.

Those who aren't crazy about sandwiches can still have a nutritious portable lunch. Halve an apple, remove the core, then spread the cut sides with peanut butter and top with sliced banana. Fill celery sticks with cheese cubes, cream cheese or peanut butter. A bran muffin and a few slices of cheese are all the nutrition needed for a quick lunch. Even popcorn, sprinkled with grated cheese and yeast, can become part of lunch away from home.

Sandwiches & Snacks

MARINATED YOGURT CHEESE

This delicate fresh cheese is a sensational appetizer or snack spread on lightly toasted baguette medallions and topped with grilled red peppers.

32 oz.	yogurt	1 kg
¼ cup	olive oil, preferably extra-virgin	50 mL
2	cloves garlic, finely minced	2
½ tsp.	thyme	2 mL
½ tsp.	rosemary	2 mL
½ tsp.	basil	2 mL
1 Tbsp.	fresh dill, chopped	15 mL

To make yogurt cheese, line a colander with a large cotton tea towel or a double thickness of cheesecloth, and place the colander in the sink. Pour in yogurt. After 15 minutes, transfer colander to a bowl. Cover with plastic wrap, and refrigerate overnight.

Gather the edges of the towel together, and gently squeeze out any remaining liquid. Transfer cheese to a separate container. Refrigerate until ready to use. Keeps for one week.

Divide into 4 rounds, shaping patties with your hands. Place in a wide, shallow bowl.

Mix together remaining ingredients, and pour over cheese. Let stand at room temperature for 30 minutes before serving. Serve with crusty French bread or crackers.

Makes 4 small cheeses.

SEASONED CRACKERS

Cut these crackers into animal shapes with cookie cutters to make them more appealing to children.

1 cup	Good Tasting Yeast	250 mL
1⅓ cups	flour	400 mL
2 tsp.	baking powder	10 mL
1	clove garlic, minced	1
½ tsp.	cayenne pepper	2 mL
½ tsp.	dried chili peppers	2 mL
¼-½ cup	water	50-125 mL
2 tsp.	soy sauce	10 mL
1 tsp.	sherry	5 mL
1 Tbsp.	oil	15 mL
	Salt	

Combine yeast, flour, baking powder, garlic, cayenne and chili peppers. Combine water, soy sauce and sherry, then stir into flour mixture to make a stiff dough.

Roll out ⅛ inch (3 mm) thick. Brush top of dough with oil, then cut into desired shapes. Sprinkle lightly with salt.

Bake at 400°F (200°C) until golden brown, about 10 minutes.

Makes 3 dozen crackers.

Sandwiches & Snacks

PRETZELS

Pretzels are fun and easy to make (even for kids), and they are delicious to eat warm from the oven, especially with mustard and sauerkraut.

1 Tbsp.	yeast	15 mL
1 Tbsp.	sugar	15 mL
$1\frac{1}{2}$ cups	lukewarm water	375 mL
4 cups	flour	1 L
1	egg, beaten	1
	Coarse salt	

Dissolve yeast and sugar in water. Stir in flour, and knead until shiny and elastic, about 10 minutes. Cover, and let rise in a warm place for approximately 1 hour, until doubled. Punch down, knead briefly, and tear dough into 24 pieces. Roll by hand into 12-inch-long (30 cm) ropes, and twist into pretzel shapes. (You can make some in the shapes of letters too.) Brush pretzels with egg, and sprinkle with salt.

Bake at 425°F (220°C) for 25 to 30 minutes.

Makes 24 pretzels.

POPCORN PLUS

This basic recipe for popcorn with yeast can be dressed up in a number of ways. For a somewhat different flavor, use garlic butter instead of melted butter; or a little soy sauce ($\frac{1}{4}$ cup/50 mL) can be added to the melted butter and the salt eliminated. A sprinkling of grated Parmesan cheese is also tasty.

	Oil	
1 cup	popcorn kernels	250 mL
$\frac{1}{3}$ cup	butter	75 mL
	Salt	
$\frac{1}{3}$ cup	Good Tasting Yeast	75 mL

Heat enough oil to cover the bottom of a heavy saucepan. Pour in popcorn, and cover, leaving lid slightly ajar to allow steam to escape. Shake and cook over medium-high heat until kernels are popped, then pour into a large bowl.

Melt butter in the same saucepan, then drizzle over popcorn, stirring it in as you do so. Add salt to taste. Sprinkle with yeast, and stir well. Eat immediately.

Makes 4 cups (1 L).

Chapter 2

SOUPS & CHOWDERS

heir steamy, mouth-watering aromas draw people from the most remote corners of the house on gloomy winter afternoons. Their chilled tastes and icy textures revive the most apathetic appetites during the dog days of summer. Modest and unassuming in presentation, no dish is more richly versatile or more universally appreciated than soup.

Jealously guarded secrets in many households, soup recipes are, in reality, as individual as the cook who creates them. All good soups come from a stock with integrity, which acts as the first essential stroke on the cook's canvas. Quality ingredients, such as mature vegetables (otherwise past their peak for fresh or steamed preparations) and aged and strong-flavored cuts of meat, make the heartiest varieties. Fresh herbs, black pepper, celery, carrots and onions are broth basics that may be added whole for taste and strained out later. Virtually anything—except bitter-tasting broccoli, cabbage, cauliflower and organ meats—sweetens the pot that, created layer upon layer, increases in interest and appeal with each new ingredient. After patiently simmering on the back burner of the stove, the stockpot is reinvented in traditional favorites such as Fresh Tomato and Cream of Mushroom and in such innovative combinations as Leek & Butternut-Squash, Gingery Almond-Carrot and Chicken Tortilla Soup With Lime.

From thick chowders to cool consommés, our soups—many of which can be deliciously cobbled together from ingredients you have on hand—offer a rich assortment of wholesome tastes that can be ladled out at lunch or at dinner. Some like it hot, others like it cold, but no matter how you serve it up, soup makes good food.

29

VEGETABLE STOCK

Vegetarians will welcome this recipe as a tasty alternative to a meat-based stock. It is a suitable starter for all soups.

	Scrubbed potato peels	
4	carrots, peeled & cut into chunks	4
2	celery stalks, including leaves, cut into chunks	2
3	onions, peeled & quartered	3
3-4	tomatoes, quartered	3-4
	Salt	
8	peppercorns	8
10-12 cups	cold water	2.5-3 L

Combine all ingredients in a stockpot, and cover with water. Bring to a boil, reduce heat, cover, and simmer for 40 minutes. After cooling slightly, strain, then store in an airtight container in the refrigerator or freezer.

Makes 8 cups (2 L).

STOCK SECRETS

Virtually all good soup is based on stock, a nutrient- and flavor-rich broth slowly simmered on the back of the stove. Unlike most recipes, stock calls for not the young, tender and freshest vegetables and meats but, rather, the fully ripe, even overripe, vegetables and the most aged—often very tough—meat. The stock maker covets a strange array of culinary oddments: fowl carcasses, tomato skins, mushroom stems, knucklebones, chicken feet and fish heads.

Stocks are by no means all based on meat; the vegetarian versions rely on fish and vegetables to produce a broth used in meatless au maigre *cooking. Those derived from poultry and red meats are known as* au gras. *Either type allows one to make full use of kitchen by-products that might otherwise go to waste, and the resulting stock is the foundation upon which great soups, sauces, gravies and stews are built. The kitchen in which good stock can be substituted for water in all manner of dishes is a kitchen with a loyal following.*

Remember that the cooking time for stocks varies, with beef requiring the longest (up to 12 hours), followed by chicken (up to 8 hours) and, finally, fish and vegetable stocks. The latter two deteriorate rapidly and, in most cases, should be ready in less than an hour.

Stocks

CHICKEN STOCK 1

Simple and flavorful, this will serve as a great foundation for any soup that calls for chicken stock.

7-8 lb.	stewing hen	3-3.5 kg
4 qt.	cold water	4 L
1	large onion, studded with 3 whole cloves	1
2	carrots	2
1	whole clove garlic, flattened	1
	Bouquet garni: bay leaf, parsley, lovage & thyme	
1 tsp.	coarse salt	5 mL

Put everything but the salt in a large stockpot, and bring to a boil. Skim off the foam that rises to the surface. Lower to a gentle boil, add salt, and simmer, partially covered, for 2 to 3 hours. Strain, and cool. The fat will rise to the top during chilling. When stock is completely cold, skim fat from surface.

Makes about 3 quarts (3 L).

CHICKEN STOCK 2

This stock recipe is a variation that adds vegetables for extra flavor and is recommended for Chicken Soup With Matzo Balls (page 45).

1	chicken carcass	1
2	carrots, peeled & cut into chunks	2
1	celery stalk, including leaves, cut into chunks	1
3	onions, peeled & quartered	3
	Salt	
12	peppercorns	12
10	sprigs parsley	10
10-12 cups	cold water	2.5-3 L

Place all ingredients in a stockpot, and cover with water. Bring to a boil, reduce heat, cover, and simmer for 3 to 4 hours, periodically skimming foam from the top. Cool slightly, and strain out solids. Cool completely in the refrigerator, then skim off surface fat. Store in an airtight container in the refrigerator or freezer.

Makes 8 cups (2 L).

Stocks

TURKEY STOCK

A great way to make use of the carcass from a holiday turkey, this stock is good for any soup and can be stored, covered, in the refrigerator for up to two days or in the freezer for six months.

1	turkey carcass	1
2	large onions, quartered	2
2	carrots, cut into thirds	2
2	celery stalks with leaves, cut into thirds	2
1	bunch parsley	1

Break turkey carcass into several pieces, and place in a large soup kettle with 3 quarts (3 L) water. Bring to a boil, then reduce heat to low. Partially cover the pot, and simmer for about 1 hour. Skim off any foam that rises to the top. Add onions, carrots, celery and parsley; continue to simmer for 2 hours. Strain stock. Skim off fat. Simmer stock until it is reduced to 6 cups (1.5 L).

BEEF STOCK

This rich, hearty stock can be used as the base for other heavy sauces such as espagnole and Madeira. When using beef stock for a soup base, dilute its intense flavor first.

5 lb.	lean beef bones	2.2 kg
5 Tbsp.	oil or butter	65 mL
10	peppercorns	10
2	bay leaves	2
2	sprigs thyme	2
5	celery stalks, chopped	5
2	carrots, peeled & chopped	2
2	onions, quartered	2
1 qt.	tomatoes	1 L
12 cups	cold water	3 L

In a stockpot, brown beef bones in oil. Cover with water, and bring to a boil. Reduce heat, and simmer, uncovered, for 20 minutes, then skim foam off the top. Add remaining ingredients, cover, and cook for 4 to 5 hours. Cool slightly, and strain. Refrigerate, then remove fat from the surface. Store in the refrigerator or freezer in an airtight container.

Makes 10 cups (2.5 L).

Roasted Garlic Soup

Soups & Chowders, page 44

Classic Pound Cake

Desserts & Sweets, page 209

Stocks

MANHATTAN-STYLE FISH STOCK

The addition of tomato to the basic stock gives cooks a Manhattan-style broth for seafood soups and stews.

2	medium onions, chopped	2
2	celery stalks, chopped	2
4	cloves garlic, crushed	4
1 tsp.	fennel seeds	5 mL
½ cup	fresh parsley, chopped	125 mL
¼ cup	olive oil	50 mL
1	plum tomato	1
	Shrimp shells	
2	fish heads from white-fleshed fish	2
1	bay leaf	1
½ tsp.	thyme	2 mL
1	strip orange zest	1
2 cups	dry white wine	500 mL
	Salt & freshly ground pepper	

Sauté onions, celery, garlic, fennel and parsley in oil in a stockpot. Stir in remaining ingredients and 6 cups (1.5 L) water. Simmer, covered, for 30 minutes, and strain.

Makes 2 quarts (2 L).

CHOWDER STOCK

This stock makes a great start for any New England-style chowder.

2½ lb.	bones from white-fleshed fish, such as cod, rinsed	1.1 kg
1 cup	dry white wine	250 mL
1	medium onion, sliced	1
1	celery stalk, chopped	1
5	peppercorns	5
3	cloves garlic, unpeeled & crushed	3
⅓ cup	mushroom stems (opt.)	75 mL
	Bouquet garni: 10 sprigs parsley, 3 sprigs thyme, 1 bay leaf	

Place all ingredients in a large stockpot; add enough cold water to cover bones (about 5 cups/1.25 L). Bring almost to a boil, lower heat, and simmer, uncovered, for 30 minutes. Skim foam from surface. Strain stock, and discard solids.

Makes about 5 cups (1.25 L).

Cold Soups

CONSOMMÉ MADRILÈNE

The tomato gives this clear, shimmering soup a rosy hue. It is lightly gelatinous, elegant and refreshing.

3 qt.	chicken stock	3 L
1½ lb.	lean beef chuck, cut into small chunks	750 g
2	carrots, finely diced	2
1	leek, white part only, finely diced	1
6	tomatoes, seeded & chopped	6
1 tsp.	coarse salt	5 mL
	Chives for garnish	

Put all ingredients into a stockpot, and bring to a gentle boil. Remove foam from surface, and lower heat to keep soup at a gentle simmer, uncovered, for 1½ hours. You should have about 3 cups (750 mL) of liquid when finished. Strain consommé through a double thickness of dampened cheesecloth, then chill until lightly set, about 2 hours. Garnish with chives.
  Serves 2.

AVOCADO-CORIANDER SOUP

No vegetable is as creamy as an avocado, and it is shown off at its best in this delicate, pale soup.

2	ripe avocados, peeled & halved	2
2	scallions, roughly chopped	2
2 cups	light cream	500 mL
	Juice of ½ lime	
½ cup	chicken stock	125 mL
¼ tsp.	salt	1 mL
¼ tsp.	cayenne pepper	1 mL
¼ cup	fresh coriander leaves, plus extra for garnish, or 1 Tbsp. (15 mL) dried	50 mL
	Salt & freshly ground pepper	

Put all ingredients in a food processor or a blender, and process until smooth. Refrigerate for 3 hours, until completely chilled. Thin with more chicken stock if necessary, and season to taste with salt and pepper. Garnish with fresh coriander leaves.
  Serves 4.

Cold Soups

AVGOLEMONO SOUP

Golden yellow and zingy with lemon, this soup is an ideal addition to a summer-soup repertoire.

6 cups	chicken stock	1.5 L
1 cup	rice, uncooked	250 mL
	Juice of 2 lemons	
3	egg yolks	3
	Salt & freshly ground pepper	
	Parsley, chopped, for garnish	

Bring chicken stock to a boil, and add rice. Partially cover the pot, and cook rice until tender, about 20 minutes. Meanwhile, beat lemon juice and egg yolks together until smooth. Whisk 1 cup (250 mL) hot broth into lemon-and-yolk mixture, then slowly add to stock and rice. Stir soup gently over low heat for 3 to 5 minutes until soup thickens slightly. Be careful not to curdle the egg yolks. Chill for 3 hours; stir well to circulate the rice, and season to taste with salt and pepper. Garnish with parsley.

Serves 4.

GREEN VICHYSSOISE

This cool but hearty soup is ideal for a light meal. Serve with a crisp green salad and fresh bread.

2 Tbsp.	butter	25 mL
5	small leeks, white part only, chopped	5
6 cups	chicken stock	1.5 L
2	medium baking potatoes, peeled & diced	2
4 cups	watercress, leaves & tender stems, or fresh spinach leaves	1 L
1 cup	heavy cream	250 mL
	Salt & freshly ground pepper	
	Sprigs of watercress or parsley for garnish	

Heat butter, and gently sauté leeks for 10 minutes, then add chicken stock and potatoes, and simmer until potatoes are tender, about 20 minutes. Add watercress, and simmer for 5 minutes longer. Puree soup, leaving flecks of green, and chill for at least 3 hours. Add cream, and season to taste with salt and pepper. Garnish with sprigs of watercress, and serve.

Serves 6.

Cold Soups

CAPE HOUSE INN ICED BUTTER-MILK WITH SHRIMP SOUP

This exhilarating soup was one of the all-time favorites from *The Harrowsmith Cookbook, Volume Two*. It was generously shared by the owners of the Cape House Inn on Mahone Bay, Nova Scotia.

3 cups	fresh shrimp	750 mL
3 qt.	buttermilk	3 L
$1\frac{1}{2}$	English cucumbers, coarsely chopped, plus thin slices for garnish	$1\frac{1}{2}$
3 Tbsp.	fresh dill	45 mL
2 Tbsp.	dry mustard	25 mL
3 Tbsp.	dill pickle, chopped	45 mL
1 tsp.	freshly ground pepper	5 mL
	Cayenne pepper	
	Salt	

Cook shrimp in boiling water until tender. Peel, and chop into pieces. Combine all ingredients, adding cayenne and salt to taste. Mix well, and chill. Serve garnished with cucumber slices.
   Serves 12.

ANDALUSIAN GAZPACHO

An authentic but simply made version of the zesty Spanish classic. Most northern vegetable gardens will yield all the required fresh ingredients.

$2\frac{1}{2}$ cups	chicken stock	625 mL
$1\frac{1}{2}$ cups	white bread, crust removed, cubed	375 mL
4 cups	concentrated crushed tomatoes, strained to remove seeds	1 L
1	small white onion, quartered	1
1	green pepper, quartered	1
$\frac{1}{2}$	large cucumber, peeled & seeded	$\frac{1}{2}$
1	clove garlic	1
$\frac{1}{4}$ cup	red wine vinegar	50 mL
2 Tbsp.	mayonnaise	25 mL
1 cup	light cream	250 mL
	Salt & freshly ground pepper	

Garnish

1 cup	each white onion, green pepper & cucumber, diced	250 mL
	Toasted croutons	

Pour $\frac{1}{2}$ cup (125 mL) chicken stock over bread cubes, and let soak. Put all other ingredients, except mayonnaise, cream and salt and pepper, in a food processor or a blender, and puree until smooth. Add bread cubes, and continue pureeing. Put mixture through a food mill to remove pepper skins and remaining tomato seeds. Chill for at least 3 hours, until flavors blend. Whisk in mayonnaise and cream. Season to taste with salt and pepper. Serve with garnishes.
   Serves 6 to 8.

Cold Soups

CHILLED BORSCHT

Good borscht has an intensity of color and taste all its own. It is, to be sure, for beet lovers only. The taste is sweet and earthy. Serve with wedges of black bread.

8	whole fresh beets	8
1	small onion, diced	1
2 Tbsp.	butter	25 mL
4 cups	chicken stock	1 L
2	medium potatoes	2
1½ cups	sour cream, plus extra for garnish	375 mL
	Salt & freshly ground pepper	

Boil unpeeled beets for 30 minutes or until tender. In a large pot, sauté onions in butter for 5 minutes or until transparent. Add chicken stock, potatoes and beets, and simmer for 20 minutes or until potatoes are soft. Puree, and chill for at least 3 hours. Whisk sour cream into soup just before serving, and season to taste with salt and pepper. Garnish each bowl with a dollop of sour cream.

Serves 6.

CHILLED BORSCHT WITH TOMATO JUICE

Tomato juice adds zing to this light summertime soup. Cook the beets in the cool of the evening, and serve chilled borscht for lunch the next day. For fullest flavor, use tender, fresh baby beets.

2 cups	tomato juice	500 mL
1 cup	chicken stock, chilled	250 mL
8	medium beets, cooked, peeled & chopped	8
½	onion, chopped	½
1	clove garlic, peeled	1
2 Tbsp.	prepared horseradish	25 mL

Place tomato juice, chicken stock and beets in a food processor, and blend until beets are smooth. Add remaining ingredients, and blend until all are well combined. Chill for 3 hours.

Serves 6 to 8.

Hot Soups

FRESH TOMATO SOUP

Anyone who has handled first-class American globe tomatoes at the peak of ripeness knows that these tomatoes really want to be soup. So, on occasion, do American plum tomatoes. Proportions are unimportant as long as the tomatoes are the real thing.

3	medium onions or 3 or 4 large shallots, minced	3
4	medium or 2 large cloves garlic, minced	4
3-4 Tbsp.	olive oil, plus extra for flavoring	45-50 mL
5 lb.	fresh, very ripe tomatoes	2.2 kg
	Salt & freshly ground pepper	
	Large pinch dried oregano or marjoram or small sprig basil	
1 Tbsp.	balsamic or other mild vinegar (opt.)	15 mL
	Pinch sugar (opt.)	

In a large non-aluminum saucepan or stockpot, sauté onions and garlic in oil until soft and translucent, about 7 to 8 minutes. Cut unpeeled tomatoes into quarters or eighths straight into the pot. Cover, and simmer over low to medium heat until tomatoes begin to give off their juice, about 5 minutes. Raise heat slightly, and continue to simmer, stirring occasionally, until tomatoes are completely soft and swimming in juice. Depending on the quantity and on how crowded your pot is, this process may take from 15 to 45 minutes.

Put the soup through a food mill, being careful to watch for splatters of hot sauce. Force through as much of the tomato mixture as possible. (Alternatively, the tomatoes can be pureed in batches in a food processor, but the texture will not be as good.)

Return the pureed tomatoes to the pot, and bring back to a simmer. Season to taste with salt and pepper and oregano. Simmer for 5 to 10 minutes to blend the flavors, and taste again. If it is bland, add vinegar. If it has an acidic edge, add a pinch of sugar and whisk in another 1-2 Tbsp. (15-25 mL) oil just before serving.

Serves 6 to 8.

Hot Soups

CREAM OF MUSTARD SOUP

Chopped green onions and diced chicken make the perfect taste complement for this savory cream soup.

1	whole chicken breast	1
1	carrot, cut into thirds	1
1	celery stalk, cut into thirds	1
1	onion, cut in half	1
6 cups	water	1.5 L
	Salt & freshly ground pepper	
2 Tbsp.	butter	25 mL
1 Tbsp.	flour	15 mL
1 Tbsp.	dry mustard	15 mL
2	egg yolks	2
1 cup	heavy cream	250 mL
4 Tbsp.	Pommery Mustard (page 141)	50 mL
2	green onions, chopped, for garnish	2

Place chicken breast, carrot, celery and onion in a heavy pot. Cover with water. Add salt and pepper. Bring to a boil, reduce heat, and simmer until chicken is cooked, about 20 minutes. Remove chicken from stock, dice, and set aside, keeping warm. Continue to cook stock for 20 minutes. Strain, and reserve 4 cups (1 L).

Melt butter, stir in flour and dry mustard, and cook over medium-low heat for 2 minutes. Gradually stir in stock, and warm over low heat.

Meanwhile, whisk together egg yolks, cream and mustard. Stir a little of the hot mixture into the cream mixture, then whisk it all back into the stock. Cook over low heat, stirring, for 5 minutes. Add salt and pepper to taste.

Ladle into bowls, and garnish with diced chicken and green onions.

Serves 4.

GINGERY ALMOND-CARROT SOUP

Fresh gingerroot adds just the right spicy touch to this colorful, invigorating soup.

1½ lb.	carrots, peeled & shredded	750 g
1 cup	white wine	250 mL
3 cups	water	750 mL
1 Tbsp.	lemon juice	15 mL
½	small yellow onion, chopped	½
1	clove garlic, minced	1
1 tsp.	gingerroot, peeled & grated	5 mL
2 Tbsp.	almonds or almond pieces	25 mL
	Oil to coat bottom of pan	
¼ tsp.	curry powder	1 mL
1½ tsp.	salt	7 mL
¼ tsp.	freshly ground pepper	1 mL
	Sliced, toasted almonds for garnish	

Simmer carrots, wine, water and lemon juice until carrots are tender, about 15 minutes.

Meanwhile, sauté onion, garlic, gingerroot and almonds in oil until onion softens and garlic turns golden. Take care not to scorch. Stir in spices.

Add the sautéed mixture to the carrots, and puree until smooth. Serve hot or chilled. Garnish with sliced, toasted almonds.

Serves 8.

CREAM OF MUSHROOM SOUP

Taste this soup, and you will never again desire canned or dried mushroom soups. It is rich, full of flavor and easy to make.

2 lb.	mushrooms	1 kg
2	onions	2
2	cloves garlic	2
$\frac{1}{3}$ cup	butter	75 mL
$\frac{1}{3}$ cup	flour	75 mL
1 Tbsp.	thyme	15 mL
	Freshly ground pepper	
$\frac{1}{2}$ cup	soy sauce	125 mL
2 cups	vegetable or chicken stock	500 mL
4 cups	cream or milk	1 L

Wash and slice mushrooms. Chop onions and garlic. Melt butter in a stockpot, then sauté mushrooms, onions and garlic for approximately 5 minutes, until mushrooms are cooked but not limp. Remove vegetables from pan with a slotted spoon, leaving behind as much butter as possible. If there is no butter left in the pot, melt 4 Tbsp. (50 mL) butter before proceeding.

Stir flour into butter over medium heat. Add thyme, pepper and soy sauce, and cook, stirring, for 3 to 4 minutes. Slowly stir in stock, then cream, cooking until the mixture is thickened and heated through. Return vegetables to pot, stir to mix thoroughly, and serve.

Serves 8.

TRADITIONAL BORSCHT

Every cook has a favorite borscht recipe. The ingredient common to each is beets; everything else depends on the cook and the culture. Some omit meat, others cabbage, while many add vinegar. With its hearty consistency, this variation sticks to your ribs and is not powerfully cabbagy in flavor.

1 lb.	lean stewing beef	500 g
3	onions	3
4 Tbsp.	oil	50 mL
7 cups	beef stock	1.75 L
10	beets	10
5	carrots	5
$\frac{1}{4}$	turnip	$\frac{1}{4}$
4 Tbsp.	butter	50 mL
3 Tbsp.	red wine	45 mL
1	can (6 oz./156 mL) tomato paste	1
$\frac{1}{2}$	head cabbage	$\frac{1}{2}$
	Salt & freshly ground pepper	
	Sour cream for garnish	

Cut beef into small cubes. Chop onions. Heat oil in a heavy soup pot, then sauté beef and onions until beef is browned on all sides. Add 3 cups (750 mL) stock, bring to a boil, cover, reduce heat, and simmer for 30 minutes.

Meanwhile, grate beets, carrots and turnip—this is one recipe where a food processor is invaluable. Melt butter in a heavy skillet, and sauté vegetables until they are limp. When beef has simmered for 30 minutes, add vegetables to soup pot. Stir in remaining stock, wine and tomato paste, and simmer for 20 minutes. Grate cabbage, and stir into soup. Season to taste with salt and pepper, and cook for 15 minutes. Serve with a dollop of sour cream.

Serves 10.

TO CLEAN LEEKS

Trim off the root end and the tough outer leaves. Remove green tip, leaving the light green portion. (The green leaves can be used to flavor stocks.) Make 2 lengthwise cuts to within 1 inch (2.5 cm) of the root end. Wash carefully in several changes of water, separating the layers of the fanned end to release any dirt from the interior.

LEEK & BUTTERNUT-SQUASH SOUP

A perfect soup to prepare in the fall, when both leeks and squash are at their peak.

1	medium butternut squash	1
2 Tbsp.	butter	25 mL
5 cups	leeks, trimmed, cleaned & chopped	1.25 L
2	cloves garlic, minced	2
4 cups	chicken stock	1 L
$\frac{1}{4}$ tsp.	thyme	1 mL
1	bay leaf	1
	Salt & freshly ground pepper	
	Crème fraîche or sour cream	
	Chives, chopped	

Preheat oven to 400°F (200°C). Cut squash in half lengthwise. Remove seeds. Place squash, cut side down, in a shallow baking dish. Bake for 35 to 45 minutes or until flesh is tender. Let stand until cool enough to handle. Scoop out flesh, and set aside.

In a large, heavy saucepan or Dutch oven, melt butter over low heat. Add leeks, and sauté for 5 to 7 minutes or until softened. Add garlic, and sauté for 1 minute longer. Stir in chicken stock, thyme and bay leaf, and bring to a boil. Reduce heat to low, and simmer, covered, for 30 minutes. Add reserved squash, and simmer for 10 minutes longer. Discard bay leaf.

Let cool slightly, and puree in batches in a food processor or a blender. Return to the saucepan, and heat through. Season with salt and pepper. Ladle into soup bowls, and garnish with a dollop of crème fraîche and chives.

Serves 4.

TOMATO CHICKEN SOUP PROVENÇAL

The characteristic flavors of the sunny Mediterranean—tomato, olive oil, garlic, chicken and rosemary—abound in this delightful soup.

1 Tbsp.	olive oil	15 mL
2 cups	mushrooms, sliced	500 mL
1	onion, thinly sliced	1
1	green pepper, diced	1
3	large cloves garlic, minced	3
1	can (28 oz./796 mL) tomatoes with juice, chopped	1
4-5 cups	chicken stock	1-1.25 L
1 tsp.	basil	5 mL
$\frac{1}{2}$ tsp.	rosemary	2 mL
$\frac{1}{2}$ tsp.	thyme	2 mL
$1\frac{1}{2}$-2 cups	cooked chicken, diced	375-500 mL
	Salt & freshly ground pepper	

Heat oil in a large soup pot over medium-high heat. Add mushrooms, onion and green pepper, and sauté for about 4 minutes. Add garlic, and sauté for 1 minute. Add tomatoes, chicken stock and herbs. Bring to a boil, then reduce heat, and simmer, uncovered, for 30 to 45 minutes. Add chicken, and heat through. Season with salt and pepper.

Serves 4 as a main course.

ROASTED GARLIC SOUP WITH HERBED CROUTONS

This is meant to be a first course or a light lunch. Adding cooked chicken to the broth will make the soup more substantial.

2	heads garlic, left whole & unpeeled	2
$4\frac{1}{2}$ cups	chicken stock, preferably reduced	1.1 L
2 Tbsp.	butter	25 mL
1 Tbsp.	fresh dill weed, chopped	15 mL
3	slices whole wheat bread, cut into cubes	3
$\frac{1}{4}$ cup	dry white wine	50 mL
	Salt	
$\frac{1}{2}$ cup	grated provolone cheese	125 mL

Preheat oven to 350°F (180°C). Cut off the tops of garlic heads so that the tops of most of the cloves can be seen. Place upright in a shallow 8-cup (2 L) casserole dish, and pour $\frac{1}{2}$ cup (125 mL) chicken stock over garlic. Bake for 1 hour. Allow garlic to cool, then squeeze the garlic puree from the papery skins.

Melt butter in a large frying pan. Stir in dill. Add bread cubes, and toss. Cook for 5 minutes, flipping occasionally, until crisp. Set aside.

In a saucepan, combine remaining chicken stock, garlic puree, wine and salt to taste. Bring to a boil. Preheat the broiler.

Pour hot soup into ovenproof soup bowls. Add croutons, and sprinkle cheese on top. Broil for 3 minutes, until the cheese is bubbly, and serve.

Serves 4.

Hot Soups

CHICKEN BARLEY SOUP

This hearty soup welcomes ingredient substitutions. Just be sure you chop the vegetables finely so that the pieces are only slightly bigger than the barley grains.

1 Tbsp.	olive or canola oil	15 mL
2 cups	mushrooms, finely chopped	500 mL
1	onion, finely chopped	1
10 cups	chicken stock	2.5 L
2	medium carrots, finely chopped	2
⅔ cup	medium barley	150 mL
½ tsp.	thyme, plus more to taste	2 mL
2 cups	cooked chicken, diced	500 mL
¼ cup	fresh parsley, chopped	50 mL
	Salt & freshly ground pepper	

Heat oil in a large soup pot over medium heat. Add mushrooms and onion, and sauté until mushrooms are limp, about 5 minutes. Add chicken stock, carrots, barley and thyme. Bring to a boil, reduce heat, and simmer, uncovered, for 45 minutes, stirring occasionally.

Add chicken and parsley; simmer for 5 minutes. Season with salt, pepper and more thyme, if desired.

Serves 4 to 5 as a main course.

CHICKEN SOUP WITH MATZO BALLS

Some say the lighter and fluffier the matzo ball, the better. This recipe makes a middle-of-the-road variety—neither too heavy nor too light. To make a lighter matzo ball, add one more egg. To make a "cannonball," add more matzo meal.

2 Tbsp.	light vegetable oil, preferably canola	25 mL
2	large eggs	2
1 tsp.	salt	5 mL
½ cup	matzo meal	125 mL
6 cups	chicken stock, preferably reduced	1.5 L
10	sprigs parsley	10
3	sprigs dill weed or 1 Tbsp. (15 mL) dill seeds (opt.)	3
4 cups	shredded greens (bok choy, kale, chard, Chinese mustard greens)	1 L

In a medium-sized bowl, whisk together oil, eggs, salt and 2 Tbsp. (25 mL) water. Stir in matzo meal with a wooden spoon. Refrigerate for 15 minutes.

Meanwhile, bring a large pot of salted water to a boil. Reduce heat to medium-low to keep water gently boiling. Form the matzo batter into 1-inch-diameter (2.5 cm) balls, and drop into water. Cover the pot, and boil gently for 30 to 40 minutes. The balls will fluff up and float to the top as they cook. The only way to tell whether a matzo ball is cooked through is to remove it from the water and cut it in half. It should be firm and no longer doughy.

While the matzo balls cook, heat the chicken stock in a soup pot. Add parsley, dill, if desired, and greens, and simmer, covered, for about 30 minutes.

To serve, place 1 or 2 matzo balls in each bowl and add the soup.

Serves 4 to 6.

Hot Soups

CHICKEN TORTILLA SOUP WITH LIME

This delicate broth has bits of tomato and green pepper, a slice of lime and tortilla strips. If you don't want to deep-fry the tortillas, crisp them in an ungreased skillet, stirring frequently to avoid scorching.

1	jalapeño pepper	1
3	corn tortillas	3
	Vegetable oil for frying	
6 cups	chicken stock	1.5 L
2	tomatoes, diced	2
4 tsp.	fresh lime juice	20 mL
¾ tsp.	ground cumin	4 mL
¼ tsp.	salt	1 mL
1 cup	cooked chicken, diced	250 mL
1-2 Tbsp.	fresh cilantro, chopped	15-25 mL
4-6	thin lime slices	4-6

Place jalapeño pepper directly over the flame of a gas burner. When one side is slightly charred, turn and continue charring until blistered and blackened all over, 4 to 5 minutes. (Alternatively, broil about 4 inches/10 cm from the heat for 5 to 6 minutes.) Place the pepper in a paper bag for about 15 minutes. Slip the skin off the flesh, cut away the stalk end, and dice. Set aside.

Cut tortillas into strips approximately ½ by 2 inches (1 x 5 cm). Heat 2 inches (5 cm) of oil in a frying pan to 365°F (185°C). Fry the tortilla strips, in two or three batches, until golden and crisp, about 3 minutes. Drain on paper towels.

In a soup pot, combine chicken stock, tomatoes, lime juice, cumin, salt and jalapeño pepper.

Simmer, uncovered, for about 1 hour. Add chicken, and heat through. To serve, ladle the soup into bowls. Add a few tortilla strips, a sprinkling of cilantro and a slice of lime.

Serves 4 to 6.

PORK WITH CHILIES SOUP

Pickled chilies add an interesting flavor to this dish. Barbecued or salted pork, which is available at Chinese specialty stores, can be used in place of the pork tenderloin.

½ lb.	pork tenderloin, julienned	250 g
2 Tbsp.	cornstarch, plus ½ tsp.- (2 mL)	25 mL
2 Tbsp.	oil	25 mL
2	pickled chilies, diced	2
2	slices gingerroot, minced	2
2	cloves garlic, chopped	2
2	green onions, chopped	2
4 cups	chicken stock	1 L
2 Tbsp.	soy sauce	25 mL
2 tsp.	vinegar	10 mL
1 tsp.	sesame oil	5 mL

Toss pork with 2 Tbsp. (25 mL) cornstarch. Heat oil in a wok, then stir-fry pork for 3 minutes. Remove pork, and stir-fry chilies, gingerroot, garlic and onions for 1 minute. Return pork to wok. Combine ½ tsp. (2 mL) cornstarch with remaining ingredients, add to wok, and heat through.

Serves 6.

Hot Soups

HOT & SOUR SOUP

After everyone is tired of eating holiday leftovers, this soup will perk up the most jaded palates.

6 cups	turkey stock	1.5 L
2	slices gingerroot, peeled & minced	2
4	cloves garlic, minced	4
¼ cup	dried oyster or shiitake mushroom caps, chopped	50 mL
3 Tbsp.	soy sauce	45 mL
1 Tbsp.	ketchup	15 mL
1	carrot, julienned	1
1	turnip, peeled & julienned, or one can (8 oz./213 mL) bamboo shoots, drained	1
½ cup	white vinegar	125 mL
1 lb.	firm tofu, diced	500 g
4	green onions, trimmed & chopped	4
1 cup	cooked turkey, shredded	250 mL
½ tsp.	white pepper	2 mL
½ tsp.	freshly ground black pepper	2 mL
3 Tbsp.	cornstarch dissolved in ¼ cup (50 mL) water	45 mL
2	large eggs, slightly beaten	2
	Dark sesame oil (opt.)	

In a large saucepan, bring turkey stock to a boil. Add gingerroot, garlic, mushrooms, soy sauce and ketchup. Simmer for about 10 minutes. Then add carrot and turnip, and simmer for 2 minutes. Add vinegar, tofu, green onions, turkey and pepper. Return to a simmer, and stir in the cornstarch mixture. Simmer for about 2 minutes or until the soup is thickened. With the soup still boiling, slowly stir in eggs. Remove from heat immediately. Taste and adjust seasonings by adding more vinegar or pepper. Pour soup into serving bowls. Drizzle a little sesame oil over each serving, if you wish.

Makes 8 cups (2 L).

ORIENTAL CHICKEN SOUP WITH NOODLES

This soup is the perfect accompaniment to a stir-fry. (Note: Fish sauce, called *nam pla* in Thai and *nuoc mam* in Vietnamese, is available in Asian food stores.)

8 cups	chicken stock	2 L
1	piece fresh gingerroot, about ½ inch (1 cm) long, peeled & thinly sliced	1
3	cloves garlic, sliced	3
2-3 tsp.	fish sauce	10-15 mL
	Salt	
2 Tbsp.	dry sherry	25 mL
3 cups	bok choy, Chinese mustard greens, chicory or other greens, shredded	750 mL
1 cup	cooked chicken, shredded	250 mL
1	can (14 oz./398 mL) baby corn, drained & cut into pieces	1
⅓ lb.	fresh Chinese egg noodles or ¼ lb. (125 g) dry vermicelli	170 g
	Sesame oil	
3	whole scallions, thinly sliced	3

In a large soup pot, combine chicken stock, gingerroot, garlic and fish sauce. Bring to a boil, reduce heat, and simmer, uncovered, for 40 to 60 minutes. Remove garlic and gingerroot. Season with salt, then add sherry, greens, chicken and corn. Simmer (do not boil) for about 15 minutes.

Meanwhile, cook noodles in plenty of boiling salted water until just tender. Drain, and toss with a few drops of sesame oil.

To serve, place a small portion of noodles in each bowl, and pour the soup over them. Sprinkle with scallions, and serve immediately.

Serves 4 to 6.

Hot Soups

WON TON SOUP

This recipe requires few ingredients, relying for its flavor on rich-tasting chicken stock.

6 cups	chicken stock	1.5 L
4 Tbsp.	Chinese rice wine or dry sherry	50 mL
4	slices gingerroot, crushed	4
18	filled won tons, uncooked	18
2	bok choy stalks, white with green parts, cut in half lengthwise & sliced diagonally into pieces	2
1	scallion, cut diagonally into pieces	1
½ tsp.	soy sauce	2 mL

In a large pot, combine chicken stock, wine and gingerroot. Simmer for 10 to 15 minutes. Remove and discard gingerroot. Add won tons to broth, and simmer, uncovered, stirring occasionally, for about 5 minutes. Add bok choy, scallion and soy sauce. Simmer for 2 to 4 minutes or until won ton filling is no longer pink and vegetables are tender-crisp. Serve immediately.

Serves 6.

WON TONS

Frozen won ton wraps are available in most supermarkets, but try to find a Chinese market that carries fresh wraps. Serve fried won tons as an appetizer with sweet-and-sour or plum sauce.

1 lb.	ground pork	500 g
¼ lb.	shrimp, peeled, deveined & finely chopped	125 g
½ cup	bok choy or cabbage, finely chopped	125 mL
2	scallions, minced	2
1½ tsp.	gingerroot, peeled & minced	7 mL
2	cloves garlic, minced	2
2 Tbsp.	soy sauce	25 mL
1 Tbsp.	Chinese rice wine or dry sherry	15 mL
1½ tsp.	cornstarch	7 mL
1 lb.	package won ton wraps	500 g

In a large bowl, mix pork, shrimp, bok choy, scallions, gingerroot, garlic, soy sauce, wine and cornstarch with a wooden spoon.

Place 1 tsp. (5 mL) pork mixture in center of each won ton wrapper. Brush one corner and the two adjacent sides of each wrapper with a little water. Fold the opposite sides over to form a triangle, then press to seal edges. Bring the outside corners together, overlapping slightly. Moisten, and press to seal.

Won tons can be prepared ahead: Arrange in a single layer on a baking sheet lined with wax paper, cover well with plastic wrap, and refrigerate for up to 8 hours or freeze for a month. Once the won tons are frozen, you can layer them in an airtight container. Do not thaw before cooking.

Steam won tons in a covered steamer basket over boiling water for about 10 minutes. To check whether they are done, remove one won ton and cut in half. When center is no longer pink, the filling is cooked. Fry in hot peanut oil, if desired, and serve with sweet-and-sour or plum sauce.

Makes about 80 won tons.

GOING FISHIN'

Low in fat and high in protein, fish is a delicious dietary dream. Freshness, however, is everything when it comes to buying and cooking fish and seafood, and the easiest and most dependable method for determining its age is to rely on your senses. Number one is smell. Fresh fish will have the faint and decidedly unfishy smell of your favorite freshwater lake. The eyes should be bright, clear and round, not sunken. The skin should feel firm and appear moist and shiny; the gill area should be a bright red color. Freshly purchased fish should be refrigerated immediately, preferably on ice, and eaten the day you bring it home.

NORTH AMERICAN BOUILLABAISSE

Monkfish, a firm white-fleshed fish readily available in winter, takes on the flavor of shellfish in this fennel-scented stew. Top with a slice of crisply fried French bread, a spoonful of Garlic Mayonnaise generously seasoned with red pepper and a sprinkling of Parmesan cheese.

4	large cloves garlic, crushed	4
1	medium onion, chopped	1
1	green pepper, cut into chunks	1
1	red bell pepper, cut into chunks	1
2 Tbsp.	olive oil	25 mL
$\frac{1}{4}$ cup	parsley, chopped	50 mL
$\frac{1}{4}$ tsp.	red pepper flakes	1 mL
$\frac{1}{2}$ tsp.	thyme	2 mL
$\frac{1}{2}$ tsp.	salt	2 mL
$\frac{1}{4}$ tsp.	freshly ground pepper	1 mL
2 qt.	fish stock	2 L
3	plum tomatoes, chopped	3
2 lb.	monkfish fillets, cut into bite-sized pieces	1 kg
$1\frac{1}{2}$ lb.	mussels, washed & debearded	750 g
$1\frac{1}{2}$ lb.	shrimp, shelled & deveined	750 g
6	slices French bread fried in olive oil	6
	Garlic Mayonnaise (page 140), seasoned with hot pepper sauce	
	Grated Parmesan cheese	

In a heavy stockpot, sauté garlic, onion and green and red peppers in oil until softened. Stir in seasonings, and sauté briefly. Add fish stock, tomatoes and monkfish, and simmer until monkfish is opaque. Steam mussels in 1 cup (250 mL) water, then add water to stockpot, and shell mussels. When monkfish is done, add shrimp, and simmer just until they turn pink. Stir in mussels. Serve in bowls topped with bread, Garlic Mayonnaise and cheese.
Serves 6.

Chowders

MRS. HUSSEY'S CHOWDER

This most basic of all chowders is constructed according to Ishmael's description in Herman Melville's *Moby-Dick*. Make it using unsalted soda crackers. (Note: An easy way to shuck clams is to spread them on a baking sheet and place them in the freezer just long enough for the shells to begin opening. Then use a clam knife to separate the shells.)

4-6 doz.	Manila or small littleneck clams, scrubbed, then shucked over a bowl to catch clam juice	4-6 doz.
$\frac{1}{4}$ cup	salt pork, cut into small pieces	50 mL
1 cup	cracker crumbs, such as Carr's Table Water Crackers, crushed with a rolling pin	250 mL
4 tsp.	unsalted butter Cayenne pepper	20 mL

Strain the clam juice. Measure the clams and their liquid, and add enough water to make 4 cups (1 L). In a large saucepan, cook salt pork over medium heat for 3 to 5 minutes or until the fat is rendered and the pork is browned. Stir in the clams and liquid. Bring to a gentle boil, stirring, over medium heat, and cook until clams are tender, about 5 minutes.

Spread a layer of cracker crumbs in the bottom of 4 bowls. Cut butter into small pieces, and divide evenly among bowls. Season the chowder with cayenne to taste. With a slotted spoon, distribute the clams evenly among the bowls. Ladle the hot broth over the clams.

Serves 4.

NEW ENGLAND POTATO & CLAM CHOWDER

Drawing its flavor from the juices of the clams and celery, this no-nonsense chowder can be on the dinner table in 30 minutes.

1	small onion, halved	1
1	bay leaf	1
1	leafy celery top	1
$\frac{1}{2}$ tsp.	salt	2 mL
18-24	cherrystone or steamer clams, scrubbed	18-24
3 cups	potatoes, peeled, halved & thinly sliced	750 mL
$\frac{1}{2}$ cup	celery, thinly sliced	125 mL
2 cups	milk or half-and-half Salt & freshly ground pepper Cayenne pepper	500 mL

In a large saucepan with a tight-fitting lid, combine 1 cup (250 mL) water, onion, bay leaf, celery leaves and salt. Bring to a boil, and add clams. Cover, and cook over high heat until all the clams have opened, about 5 minutes. (Discard any clams that do not open.) With a slotted spoon, transfer clams to a dish to cool. Strain the broth, and add enough water to make 2 cups (500 mL). Set aside.

Rinse out the saucepan. Add the clam broth, potatoes and celery, and heat to boiling. Cover, and cook over low heat until the potatoes are tender, about 10 to 12 minutes.

Meanwhile, shell clams, and mince with kitchen shears or a knife. Pour milk into a bowl, and spoon a little of the hot broth into it. Stir the mixture back into the saucepan. Stir in the clams. Gently heat, stirring. Do not boil, or the milk may curdle. Season to taste with salt and pepper and a little cayenne.

Serves 4.

Chowders

CODFISH CHOWDER

The savory flavor of this traditional nor'easter chowder comes mostly from its fish stock.

2 Tbsp.	salt pork, diced	25 mL
1	medium onion, diced	1
1½ tsp.	butter	7 mL
1 tsp.	fresh thyme, chopped, or ¼ tsp. (1 mL) dried	5 mL
2 Tbsp.	flour	25 mL
2	large potatoes, diced	2
2 cups	fish stock	500 mL
2	bay leaves	2
1½ lb.	cod fillets, cut into large chunks	750 g
1½ cups	skim milk	375 mL
	Salt & freshly ground pepper	

In a large saucepan, sauté salt pork over low heat, stirring, for about 3 minutes or until the fat is rendered and the pork browned. Add onion, butter and thyme, and sauté, stirring, for 3 to 4 minutes or until onion is soft. Add flour, and sauté, stirring, for 1 minute. Add potatoes, fish stock and bay leaves, and simmer for 15 to 20 minutes or until the potatoes are tender. Remove bay leaves, and add cod and milk. Simmer for 8 to 10 minutes or until fish is cooked through. Season with salt and pepper.

Serves 4.

SALMON CORN CHOWDER

Simmering the corncobs in the broth and adding the corn kernels and salmon later leaves the corn crisp and the fish tender but not overdone.

3	cobs of corn	3
1 Tbsp.	unsalted butter	15 mL
⅓ cup	shallots, chopped	75 mL
2 cups	chicken stock	500 mL
½	bay leaf	½
1	sprig thyme or ¼ tsp.(1 mL) dried, plus extra fresh thyme for garnish	1
¼ cup	long-grain white rice, uncooked	50 mL
1 tsp.	salt	5 mL
2 cups	half-and-half	500 mL
12 oz.	fresh salmon, cut into 2-inch (5 cm) pieces, skin & bones discarded	375 g
	Hot pepper sauce	
¼ cup	red bell pepper, finely minced	50 mL
	Freshly ground pepper	

Cut the corn from the cobs (there should be about 2½ cups/625 mL), and set both aside. Heat butter in a large, heavy saucepan over medium heat. Add shallots, and sauté, stirring, until tender, about 3 to 5 minutes. Add chicken stock, bay leaf, thyme and corncobs. Heat to boiling, reduce heat, cover, and simmer for 20 minutes. Remove corncobs, and discard. Stir in rice and salt. Cover, and cook over low heat until rice is soft, about 20 minutes.

Stir in half-and-half and corn kernels. Cook, uncovered, over medium heat until hot; do not boil. Reduce heat to low, and simmer, stirring occasionally, for 10 minutes. Add salmon, cover, and cook for 5 minutes or until fish is cooked through. (Do not boil.) Remove bay leaf. Add additional salt, if desired, and hot pepper sauce to taste. Ladle into bowls, and sprinkle each with red pepper, fresh thyme, if available, and black pepper.

Serves 4.

Chowders

ITALIAN-STYLE SEAFOOD CHOWDER

A simple version of Mediterranean fish soup, this dramatic-looking chowder can be varied by omitting the licorice-flavored fennel and adding a pinch of saffron, soaked in $\frac{1}{2}$ cup (125 mL) water for 15 minutes, along with the tomatoes.

2	cloves garlic	2
8	slices Italian bread	8
1 Tbsp.	olive oil, plus extra for brushing bread	15 mL
2	strips orange zest	2
	Pinch fennel seeds	
$\frac{1}{2}$ cup	dry white wine	125 mL
1	can (28 oz./796 mL) plum tomatoes, chopped, with juice	1
1	sprig basil, plus 2 Tbsp. (25 mL), chopped, or 2 tsp. (10 mL) dried	1
1	sprig parsley, plus 2 Tbsp. (25 mL), chopped	1
12	littleneck, mahogany, Manila or steamer clams, scrubbed	12
12	mussels, scrubbed, beards removed	12
12	extra-large shrimp, peeled & cleaned	12
	Salt & freshly ground pepper	

Preheat oven to 350°F (180°C). Cut 1 clove garlic in half, and rub halves over bread slices. Brush lightly with oil, place on a baking sheet, and bake until golden, about 20 minutes, turning once halfway through. Set aside.

Heat remaining 1 Tbsp. (15 mL) oil in a large saucepan or a deep skillet with a tight-fitting lid. Crush the second garlic clove, and add to the pan along with orange zest and fennel. Sauté over low heat, stirring, for about 3 to 4 minutes or until garlic is soft but not browned.

Add wine to the garlic mixture, and boil over high heat, stirring, for about 3 minutes or until reduced by half. Add tomatoes and sprigs of basil and parsley. Cover, and heat to boiling, reduce heat, and simmer for about 10 minutes.

Add clams, mussels and shrimp, cover, and cook over medium-high heat until the clams and mussels have opened, about 5 minutes. (Discard any that do not open.)

Place 1 or 2 slices of toast in the bottom of 4 soup bowls (serve any extra on the side). Divide the seafood evenly among the bowls. Remove orange zest and sprigs of basil and parsley. Season broth with salt and pepper, and add half the chopped basil and parsley. Ladle all the broth over the seafood, and sprinkle with remaining chopped basil and parsley.

Serves 4.

Chowders

CURRIED MUSSEL CHOWDER

The subtle curry flavor in this contemporary chowder brings out the slightly sweet taste of the mussels.

1 Tbsp.	olive oil	15 mL
1	medium onion, chopped	1
1	clove garlic, crushed	1
1 cup	dry white wine	250 mL
1	leafy celery top, coarsely chopped	1
1	strip orange zest	1
1	bay leaf	1
1	sprig parsley	1
½ tsp.	salt	2 mL
2 lb.	small mussels, scrubbed, beards removed	1 kg
2 Tbsp.	unsalted butter	25 mL
2 tsp.	curry powder	10 mL
¼ tsp.	turmeric	1 mL
2 Tbsp.	flour	25 mL
2 cups	half-and-half or milk	500 mL
⅔ cup	potatoes, peeled & diced	150 mL
⅓ cup	carrots, peeled & diced	75 mL
¼ cup	frozen baby peas	50 mL
	Hot pepper sauce	

In a large saucepan with a tight-fitting lid, heat oil over medium heat. Add onion, and sauté, stirring, for 3 to 5 minutes or until tender. Add garlic, and sauté for 2 minutes. Add wine, celery, orange zest, bay leaf, parsley and salt. Boil over high heat until wine is reduced by half, about 5 minutes. Add 1 cup (250 mL) water, and bring to a boil again. Add mussels, cover, and cook over high heat until all the mussels have opened. (Discard any that do not open.)

With a slotted spoon, transfer mussels to a colander set over a bowl. Strain the broth, and set aside. Shell the mussels, and add to the reserved broth. Melt butter in another large saucepan over medium heat. Stir in curry powder and turmeric until blended, and sauté for 1 minute. Add flour, and sauté, stirring, for 2 minutes. Gradually stir in half-and-half, and whisk for 3 to 5 minutes, until the mixture is smooth and slightly thickened. Add the mussels and broth, and set aside.

In a small saucepan, boil potatoes and carrots for 5 minutes. Add peas, boil 1 minute longer, and drain. Stir vegetables into the thickened broth. Add more salt, if desired, and hot pepper sauce to taste. Heat through.

Serves 4.

SCALLOP CHOWDER

Delicate scallops benefit from their association with fresh fennel and pancetta (Italian bacon that is cured, not smoked). The scallops must be only *lightly* poached, or they will become rubbery.

1	red bell pepper	1
¼ cup	pancetta or lightly smoked bacon, diced	50 mL
1	bulb fennel, cored & coarsely chopped, plus green top, chopped	1
1	medium onion, chopped	1
2 tsp.	fresh thyme leaves or ½ tsp. (2 mL) dried	10 mL
	Salt	
4 cups	milk or half-and-half	1 L
1 lb.	bay or sea scallops, cut into uniform pieces, if large	500 g
	Freshly ground pepper	

Roast red pepper directly over the flame of a gas burner or under an electric broiler. When one side is charred, turn, and continue roasting until pepper is blackened and blistered all over, about 10 minutes. Place in a paper bag, and set aside for about 15 minutes so that it softens. Peel off skin, rinse, remove seeds, and dice finely. Set aside.

Fry pancetta in a large saucepan over medium-low heat for 3 to 5 minutes or until the fat is rendered and the meat is golden. Stir in fennel and onion, add ¼ cup (50 mL) water and half of the thyme, and sprinkle with salt. Cover, and cook over medium-low heat until the fennel and onion are very tender, about 20 minutes.

Gradually stir milk into the skillet, and heat until steaming, but do not boil. Add scallops, cover, and cook over low heat just until cooked through, about 3 to 5 minutes, depending on their size. Stir in red pepper. Add pepper to taste. Ladle the chowder into bowls, and garnish each with a sprinkling of thyme. Serves 6.

Chapter 3

SALADS & DRESSINGS

he day of reckoning for the old-style tossed salad has come and gone. Weighed in the balance and found wanting, this once tasteless green course has surrendered its established place on North American dining tables and been reinvented with style as the dietary backbone of a health-conscious continent.

Freed from the slavish bonds of iceberg lettuce and unseasonable tomatoes, cooks can never have too many salad recipes in their repertoires. Endless combinations of nutritious ingredients—including grains, legumes, herbs, greens, vegetables, pasta, bread, meat, fish and seafood—all play a role in the sophisticated postmodern salad. Much more than wholesome low-calorie starters, these combinations, rich in both texture and flavor, can introduce a welcome versatility to a special lunch or an evening meal. Warm chicken and baby greens, pasta and olives, glass noodles, chicken and mint, warm chicken and greens or grainy mixtures accented with citrus fruit and parsley, each garnished with savory chopped herbs, are all delicious dining experiences. While many earn status as main-course meals, the most indulgent of the lot can work as a fine starter when offered in delicate servings.

No longer exclusively dependent on leafy greens, most of these recipes are suited to lasting a few days, which makes many perfect for brown-bag lunches or no-fuss midday meals. Some, like the classic Greek Salad, are actually tastier after a day or two in the refrigerator, which allows the vegetables, cheese and dressing to marinate longer. Some can be successfully prepared year-round, although we repeat our standing advice that you adjust your salad fixings to suit what's in season, enjoying as much as possible the natural succession of harvests.

WARM WATERCRESS & PINE NUT SALAD

Bacon and warmed hazelnuts give an earthy flavor to this satisfying salad.

8 cups	watercress	2 L
4	slices bacon, diced	4
¼ cup	olive oil	50 mL
1	large clove garlic, peeled & halved	1
¼ cup	pine nuts	50 mL
¼ cup	finely chopped hazelnuts	50 mL
2 Tbsp.	cider vinegar	25 mL
	Salt & freshly ground pepper	

Trim watercress stems. Wash and dry leaves, then place in a large salad bowl, and set aside. In a small skillet, cook bacon over medium heat, stirring, until crisp, 2 to 3 minutes. Drain bacon on paper towels, and set aside.

In a large skillet, heat oil over medium heat. Add garlic, and cook, stirring, until golden, about 2 minutes. Remove garlic, and discard. Add pine nuts and hazelnuts to the skillet, and cook, stirring, until lightly browned, 5 to 6 minutes. Pour over watercress. Add vinegar, and toss well. Season with salt and pepper. Sprinkle with reserved bacon, and serve immediately.

Serves 4.

SPINACH & ARTICHOKE-HEART SALAD

Artichokes—rich in both flavor and texture—are the centerpiece of this salad, which can be made all winter long.

3	cans (14 oz./398 mL each) artichoke hearts	3
1	red onion	1
½ cup	oil	125 mL
⅓ cup	cider vinegar	75 mL
2 Tbsp.	honey	25 mL
1 Tbsp.	grated onion	15 mL
½ tsp.	mustard	2 mL
	Salt & freshly ground pepper	
1	package spinach, washed & torn	1

Drain and thoroughly rinse artichoke hearts, and cut into quarters. Peel and slice red onion into thin rings. Combine oil, vinegar, honey, onion, mustard and salt and pepper in a glass jar, and shake to blend well.

Mix artichokes and red onion in a salad bowl, then pour dressing over, and mix well. Let sit at room temperature for 2 hours. Just before serving, add spinach and toss gently.

Serves 6.

Salads & Dressings

ORANGE NAPA SALAD

Napa is Chinese cabbage and is available in large supermarkets or Asian food stores. The quantity of gingerroot can vary depending on individual taste.

1	small head napa	1
6	oranges	6
1 cup	orange juice	250 mL
½ cup	oil	125 mL
⅓ cup	malt or cider vinegar	75 mL
3 Tbsp.	soy sauce	45 mL
2 tsp.	black bean sauce	10 mL
2 Tbsp.	grated gingerroot	25 mL
	Salt & freshly ground pepper	

Slice napa in half lengthwise. Remove core, and chop cabbage into strips. Remove skin and pith from oranges, and chop into rounds. Toss with cabbage. Whisk remaining ingredients together, pour over salad, and toss.

Serves 6 to 8.

GREEK SALAD

Prepare this salad a few hours ahead of time—the longer it marinates, the better it tastes. Enjoy it during the peak of the growing season, when vine-ripened tomatoes fill the local markets.

Dressing

½ cup	olive oil	125 mL
¼ cup	red wine vinegar	50 mL
1 tsp.	rosemary	5 mL
1 tsp.	oregano	5 mL
½ tsp.	dry mustard	2 mL
1	clove garlic, crushed	1
¼ tsp.	marjoram	1 mL
	Salt & freshly ground pepper	

Salad

4	large tomatoes, cut into wedges	6
½ cup	marinated black olives	125 mL
½	English cucumber, halved lengthwise & sliced	½
1	green pepper, chopped	1
½	red onion, sliced into rings	½
⅓ lb.	feta cheese	170 g

Shake dressing ingredients in a jar to blend. Place salad ingredients in a bowl, pour dressing over, and toss. Cover, and refrigerate until ready to use.

Serves 4 to 6.

Salads & Dressings

PANZANELLA
(Tomato Salad With Croutons)

Vine-ripened tomatoes that have never been refrigerated are essential to this sweet-tasting salad. Traditional versions allow the croutons to steep in the salad for 30 minutes, but tossing the mixture together at the last moment helps the croutons retain their crunch.

1½ cups	peasant-style Italian bread, crusts removed, cut into cubes	375 mL
1 cup	tomatoes, cubed	250 mL
¾ cup	cucumber, peeled, seeded & diced	175 mL
⅓ cup	chopped red onion	75 mL
6	fresh basil leaves or ½ tsp. (2 mL) dried	6
3 Tbsp.	olive oil	45 mL
1 Tbsp.	red wine vinegar	15 mL
¼ tsp.	freshly ground pepper	1 mL

Preheat oven to 425°F (220°C). Toast bread cubes on a baking sheet for 15 minutes or until golden and crisp. Set aside to cool. In a medium-sized bowl, combine tomatoes, cucumber, onion and basil with oil, vinegar and pepper. Add croutons, and toss to coat evenly. Serve immediately.
    Serves 4.

CHICKEN WITH CUCUMBER & CASHEWS

This delicious salad can be served as a starter or as a main course.

1 Tbsp.	gingerroot, chopped	15 mL
2 tsp.	Szechuan peppers, chopped	10 mL
2 Tbsp.	sherry	25 mL
2	chicken breasts, skinned & boned	2
½ cup	roasted cashews	125 mL
½ cup	cucumber, diced	125 mL
1	green onion, chopped	1
1 Tbsp.	hoisin sauce	15 mL
1 Tbsp.	vinegar	15 mL
3 Tbsp.	tahini	45 mL
1 tsp.	chili oil	5 mL

Combine gingerroot, peppers and sherry, then toss gently with chicken, and marinate for 1 hour. Sauté chicken in a little butter, cool, and cube.
    Toss chicken with cashews, cucumber and onion. Combine hoisin sauce, vinegar and tahini, and toss with chicken mixture. Drizzle oil over salad when ready to serve.
    Serves 6.

ORANGE-WALNUT CHICKEN SALAD

Serve this salad on a bed of lettuce as a healthy main course at lunch with freshly baked muffins.

8	oranges	8
3 cups	cooked chicken, diced	750 mL
1	red onion, thinly sliced	1
1 cup	chopped walnuts	250 mL
2 Tbsp.	parsley, chopped	25 mL
2 Tbsp.	mayonnaise	25 mL

Peel oranges, and remove pith. Slice into rounds, removing seeds. Add remaining ingredients, and toss.
    Serves 4 to 6.

TUSCANY CHICKEN & BREAD SALAD

The inspiration for this savory salad comes from Tuscany, where fresh herbs, tomatoes and bread are a feature of every meal.

3	chicken breasts, split, skinned & boned	3
2 Tbsp.	olive oil	25 mL
$\frac{1}{2}$ tsp.	fresh rosemary, chopped	2 mL
1	clove garlic, minced	1
	Salt & freshly ground pepper	
8	thick slices Italian bread	8
3	tomatoes, diced	3
1	English cucumber, diced	1
2	celery stalks, diced	2
$\frac{1}{3}$ cup	black olives	75 mL
$\frac{1}{4}$ cup	fresh parsley, chopped	50 mL
$\frac{1}{4}$ cup	fresh basil, chopped	50 mL
$\frac{1}{4}$ cup	green onions, chopped	50 mL

Dressing

$\frac{2}{3}$ cup	olive oil	150 mL
$\frac{1}{4}$ cup	red wine vinegar	50 mL
1 tsp.	salt	5 mL
$\frac{1}{2}$ tsp.	freshly ground pepper	2 mL
$\frac{1}{4}$ tsp.	hot pepper sauce	1 mL
2	cloves garlic, minced	2
	Fresh lemon juice (opt.)	

Pat chicken breasts dry. In a shallow dish, combine oil, rosemary, garlic and salt and pepper to taste. Add chicken breasts, and turn to coat well. Marinate chicken in refrigerator for at least 15 minutes or up to 8 hours.

Toast bread until lightly browned, and cut into 1-inch (2.5 cm) cubes. In a large serving dish, combine bread cubes, tomatoes, cucumber, celery, olives, parsley, basil and onions.

To make dressing, blend oil, vinegar, salt, pepper, hot pepper sauce and garlic. Pour over bread-vegetable mixture, and toss to coat. Taste and adjust seasoning with salt, pepper and a dash of lemon juice, if desired.

Grill chicken breasts over medium-high heat for 6 to 8 minutes per side or until no longer pink inside. Slice thinly on the diagonal, and serve on top of the bread salad.

Serves 6.

TURKEY & GREENS WITH CRANBERRY VINAIGRETTE

A natural for holiday leftovers, this salad is delicious anytime during the year.

Vinaigrette

½ cup	cranberry sauce	125 mL
2	shallots, finely chopped	2
2 Tbsp.	balsamic vinegar	25 mL
2 Tbsp.	fresh orange or grapefruit juice	25 mL
6 Tbsp.	extra-virgin olive oil	75 mL

Salad

2	pink grapefruit	2
12 cups	mixed salad greens	3 L
3 cups	cooked turkey, diced	750 mL
1 cup	toasted walnut pieces	250 mL
¼ cup	dried cranberries (opt.)	50 mL

To make vinaigrette, combine cranberry sauce, shallots, vinegar and juice in a food processor or a blender, and process until smooth. Slowly drizzle in oil, with the motor running, until the oil is completely incorporated.

To make salad, peel grapefruit with a sharp knife, removing all pith. Cut grapefruit segments away from surrounding membranes. Combine greens and turkey in a large salad bowl. Add vinaigrette, and toss. Arrange grapefruit sections over tossed salad, and sprinkle with walnuts and dried cranberries, if desired. Serve immediately.

Serves 4 to 6.

HOW TO ROAST & PEEL PEPPERS

To roast peppers, broil or grill 4 inches (10 cm) from heat, turning to brown all over, for 15 minutes or until puffed and charred. (Or roast in a 375°F/190°C oven for 30 minutes or until lightly browned.) Let cool. (Roasted peppers may be placed in a paper bag for 15 minutes to cool, making the skins easier to remove.) Peel and seed, then dice or cut into strips as recipe directs.

Julienned strips of roasted red, green and yellow bell peppers tossed with a few splashes of balsamic vinegar make a simple summer salad.

SHRIMP QUESADILLA SALAD

Fresh garden greens, shrimp, corn and sweet peppers offer a medley of colors, flavors and textures in this Mexico-inspired dish. Pita bread split horizontally can be used instead of the flour tortillas.

Filling

¾ lb.	cooked shrimp, diced	375 g
2	red bell peppers, roasted, peeled & chopped (facing page)	2
2	jalapeño peppers (or other hot peppers), seeded & diced	2
1 cup	cooked kernel corn	250 mL
½ cup	fresh cilantro, chopped	125 mL
½ cup	fresh chives or green onions, chopped	125 mL
1	small red onion, diced	1
2	cloves garlic, minced	2
1 tsp.	cumin	5 mL
¼ tsp.	cayenne pepper	1 mL
3 cups	grated Monterey Jack cheese	750 mL
9	flour tortillas	9

Salad

8 cups	mixed salad greens	2 L
⅓ cup	olive oil	75 mL
2 Tbsp.	red wine vinegar	25 mL
2 Tbsp.	fresh cilantro, chopped	25 mL
2 Tbsp.	fresh basil, chopped	25 mL
½ tsp.	salt	2 mL
¼ tsp.	freshly ground pepper	1 mL

To make filling, combine shrimp, red and jalapeño peppers, corn, cilantro, chives, onion, garlic, cumin, cayenne and cheese.

Arrange 3 tortillas on a baking sheet, and top with half the filling. Place a second tortilla on each, and spread with rest of filling. Top with the 3 remaining tortillas. Just before serving, bake the tortilla "cakes" in a 400°F (200°C) oven for 10 to 15 minutes or until crisp and brown.

To make salad, place greens in a large bowl. Whisk together oil, vinegar, cilantro, basil, salt and pepper. Just before serving, pour dressing over greens and toss. Divide greens among 6 serving plates. Cut each tortilla cake into 8 wedges using your sharpest kitchen knife. Place 4 wedges on top of each salad.

Serves 6.

GRILLED VEGETABLE SALAD WITH CHÈVRE DIP & GARLIC TOAST

The earthy taste of grilled vegetables is a perfect foil for the tart bite of creamy goat cheese.

1 lb.	eggplant	500 g
	Salt	
2 Tbsp.	olive oil	25 mL
2	small zucchini	2
1	red onion	1
2	red bell peppers	2
2	yellow bell peppers	2
1 lb.	asparagus	500 g
1	bulb fennel	1

Chèvre Dip

¼ lb.	chèvre or cream cheese	125 g
½ cup	yogurt or sour cream	125 mL
¼ cup	mayonnaise	50 mL
1 Tbsp.	fresh chives, chopped	15 mL
½ tsp.	fresh thyme, chopped	2 mL
½ tsp.	fresh rosemary, chopped	2 mL
¼ tsp.	freshly ground pepper	1 mL

Garlic Toast

2 Tbsp.	olive oil	25 mL
2	cloves garlic, minced	2
½ tsp.	salt	2 mL
	Small loaf crusty Italian bread, sliced ½ inch (1 cm) thick	

Cut eggplant into ½-inch (1 cm) slices. Sprinkle lightly with salt, and place in a colander; let drain for 30 minutes. Pat dry, brush with oil, and grill for 5 to 8 minutes on each side, until tender and well browned. Cut slices in half.

While eggplant is draining, slice zucchini lengthwise into ½-inch (1 cm) strips; peel onion, and slice into ½-inch (1 cm) rounds. Brush zucchini and onion with oil, and grill for about 5 minutes, until lightly browned on both sides.

Grill red and yellow peppers until blackened all over. Let cool. Remove and discard peel, core, ribs and seeds. Cut peppers into strips.

Trim asparagus, and if it's tough, peel about 2 inches (5 cm) up the stalk. Brush with oil, and grill, turning frequently, just until tender. Trim fennel, and slice; brush with oil, and grill until tender and lightly browned on both sides.

To make chèvre dip, combine chèvre, yogurt, mayonnaise, chives, thyme, rosemary and pepper in a blender or a food processor; blend until smooth. Divide dip among 6 small ramekins.

To make garlic toast, combine oil, garlic and salt; brush both sides of bread slices. Place on a baking sheet, and broil until lightly browned on both sides.

To serve, place one ramekin of chèvre dip on each serving plate. Divide vegetables among plates, and serve with garlic toast.

Serves 6.

Salads & Dressings

HOT POTATO & BEET SALAD

With the addition of beets, this variation on a traditional German hot potato salad is full of extra color and flavor. Handle the potatoes and beets carefully to prevent the color from running.

6	medium beets, scrubbed	6
10	small potatoes, peeled & sliced	10
2	eggs	2
$\frac{1}{4}$ cup	butter	50 mL
$1\frac{1}{2}$ cups	sour cream	375 mL
	Salt & freshly ground pepper	
4 Tbsp.	fresh dill, chopped	50 mL

Cook beets and potatoes separately until tender. Peel and slice beets. Arrange potatoes and beets in alternating overlaps in a shallow bowl, and keep warm.

In the top of a double boiler, beat eggs, then add butter and sour cream. Cook and stir over simmering water until all are well combined. Season with salt and pepper to taste. Pour over vegetables, and top with dill. Serve immediately.

Serves 6.

SPAGHETTI SALAD WITH TUNA

A fast warm-weather meal, this is pasta salad with a difference. Tuna packed in olive oil has extra flavor, but tuna packed in water is for the health-conscious.

$\frac{1}{3}$ cup	olive oil	75 mL
$\frac{1}{2}$ cup	extra-large black olives, pitted & quartered	125 mL
$\frac{1}{3}$ cup	fresh parsley, chopped	75 mL
$\frac{1}{3}$ cup	fresh basil, chopped	75 mL
$\frac{1}{3}$ cup	fresh chives, chopped	75 mL
2 Tbsp.	drained capers	25 mL
$\frac{1}{4}$ tsp.	red pepper flakes	1 mL
1	red or yellow bell pepper, roasted, peeled & diced (page 60)	1
2	cloves garlic, minced	2
2	cans tuna, drained & flaked	2
2 Tbsp.	balsamic vinegar	25 mL
1 Tbsp.	lemon juice	15 mL
1 tsp.	salt	5 mL
$\frac{1}{2}$ tsp.	freshly ground pepper	2 mL
$\frac{3}{4}$ lb.	spaghetti, fusilli or penne	375 g

In a large serving bowl, combine oil, olives, parsley, basil, chives, capers, red pepper flakes, bell pepper, garlic and tuna. Sprinkle with vinegar, lemon juice, salt and pepper. Marinate at room temperature for up to 30 minutes.

Just before serving, cook spaghetti in a large pot of boiling salted water until barely tender. Drain well, and toss with salad ingredients. Serve immediately, slightly warm or at room temperature.

Serves 4.

Salads & Dressings

PASTA SALAD WITH OLIVES & BLUE CHEESE

This salad is rich with eggs and the pungent flavor of blue cheese. More manageable penne, farfalle or rotini can be used instead of strand pasta.

2 lb.	fresh spaghetti or fettuccine	1 kg
2	cloves garlic	2
2	eggs	2
6 Tbsp.	red wine vinegar	75 mL
1 tsp.	dry mustard	5 mL
	Salt & freshly ground pepper	
2 cups	oil	500 mL
⅔ cup	crumbled blue cheese	150 mL
2	celery stalks	2
1	green pepper	1
1	bunch green onions	1
1 cup	pitted black olives	250 mL

Cook pasta in rapidly boiling salted water until just tender—2 to 3 minutes for fresh pasta. Rinse under cold running water, then drain.

To make dressing, place garlic, eggs, vinegar, mustard and salt and pepper in a blender or a food processor. Add 1 cup (250 mL) oil, and blend until all ingredients are well mixed. Slowly add remaining oil, with machine running, until a thick mayonnaise results. Add cheese, and blend until smooth.

Mince celery, green pepper and onions. Toss vegetables, olives and pasta together. Add dressing, and toss gently to blend. Chill well.

Serves 8.

VIETNAMESE NOODLE SALAD

This salad is both sweet and tangy at the same time, thanks to the unusual flavor blend of mint, shrimp, peanuts and rice noodles. It is refreshing in summer but is also a welcome addition in the cooler months, when salad greens are harder to come by.

½ lb.	rice noodles (rice sticks)	250 g
1½ cups	cucumber, peeled & diced	375 mL
½ lb.	small cooked shrimp	250 g
2	scallions, trimmed & sliced diagonally	2
¼ cup	peanut or vegetable oil	50 mL
¼ cup	white vinegar	50 mL
4 tsp.	sugar	20 mL
	Dash Chinese chili oil	
2 Tbsp.	fresh mint, chopped, or 1 Tbsp. (15 mL) dried	25 mL
½ cup	roasted, unsalted peanuts, coarsely chopped	125 mL

Soak rice noodles in warm water for 15 minutes. Drain, and cook in boiling salted water for 1 minute or until tender but still firm. Drain, and rinse thoroughly with cold water. Place in a serving bowl. Add cucumber, shrimp and scallions.

In a small saucepan, stir together oil, vinegar, sugar and chili oil over low heat until sugar has dissolved. Pour over the rice-noodle mixture, add mint, and toss. Sprinkle peanuts over top. Serve immediately, or refrigerate for up to 2 hours.

Serves 4 to 6.

Salads & Dressings

SUNBURST SALAD

Complex carbohydrates, fresh herbs and vegetables and refreshing oranges make this grain-based salad hearty and satisfying.

1¼ cups	wheat berries, uncooked	300 mL
1	orange, halved crosswise	1
1	cucumber, peeled, seeded & chopped	1
4	scallions, sliced	4
2 Tbsp.	fresh parsley, chopped	25 mL
½ cup	dried fruit, soaked in hot water to soften, then sliced (try apricots & peaches)	125 mL
¼ cup	toasted nuts or seeds, preferably pepitas (pumpkin seeds)	50 mL
3 Tbsp.	lemon juice	45 mL
2 Tbsp.	olive oil	25 mL
1 Tbsp.	Dijon mustard	15 mL
1 tsp.	fresh mint, chopped, or ½ tsp. (2 mL) dried	5 mL
¼ tsp.	cinnamon	1 mL

Place wheat berries in 3½ cups (875 mL) water, and simmer, covered, for 1 to 1½ hours or until tender. (The wheat berries will expand when cooked to produce 3 cups/750 mL.)

Scoop the segments out of the orange as you would with a grapefruit. In a large bowl, combine wheat berries, orange segments and any remaining juice from the orange, cucumber, scallions, parsley, dried fruit and toasted nuts or seeds. (To toast nuts or seeds, place on a baking sheet in a 350°F/180°C oven for 7 to 10 minutes.)

Whisk together remaining ingredients, and pour over salad. Toss to combine. Chill salad for at least 1 hour before serving.

Serves 5.

TOASTED QUINOA SALAD

Well suited for summer salads, quinoa is lighter than other grains and tastes best when it is dry-toasted before it is simmered in water.

½ cup	pepitas (pumpkin seeds)	125 mL
¾ cup	quinoa, uncooked	175 mL
1 cup	carrot, diced	250 mL
½	red bell pepper, chopped	½
¼ cup	fresh parsley, chopped	50 mL
2	scallions, sliced	2
	Juice of 1 lemon	
4 tsp.	soy sauce	20 mL
6	drops hot pepper sauce	6
1	clove garlic, minced	1

Toast pepitas by placing them on a baking sheet in a 350°F (180°C) oven for 7 to 10 minutes.

Rinse quinoa in water. Drain, put in a pot, and dry-toast until a few grains begin to pop. Add 1½ cups (375 mL) water, bring to a boil, cover, and simmer for 15 minutes or until the quinoa has absorbed all the liquid. Remove from heat, and let stand for 10 minutes. Fluff with a fork.

Mix pepitas, carrot, red pepper, parsley and scallions in a large bowl. When quinoa has cooled, add to the bowl and stir to combine.

Whisk together remaining ingredients. Pour over salad, and toss to mix.

Serves 5.

QUINOA WITH SUN-DRIED TOMATOES

Quinoa, an ancient Peruvian grain, has a nutty, sweet flavor that is excellent with tomatoes and shallots.

1 cup	quinoa, uncooked	250 mL
1 tsp.	butter	5 mL
8	sun-dried tomatoes (not oil-packed), diced	8
2	shallots, minced	2
1	clove garlic, minced	1
2 cups	chicken stock or water	500 mL
	Pinch cayenne pepper	
2 Tbsp.	fresh parsley, chopped	25 mL
	Salt & freshly ground pepper	

Place quinoa in a fine-meshed sieve, and rinse under warm running water for 1 minute. Set aside.

Heat butter in a heavy, medium saucepan over medium heat. Add tomatoes, shallots and garlic, and sauté for 3 to 5 minutes or until the shallots are softened. Add chicken stock, and bring to a boil. Stir in quinoa and cayenne, return to a boil, then reduce heat to low, and simmer, covered, for about 30 minutes or until the liquid is absorbed. Let sit for 5 minutes, and fluff grains with a fork to separate. Stir in parsley, and season with salt and pepper.

Serves 4.

PROVENÇAL TABOULI SALAD

Every delicatessen in France has its own version of tabouli, all using couscous. Traditionalists of Middle Eastern cooking, however, prefer cracked wheat.

1 cup	couscous, uncooked	250 mL
1⅓ cups	boiling water	325 mL
1	red bell pepper, roasted, peeled & diced	1
1	yellow bell pepper, roasted, peeled & diced (page 60)	1
2	tomatoes, seeded & diced	2
1	can (19 oz./540 mL) chickpeas, drained	1
½ cup	fresh parsley, chopped	125 mL
¼ cup	fresh mint, chopped	50 mL
¼ cup	fresh basil, chopped	50 mL
¼ cup	fresh chives, chopped	50 mL
Dressing		
¼ cup	olive oil	50 mL
¼ cup	lemon juice	50 mL
1	clove garlic, minced	1
1 tsp.	salt	5 mL
½ tsp.	freshly ground pepper	2 mL
½ lb.	feta cheese, crumbled	250 g

In a 6-cup (1.5 L) casserole, combine couscous and boiling water. Cover with foil, and let stand for 15 minutes. Fluff gently with a fork.

Meanwhile, in a large serving bowl, combine red and yellow peppers, tomatoes, chickpeas, parsley, mint, basil and chives. Toss gently with couscous.

Dressing: Whisk together oil, lemon juice, garlic, salt and pepper. Drizzle over couscous mixture, sprinkle with cheese, and toss gently.

Serves 6.

Spaghetti Salad With Tuna

Salads & Dressings, page 63

Couscous Niçoise

Salads & Dressings, page 69

Salads & Dressings

CRACKED WHEAT SALAD

This healthy grain salad is an ideal solution to the problem of what to take to the office for lunch.

1 cup	bulgur or cracked wheat, uncooked, preferably medium-ground	250 mL
1	tomato, diced	1
1 cup	scallions, minced	250 mL
2	cloves garlic, minced	2
$\frac{1}{3}$ cup	lemon juice	75 mL
2 Tbsp.	olive oil	25 mL
3 Tbsp.	fresh parsley, chopped	45 mL
2 Tbsp.	fresh mint leaves, chopped, or 2 tsp. (10 mL) dried	25 mL
$\frac{1}{2}$-1 tsp.	soy sauce	2-5 mL
$\frac{1}{4}$ tsp.	freshly ground pepper	1 mL
	Pinch cayenne pepper	
	Romaine lettuce (opt.)	

Pour 2 cups (500 mL) boiling water over bulgur, and let sit for 30 to 45 minutes until tender. (Bulgur wheat varies in coarseness. The coarser the grind, the longer it needs to soak; finely ground needs only about 10 minutes.) Drain, and press out excess liquid. Combine remaining ingredients, except lettuce, then mix with the softened bulgur. Serve on a bed of romaine lettuce, if desired.

Serves 4.

COUSCOUS NIÇOISE

A colorful accompaniment to plain roast chicken or broiled fish, Couscous Niçoise can also serve as a salad if you splash on extra vinegar. Niçoise olives—tiny, dark brown salt-brine-cured olives from France—are available in specialty shops, or you can substitute another good-quality black olive, such as Kalamata or Gaeta.

1¼ cups	chicken stock or water	300 mL
½ tsp.	salt	2 mL
2	cloves garlic, minced	2
1½ tsp.	olive oil, preferably extra-virgin	7 mL
1½ cups	medium-grain couscous	375 mL
8	cherry tomatoes, cut into slivers	8
¼ cup	niçoise olives, pitted & sliced	50 mL
8	fresh basil leaves, cut into julienne strips, or 1 Tbsp. (15 mL) fresh parsley, coarsely chopped	8
1 Tbsp.	red wine vinegar	15 mL
	Salt & freshly ground pepper	

Combine chicken stock, salt, garlic and oil in a medium saucepan with a tight-fitting lid, and bring to a boil. Stir in couscous, and remove from heat. Cover, and let stand for 5 minutes. Uncover, and fluff with a fork to separate the grains.

Add tomatoes, olives, basil and vinegar, and toss until completely mixed. Season with salt and pepper. Serve warm or at room temperature.

Serves 6.

Salads & Dressings

ALL-SEASON BLACK BEAN SALAD

The ingredients for this salad are available year-round, and the preparation is simple.

1½ cups	black beans, uncooked	375 mL
1	red bell pepper, chopped	1
½	green pepper, chopped	½
¼	red onion, chopped	¼
2	whole scallions, sliced	2
1	celery stalk, finely chopped	1
2	oranges, halved crosswise	2
4 tsp.	lemon juice	20 mL
1 tsp.	olive oil	5 mL
½ tsp.	cumin	2 mL
¼ tsp.	hot pepper sauce	1 mL
¼ tsp.	salt	1 mL
¼ tsp.	coriander	1 mL

Cover beans with water, and soak overnight. Drain, and simmer, uncovered, in 6 cups (1.5 L) fresh water, for 1 to 1½ hours or until tender. Drain, rinse in cold water, and cool slightly. (The beans will expand when cooked to produce 3 cups/750 mL.)

In a large bowl, combine beans, red and green peppers, onion, scallions and celery, tossing well. Scoop out orange segments as you would with a grapefruit. Add segments to the bean mixture, and squeeze in the remaining juice from the orange. Take care not to drop in any orange seeds.

Whisk remaining ingredients together (or shake in a glass jar), pour over salad, and toss to coat.

Serves 6.

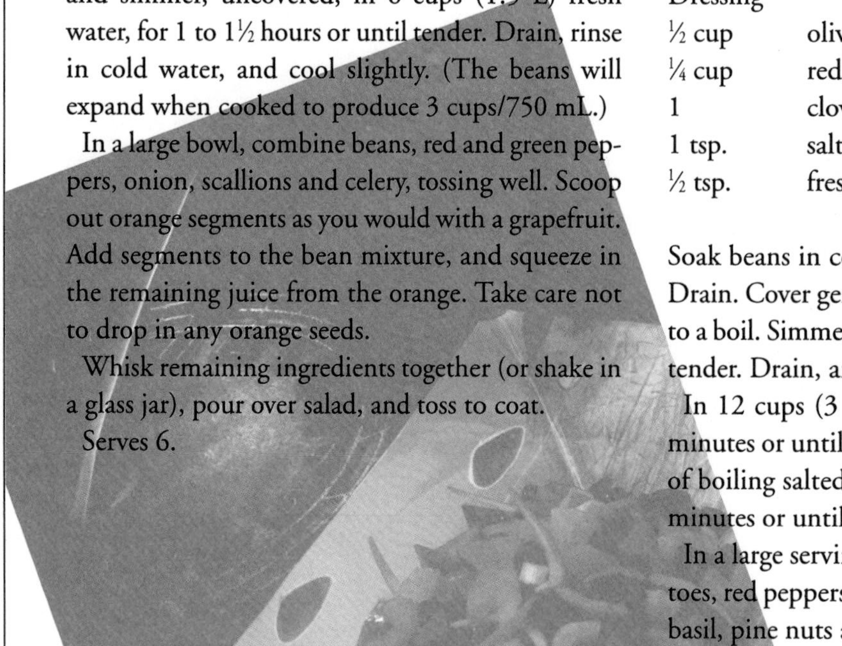

BLACK BEAN & RICE SALAD

Fresh herbs accent the wonderful flavors of this colorful vegetarian bean salad. Perfect for summer.

1 cup	black beans, uncooked	250 mL
1 cup	basmati or other scented rice	250 mL
2	new potatoes, diced	2
2	red bell peppers, roasted, peeled & diced (page 60)	2
1	jalapeño pepper, seeded & diced	1
1	bunch arugula or watercress, trimmed & chopped	1
½ cup	fresh cilantro, chopped	125 mL
⅓ cup	fresh basil, chopped	75 mL
⅓ cup	pine nuts, toasted	75 mL
2 Tbsp.	fresh mint, chopped	25 mL

Dressing

½ cup	olive oil	125 mL
¼ cup	red wine vinegar	50 mL
1	clove garlic, minced	1
1 tsp.	salt	5 mL
½ tsp.	freshly ground pepper	2 mL

Soak beans in cold water overnight in refrigerator. Drain. Cover generously with fresh water, and bring to a boil. Simmer gently for 1 hour or until beans are tender. Drain, and set aside.

In 12 cups (3 L) boiling water, cook rice for 12 minutes or until tender. Drain. Meanwhile, in a pot of boiling salted water, cook potatoes for about 10 minutes or until tender. Drain.

In a large serving bowl, combine beans, rice, potatoes, red peppers, jalapeño pepper, arugula, cilantro, basil, pine nuts and mint.

To make dressing, whisk together oil, vinegar, garlic, salt and pepper. Drizzle over black-bean mixture. Taste, and adjust seasoning, adding more vinegar, if desired.

Serves 6.

SPANISH RICE SALAD

Tofu or tempeh instead of chicken makes this a zesty vegetarian salad.

1 cup	long-grain brown rice, uncooked	250 mL
¾ cup	tomato juice	175 mL
¼ cup	red wine vinegar	50 mL
¼ cup	olive oil	50 mL
1 tsp.	thyme	5 mL
¼ tsp.	hot pepper sauce	1 mL
¼ tsp.	paprika	1 mL
1	small clove garlic, minced, or ¼ tsp. (1 mL) garlic powder	1
¼ tsp.	salt	1 mL
2	tomatoes, chopped	2
1	green pepper, chopped	1
1	red bell pepper, chopped	1
¼	red onion, thinly sliced	¼
¼ cup	fresh parsley, chopped	50 mL
1 lb.	boneless, skinless chicken breast, poached & cut into bite-sized chunks	500 g

Cook rice, covered, in ½ cup (125 mL) tomato juice and 1½ cups (375 mL) water for 40 to 45 minutes. It will be sticky but more flavorful than rice cooked in water only. Allow rice to cool to room temperature.

Whisk together remaining ¼ cup (50 mL) tomato juice, vinegar, oil, thyme, hot pepper sauce, paprika, garlic and salt. Combine rice, tomatoes, green and red peppers, onion, parsley and chicken. Pour dressing over all, and toss to coat.

Serves 6.

THE PERFECT FOOD

Made from soybeans, tofu is a complete protein and an excellent source of nutrition for vegetarians. Tofu's mild taste makes it a natural vegetarian alternative in a variety of seasoned dishes, yet inexperienced cooks working with tofu often object to its unfamiliar texture. To maximize its potential, cut tofu into small pieces before adding to stir-frys or stews, and be sure to choose a firm-textured variety when preparing a recipe that uses tofu as its featured ingredient. In salads, when you want the tofu to keep its shape, select the firm variety or increase its density by pressing out excess moisture through a sieve.

Salads & Dressings

INDONESIAN RICE SALAD

This salad can stand on its own without the chicken or tofu—just reduce the dressing or add more vegetables, such as snow peas.

½ lb.	boneless, skinless chicken breast or tofu	250 g
	Indonesian Sauce (recipe follows)	
1 cup	cooked brown rice	250 mL
½ cup	bean sprouts	125 mL
½	red bell pepper, chopped	½
½ cup	cooked peas	125 mL
2	scallions, sliced	2
1	can (8 oz./213 mL) unsweetened pineapple chunks, drained	1
½ cup	water chestnuts, sliced, or jicama, peeled, sliced & cut into bite-sized pieces	125 mL
2 Tbsp.	orange juice	25 mL
½ tsp.	soy sauce	2 mL

Cut chicken into cubes. Reserve 2 Tbsp. (25 mL) Indonesian Sauce, and marinate chicken in remainder for 1 hour (if using tofu, marinate overnight). Bake on a baking sheet lined with parchment at 350°F (180°C) for about 20 minutes (if using tofu, bake at 425°F/220°C for 15 minutes). Shake the pan several times during baking to loosen the cubes. Turn cubes over, and bake until crisp, about 15 minutes.

Combine rice, bean sprouts, red pepper, peas, scallions, pineapple and water chestnuts. When the chicken or tofu cools, add to the rice mixture. Whisk together reserved Indonesian Sauce, orange juice and soy sauce. Pour over salad, and stir gently to mix well.
Serves 4.

INDONESIAN SAUCE

4 tsp.	lime juice	20 mL
2 Tbsp.	chunky unsalted peanut butter	25 mL
2 tsp.	soy sauce	10 mL
1 Tbsp.	Dijon mustard	15 mL
1 Tbsp.	honey	15 mL
¼ tsp.	hot pepper sauce	1 mL
	Pinch red pepper flakes or cayenne pepper (opt.)	

Puree all ingredients with 4 tsp. (20 mL) water in a food processor.
Makes ⅜ cup (100 mL).

Chapter 4

MAIN COURSES

ell me what you eat, and I will tell you what you are," wrote Anthelme Brillat-Savarin in the early 19th century in *The Physiology of Taste*. It would be interesting to hear how the French gourmet would interpret the comfortably eclectic tastes that have produced the "Pantry" department in *Harrowsmith Country Life*, which are nowhere more apparent than in this chapter. We hope the recipes set out here will reacquaint you with the charm and pleasure that come from simple, unfussy cooking. They provide a wide selection of dishes that will inspire warm feelings and lively conversation, whether served at the conclusion of a hectic workday or to family and friends celebrating a special occasion.

Our inventory of main-course meals incorporates the best in family-style cooking and will please a broad range of tastes—from potpies to stews, savory Mediterranean meals infused with the earthy flavors of olive oil, garlic and herbs, Indian cooking that tickles the senses with the pungent spices of cumin and coriander and Asian cuisine with its contradictory spicy, sour and sweet sensations simultaneously teasing the palate. Each offering underscores the virtually limitless possibilities of creating something distinctive from the same natural ingredients.

That home cooks everywhere make the most of these fresh ingredients, combined in interesting and satisfying recipes, reaffirms our belief that the preparation of good food does not have to be complicated. This chapter expresses our appreciation for cooks the world over, and we trust it also reflects something of who we are, members of the fellowship of cooks whose delicious regional cuisines unite us regardless of nationality.

Main Courses

GREEN PEPPERS STUFFED WITH BACON & BASIL

Old-fashioned, rich and satisfying, these stuffed peppers are excellent alone or with a simple tomato sauce. They make a delightful meal accompanied by a refreshing salad.

3	large green peppers	3
16	slices bacon	16
1	clove garlic, crushed	1
$\frac{1}{2}$ cup	green onion, chopped	125 mL
8 Tbsp.	fine fresh breadcrumbs	100 mL
2 Tbsp.	heavy cream	25 mL
2	eggs, lightly beaten	2
$\frac{1}{2}$ cup	grated Parmesan cheese	125 mL
1 cup	chicken stock	250 mL
$\frac{1}{4}$ cup	fresh basil or $\frac{1}{2}$ cup (125 mL) fresh parsley	50 mL
$\frac{1}{2}$ tsp.	freshly grated nutmeg	2 mL
	Freshly ground pepper	

Wash, de-stem, halve and core green peppers; blanch in boiling salted water for 1 minute; drain.

Fry bacon in a large skillet until crisp, then drain on paper towels, and crumble. Discard $\frac{1}{4}$ cup (50 mL) bacon fat, then add garlic and onion, and cook until wilted. Add remaining ingredients (except $\frac{1}{2}$ cup/125 mL chicken stock), including bacon. Mix well.

Stuff peppers, pour remaining chicken stock around them, cover, and bake for 30 minutes at 400°F (200°C). Uncover, and bake for 10 minutes longer or until nicely browned.

Serves 6.

GREEK RICE & BEEF STUFFING

Dark, chunky and robust, this stuffing, which is suitable for eggplants or tomatoes, can easily stand alone as a main course.

$1\frac{1}{2}$ cups	chicken stock	375 mL
1 cup	white rice, uncooked	250 mL
5 Tbsp.	unsalted butter	65 mL
1	small onion, chopped	1
$1\frac{1}{2}$ lb.	lean ground beef	750 g
1 cup	raisins	250 mL
1 cup	toasted almonds, chopped	250 mL
$\frac{1}{2}$ cup	chestnut puree (opt.)	125 mL
1	egg, lightly beaten	1
$1\frac{1}{2}$ tsp.	cinnamon	7 mL
$\frac{1}{2}$ tsp.	cloves	2 mL
$\frac{3}{4}$ tsp.	salt	4 mL
	Freshly ground pepper	

In a small saucepan, bring chicken stock to a simmer. Add rice, cover, and simmer on low for 17 minutes.

Meanwhile, heat butter in a skillet, and sauté onion until transparent. Add ground beef, and cook until it loses its pink color. Add remaining ingredients, and toss well. Spoon into a well-greased soufflé dish or casserole, and bake at 350°F (180°C) for 25 minutes.

If you are using this stuffing for eggplants, split about three 1 lb. (500 g) eggplants in half lengthwise, and run a paring knife around the inside rim about $\frac{1}{4}$ inch (5 mm) from the outside skin. Score inside flesh of eggplants, and brush tops with olive oil. Place the halves on a greased cookie sheet, and bake at 425°F (220°C) for 30 minutes.

When eggplants are cooked, scrape out pulp (leaving a shell $\frac{1}{4}$ inch/5 mm thick), chop it, and add to beef mixture. Fill eggplant shells with equal portions of stuffing. Place eggplants in oven, and bake at 375°F (190°C) for 35 minutes.

Serves 6.

BEEF STEW WITH LEEKS & MUSHROOMS

For this voluptuously rich French stew, use beef shin, a highly flavorful cut, which becomes tender when slowly simmered in the oven.

2½ lb.	beef shin with marrowbones	1.1 kg
2	medium onions	2
6 Tbsp.	vegetable oil	75 mL
3	cloves garlic, minced	3
3	leeks, well washed & cut into pieces	3
3 Tbsp.	flour	45 mL
1½ cups	beef stock made from shin marrowbones	375 mL
1½ cups	dry red wine	375 mL
½ cup	cognac	125 mL
2 Tbsp.	tomato paste	25 mL
1	bay leaf	1
½ tsp.	rosemary	2 mL
½ tsp.	thyme	2 mL
¼ tsp.	nutmeg	1 mL
¼ tsp.	allspice	1 mL
1 tsp.	salt	5 mL
1 tsp.	freshly ground pepper	5 mL
3	carrots, sliced into rounds	3
8	small red potatoes with skins on, washed & cut into chunks	8
6	onions, quartered	6
8 oz.	mushrooms, halved	250 g
½ cup	fresh parsley, chopped	125 mL

Remove meat from marrowbones, trim excess fat, and cut meat into 1½-inch (4 cm) pieces; set aside.

Brown marrowbones in a heavy oiled pot, then add 2½ cups (625 mL) cold water and 1 onion, chopped. Simmer for 1 to 2 hours.

In a Dutch oven, brown meat on both sides in 2 Tbsp. (25 mL) oil, and set aside. Add 2 Tbsp. (25 mL) oil, or as necessary, and sauté remaining onion, chopped, garlic and leeks until soft. Stir in flour, and cook until it colors slightly.

Strain beef stock, and add 1 cup (250 mL) to the pot, along with wine, cognac, tomato paste, meat and seasonings. Simmer, covered, in a 300°F (150°C) oven for 1½ hours. Add carrots, potatoes, quartered onions and ½ cup (125 mL) stock. Simmer for 1 hour longer or until vegetables are tender. During the last 30 minutes, sauté mushrooms in 2 Tbsp. (25 mL) oil, and add to the pot. Skim fat. Stir in parsley just before serving.

Serves 6.

CHICKEN STEW WITH CORN DUMPLINGS

Dumplings add an unexpected element to this traditional dinnertime fare.

3 lb.	chicken, cut into quarters	1.5 kg
1	onion, peeled & cut into quarters	1
1	carrot, peeled & cut into chunks	1
1	celery stalk, cut into chunks	1
1	bay leaf	1
1 tsp.	whole black peppercorns	5 mL
4½ cups	chicken stock	1.1 L
3 Tbsp.	butter	45 mL
4	leeks, white & tender green parts, cut diagonally into pieces	4
6 Tbsp.	flour	75 mL
½ cup	light cream	125 mL
⅓ cup	dry sherry	75 mL
1 Tbsp.	fresh thyme, chopped, or 1 tsp. (5 mL) dried	15 mL
	Salt & freshly ground pepper	
2	large red bell peppers, cored, seeded & cut into pieces	2
½ lb.	mushrooms, thickly sliced	250 g

Dumplings

1 cup	flour	250 mL
½ cup	cornmeal	125 mL
2 tsp.	sugar	10 mL
2 tsp.	baking powder	10 mL
½ tsp.	baking soda	2 mL
½ tsp.	salt	2 mL
2 Tbsp.	butter, melted	25 mL
1	large egg	1
¾ cup	buttermilk	175 mL
1 cup	corn kernels, fresh or frozen	250 mL
½ cup	red bell pepper, diced	125 mL

Place chicken, onion, carrot, celery, bay leaf and peppercorns in a large pot. Add chicken stock and enough water to cover chicken. Bring to a boil, partially cover, reduce heat to low, and simmer for 40 to 45 minutes or until the juices run clear when chicken is pierced with a skewer. Remove chicken, and set aside to cool.

When cool enough to handle, remove skin and bones and cut chicken meat into large pieces. Set meat aside. Strain chicken broth, pressing vegetables with the back of a spoon to extract the juices. Skim off fat. Measure out 4 cups (1 L) broth, and reserve.

Melt 2 Tbsp. (25 mL) butter in a Dutch oven. Add leeks, and cook over medium heat for 5 minutes or until softened. Add flour, and cook for 1 minute, stirring. Add reserved chicken broth, and bring to a boil. Cook for 6 to 7 minutes, stirring frequently, until thickened. Add cream, sherry, thyme and chicken. Season with salt and pepper.

Meanwhile, in a large skillet, melt the remaining butter. Add red peppers, and sauté over medium-high heat for 2 minutes. Add mushrooms, and continue sautéing for 3 minutes or until mushrooms begin to brown. Add to chicken mixture. (Recipe can be prepared to this point, covered and refrigerated for up to 2 days.)

To make dumplings, bring stew to a simmer. In a large bowl, stir together flour, cornmeal, sugar, baking powder, baking soda and salt. In a small bowl, whisk together butter, egg and buttermilk. Add to flour mixture, along with corn and red pepper. Stir until just combined. Immediately drop by spoonfuls onto the simmering stew, leaving a space between each dumpling. Cover, and cook for 15 to 20 minutes or until dumplings are firm to the touch. Serve directly from the Dutch oven.

Serves 6 to 8.

CHICKEN FRICASSEE WITH DUMPLINGS

The creamy richness of this traditional chicken stew comes from the roux, which is cooked slowly to a golden brown.

4½-5 lb.	chicken, split & jointed	2.1-2.2 kg
	Nutmeg	
	White pepper	
	Paprika	
2½ Tbsp.	vegetable oil	35 mL
3 Tbsp.	flour	45 mL
1 cup	dry white wine	250 mL
2	large shallots, cut into slivers	2
1	medium onion, finely chopped	1
3	leeks, cut into pieces	3
4	carrots, cut into pieces	4
1 cup	celery, cut into pieces	250 mL
2 Tbsp.	butter	25 mL
½ tsp.	thyme	2 mL
1 Tbsp.	chervil	15 mL
1 tsp.	salt	5 mL
½ tsp.	paprika	2 mL
	Cheese-Herb Dumplings (recipe follows)	

Sprinkle chicken on both sides with nutmeg, pepper and paprika. Heat oil in a heavy stew pot, and brown chicken in batches. Set aside. Reduce heat, and add flour, scraping up browned bits with a spoon. Cook the roux, mashing lumps, until it colors to a light brown. Be careful not to let it burn. Whisk in 3 cups (750 mL) water and the wine, and return chicken to the pot. Simmer, covered, for 45 minutes to 1 hour. Strain stock through a colander, and set aside. Cool chicken in colander over a bowl.

In a Dutch oven, sauté vegetables in butter until softened. Add stock to vegetables, and simmer. Skim fat. Stir in seasonings. Prepare dumplings (recipe follows). Remove meat from chicken, and add to Dutch oven, along with any drippings. Spoon in dumplings, cover, and cook for 15 minutes, keeping stew at a slow boil. Cook, uncovered, for 5 minutes longer.

Serves 6.

CHEESE-HERB DUMPLINGS

These fluffy dumplings with crusty tops may be adapted for beef stew by substituting rosemary and thyme for the chervil and omitting the cheese.

2 cups	flour, sifted	500 mL
1 tsp.	salt	5 mL
4 tsp.	baking powder	20 mL
1 tsp.	chervil	5 mL
⅓ cup	grated Cheddar cheese	75 mL
1	egg, beaten	1
3 Tbsp.	melted butter	45 mL
⅔ cup	milk	150 mL

Sift flour, salt, baking powder and chervil together. Stir in cheese. Mix egg, butter and milk, and stir into flour mixture to make a moist, stiff batter. Using two teaspoons, drop dumplings over bubbling stew.

Makes about 2 dozen.

CURRIED VEGETABLES WITH BISCUITS

This unusual potpie is spicy but not too hot and is nicely balanced by the delicious biscuits.

1 cup	carrots, sliced	250 mL
2 cups	leeks, sliced	500 mL
1 cup	celery, sliced	250 mL
2 cups	red bell peppers, cut into chunks	500 mL
2	small cloves garlic, crushed	2
4 tsp.	peanut oil	20 mL
½ tsp.	sesame oil	2 mL
2½ cups	broccoli, chopped	625 mL
3 tsp.	curry powder	15 mL
½ cup	crushed tomatoes	125 mL
⅓ cup	water	75 mL
4 tsp.	peanut butter	20 mL
3 Tbsp.	plain yogurt	45 mL
¾ tsp.	salt	4 mL
	Cream Biscuits (recipe follows)	

Sauté carrots, leeks, celery, red peppers and garlic in oils. Transfer to a bowl, and add broccoli, curry powder, tomatoes, water and peanut butter; stir, then let sit until cool. Add yogurt and salt. Place in a soufflé dish, cover with aluminum foil, and bake at 450°F (230°C) until mixture starts to bubble—about 25 minutes. Meanwhile, prepare biscuits, and top mixture with them. Bake an additional 15 minutes or until biscuits are golden brown.

Serves 6.

CREAM BISCUITS

These biscuits are light and delicate. Since they take only minutes to prepare, they can be made when the potpie is warming in the oven.

2 cups	sifted flour	500 mL
1 Tbsp.	baking powder	15 mL
½ tsp.	salt	2 mL
⅓ cup	butter	75 mL
2	large eggs	2
½ cup	heavy cream	125 mL

Sift flour, baking powder and salt. Cut in butter with a pastry cutter. Add eggs and cream, barely mixing. Turn dough onto a floured surface, and knead briefly. Pat into a ½-inch (1 cm) thickness, and cut biscuits with a floured 2-inch (5 cm) biscuit cutter. Place them, touching, on top of hot mixture, and bake for 12 to 15 minutes longer or until biscuits are well baked.

Main Courses

CURRY LORE

Curries are as individual as the cooks who make them. The word actually describes a cooking method rather than an ingredient, and the spices do vary from one region of India to another. Fresh homemade curry spices far outshine anything you can find on a grocery-store shelf.

Traditionally, the curry spices are mixed fresh daily by grinding them with a masala stone and then adding them to the dish as it is being cooked. Many spices are mixed in different combinations, and while we recommend specific proportions in Chicken Curry With Yogurt, there is a standard recipe in the condiments section (page 144) that can be used in a variety of recipes.

With a little experience, you will be free to adapt the strength of seasoning to suit your tastes and those of the guests who join you at the table. Treat yourself to a little bit of an old-world ritual with each curry dish you prepare.

CHICKEN CURRY WITH YOGURT

The addition of apricot preserves makes this curry taste faintly of chutney. If you wish, 1 Tbsp. (15 mL) curry powder from a health-food store may be substituted for the combination of coriander, cumin, cardamom and cayenne, but don't use supermarket curry powder, which is too flat and sweet.

2	cloves garlic, minced	2
1	onion, chopped	1
1 Tbsp.	olive oil	15 mL
4	boneless chicken breasts, skinned & cubed	4
1½ tsp.	ground coriander	7 mL
¾ tsp.	ground cumin	4 mL
½ tsp.	ground cardamom	2 mL
	Pinch cayenne pepper	
1 tsp.	ground ginger	5 mL
¼ cup	apricot preserves	50 mL
½ cup	golden raisins	125 mL
2 cups	yogurt	500 mL
	Salt & freshly ground pepper	

In a large skillet, sauté garlic and onion in oil. Add chicken, and sauté until browned. Add ¼ cup (50 mL) water, seasonings, apricot preserves and raisins. Simmer, uncovered, for 30 minutes, stirring occasionally. The liquid will be mostly absorbed. Fold in yogurt, and heat briefly, but do not boil. Season with salt and pepper and more cayenne, if desired.

Serves 4.

CHICKEN FRICOT

In New Brunswick and Nova Scotia, this traditional Acadian stew, called a fricot, is made much the same way as it was centuries ago. Salt pork, which was used to brown the chicken, added flavor to the original dish, but herbs and extra vegetables are today's healthful alternative. Delicious served with dumplings or potato gnocchi.

2 tsp.	each butter & vegetable oil	10 mL
1 lb.	skinless, boneless chicken breasts, cut into cubes	500 g
½ cup	onions, chopped	125 mL
½ cup	mushrooms, halved or quartered	125 mL
3 cups	chicken stock	750 mL
2 Tbsp.	flour	25 mL
½ tsp.	thyme	2 mL
¼ tsp.	summer savory	1 mL
	Pinch freshly grated nutmeg	
	Salt & freshly ground pepper	
2	medium potatoes, cut into chunks	2
2	medium carrots, cut into chunks	2
8	small onions (about the size of pickling onions)	8
1 cup	turnip, cubed (opt.)	250 mL
1 cup	frozen lima beans	250 mL
1 cup	potato gnocchi, fresh or frozen	250 mL
⅓ cup	fresh parsley, chopped	75 mL

In a Dutch oven or a large saucepan, melt butter with oil over medium heat. Add chicken, and cook, turning frequently, until opaque. Stir in chopped onions, mushrooms and 1 Tbsp. (15 mL) chicken stock. Cover, and cook over medium-low heat for 5 to 8 minutes or until onions are transparent and liquid has evaporated.

In a small bowl, combine flour, thyme, savory, nutmeg and salt and pepper to taste. Add to Dutch oven, stirring constantly until flour starts to brown slightly. Blend in remaining chicken stock. Bring to a simmer, stirring frequently. Add potatoes, carrots, onions and turnip, if desired. Cover, and simmer gently for 30 minutes or until vegetables are almost tender. Add lima beans. Simmer, covered, for 5 minutes or until beans are tender.

Increase heat to medium, and add gnocchi. Cook for 3 to 4 minutes or until most of gnocchi have bobbed to the surface. Stir in parsley. Season with salt and pepper to taste.

Serves 4.

Main Courses

MOROCCAN LAMB TAJINE

Tajines, or tagines, are named after the Moroccan pots with cone-shaped lids in which they are cooked. Moroccan cooks often flavor lamb tajines with slices of pickled lemon and local olives. North American cooks can substitute a bowl of black, purple and green oil-cured olives and wedges of lemon to squeeze over the lamb as an accompaniment.

2 lb.	lean lamb shoulder chops	1 kg
1 tsp.	paprika	5 mL
$\frac{1}{4}$ tsp.	salt	1 mL
2	cloves garlic, minced	2
4 tsp.	olive oil	20 mL
1	onion, finely chopped	1
1	can (28 oz./796 mL) tomatoes, diced	1
1 cup	chicken stock, plus 2 Tbsp. (25 mL)	250 mL
1 tsp.	sugar	5 mL
$\frac{1}{2}$ tsp.	cinnamon	2 mL
$\frac{1}{4}$ tsp.	ginger	1 mL
$\frac{1}{4}$ tsp.	cumin	1 mL
1	sprig thyme or $\frac{1}{2}$ tsp. (2 mL) dried	1
	Pinch saffron threads (opt.)	
4	slender carrots, quartered lengthwise	4
$\frac{3}{4}$ lb.	green beans, trimmed & halved	375 g
	Salt & freshly ground pepper	
2 Tbsp.	fresh coriander leaves or parsley, chopped	25 mL
	Hot prepared couscous or cooked rice	

Trim and discard all fat and membranes from lamb. Cut meat into bite-sized pieces, reserving marrow bones and riblets; set aside.

In a small bowl, use a wooden spoon to mix paprika, salt and garlic with 1 tsp. (5 mL) oil to make a paste. Add meat, and toss well to coat.

In a large saucepan over medium-high heat, heat remaining oil. Add meat, and cook, turning frequently, until well browned, about 6 minutes. Add onion, and cook, stirring, for 2 minutes. Add tomatoes with liquid along with 1 cup (250 mL) chicken stock, reserved bones, sugar, cinnamon, ginger, cumin, thyme and saffron, if desired. Bring to a gentle simmer, and cook, covered, for 1½ hours or until meat is very tender.

With a slotted spoon, transfer meat to a shallow heatproof dish (discarding bones), and keep warm. Bring liquid in the saucepan to a boil. Add carrots and beans. Cook for 5 to 7 minutes or until vegetables are tender and sauce has thickened. With a slotted spoon, remove vegetables and arrange around outer edge of meat. Remove thyme sprig from sauce. Season with salt and pepper. Pour over meat and vegetables. Sprinkle with coriander. Serve with couscous. Serves 4.

Main Courses

LAMB-SPINACH CURRY

The rich, earthy taste of lamb combines nicely with the delicate flavor and smooth texture of spinach in this hearty Indian stew. Delicious served over fragrant basmati rice.

½ cup	oil	125 mL
4 lb.	stewing lamb, cut into cubes	1.8 kg
4	large onions, cut into eighths	4
8	large potatoes, cut into large cubes	8
8 Tbsp.	Madras-Style Curry Paste (page 144)	100 mL
1 lb.	spinach	500 g

Heat oil in a large, heavy pot. Add lamb, onions and potatoes, and cook over high heat, stirring constantly, for 7 minutes. Add curry paste, stirring well. Cook over medium-high heat, stirring occasionally, until meat is well browned. Add water to cover, bring to a boil, cover, reduce heat, and cook for 1 hour. Meanwhile, wash and tear spinach. Stir into curry as it is removed from the heat.

Serves 8.

HOT & SPICY BEAN CURD
(Szechuan Tofu)

This recipe can go anywhere the cook's imagination takes it—add more vegetables or, for variety, substitute beef or chicken for the tofu.

¾ cup	oil	175 mL
4	tofu cakes, well drained & cubed	4
3 Tbsp.	soy sauce	45 mL
3 Tbsp.	sherry	45 mL
4 Tbsp.	oyster sauce	50 mL
2 Tbsp.	black bean sauce	25 mL
3	Szechuan peppers, crumbled	3
2 tsp.	Chinese five-spice powder	10 mL
2	quarter-sized slices gingerroot, minced	2
2	cloves garlic, minced	2
2 cups	snow peas	500 mL
	Cornstarch (opt.)	

Heat oil in a wok. Deep-fry tofu until firm and golden brown. Remove tofu, drain well, and set aside. Pour off all but 1 Tbsp. (15 mL) oil.

To make sauce, combine remaining ingredients, except snow peas and cornstarch. Set aside.

Reheat oil in wok, and briefly stir-fry peas—about 30 seconds. Add tofu, and stir-fry for another 30 seconds. Add sauce, and cook for 30 seconds. Thicken with cornstarch dissolved in water, if desired.

Serves 6.

Main Courses

NOODLES WITH PEANUT SAUCE

These noodles make a tasty base for vegetable or meat dishes. Stir-fried vegetables can be added to the noodles to provide a complete dish.

6 Tbsp.	oil	75 mL
4 cups	fresh Oriental noodles	1 L
4 Tbsp.	chopped unsalted peanuts	50 mL
5 Tbsp.	peanut butter	65 mL
1 tsp.	sesame oil	5 mL
2	green onions, minced	2

Heat 5 Tbsp. (65 mL) oil in a wok. Fry noodles in 1-cup (250 mL) batches until lightly browned. Drain, and keep warm.

Combine 3 Tbsp. (45 mL) peanuts with peanut butter, remaining oil and sesame oil, and mix well. Toss with noodles (you may have to use your hands to mix thoroughly).

Garnish with remaining peanuts and green onions. Serves 8 as an accompaniment dish.

PORK WITH SWEET PEPPERS

A spicy stir-fry that is easy to make year-round.

2	red bell peppers, julienned	2
½ lb.	pork tenderloin, julienned or cut into rounds	250 g
2 Tbsp.	cornstarch, plus 2 tsp. (10 mL)	25 mL
3 Tbsp.	oil	45 mL
6	green onions, julienned	6
4	cloves garlic, julienned	4
4	slices gingerroot, julienned	4
1 cup	vegetable stock	250 mL
2 Tbsp.	soy sauce	25 mL
1 Tbsp.	sherry	15 mL
	Almonds (opt.)	

Stir-fry peppers in a wok with no oil for 2 minutes, remove, and set aside.

Coat pork with 2 Tbsp. (25 mL) cornstarch. Heat oil in the wok, then stir-fry pork for 3 minutes. Add onions, garlic and gingerroot, and stir-fry for 1 minute.

Combine vegetable stock, soy sauce, sherry and 2 tsp. (10 mL) cornstarch. Add to wok, and cook until just thickened. Stir in peppers. Garnish with almonds, if desired.

Serves 4.

Main Courses

STIR-FRIED BEEF

Beef and slivers of parsnip combine to make an unusually delicious and spicy stir-fry that is easy to prepare and quick to cook.

4	eggs	4
1 cup	cornstarch	250 mL
1 lb.	beef tenderloin, julienned	500 g
2 cups	oil	500 mL
1	large parsnip, julienned	1
2	green onions, sliced length-wise & cut into pieces	2
2	chili peppers, diced	2
3	cloves garlic, crushed	3
3 tsp.	sugar	15 mL
1 Tbsp.	soy sauce	15 mL
4 Tbsp.	rice vinegar	50 mL

Combine eggs and cornstarch, then toss beef in mixture. Heat oil in a wok, deep-fry beef for $1\frac{1}{2}$ minutes, then remove. Deep-fry parsnip for 1 minute, and set aside. Remove all but 2 Tbsp. (25 mL) oil, then stir-fry onions, chilies and garlic for 30 seconds.

Combine sugar, soy sauce and vinegar; add to wok along with meat and parsnip. Cook for 1 minute. Serves 6.

SPICY ASIAN CHICKEN

Freeze some of your summer basil crop so that you can make this recipe during the winter months. If using dried lemongrass, soak it in water for 30 minutes first, then drain. If you cannot find lemongrass, substitute lemon zest.

3 Tbsp.	peanut oil	45 mL
1 cup	blanched, unsalted, roasted or raw peanuts, plus 1 Tbsp. (15 mL), chopped, for garnish	250 mL
4	cloves garlic, chopped	4
1	dried red chili, chopped, or 1 tsp. (5 mL) red pepper flakes	1
1 lb.	boneless, skinless chicken breast, trimmed & cut into strips	500 g
¾ cup	basil leaves, lightly packed	175 mL
4	scallions, trimmed & cut into 1-inch (2.5 cm) pieces	4
2 Tbsp.	fish sauce	25 mL
2 Tbsp.	fresh lemon juice	25 mL
1 Tbsp.	fresh or dried lemongrass, chopped, or grated lemon zest	15 mL
1 tsp.	sugar	5 mL
1 Tbsp.	cornstarch dissolved in 2 Tbsp. (25 mL) water	15 mL

In a wok or a large skillet, heat oil over medium-high heat. Add 1 cup (250 mL) peanuts, and stir-fry for 1 to 2 minutes or until lightly browned. Add garlic and dried chili, and stir-fry for 1 minute. Add chicken, basil and scallions, and stir-fry for about 2 minutes or until chicken loses its pinkness. Add fish sauce, lemon juice, lemongrass, sugar and 2 Tbsp. (25 mL) water, and bring to a boil. Stir in cornstarch mixture, and toss until sauce has thickened. Garnish with chopped peanuts, and serve with noodles or rice. Serves 4.

Main Courses

HONEY-MUSTARD CHICKEN

The type of mustard selected will greatly influence the overall taste of this dish. Use Pommery mustard for a more textured taste. Both Dijon and Pommery mustards are available in a wide range of hotnesses; you can also make your own (pages 140 & 141).

¼ cup	butter	50 mL
½ cup	honey	125 mL
¼ cup	mustard	50 mL
10	chicken legs	10
	Salt & freshly ground pepper	

Melt butter, honey and mustard together. Dip chicken legs into mixture, place in a shallow casserole dish, and sprinkle with salt and pepper to taste. Bake at 350°F (180°C) for 35 minutes.

Serves 5 to 6.

LEMON-ROSEMARY CHICKEN

Chicken breasts marinated in lemon juice are the most tender, succulent meat imaginable. This dish is excellent hot or cold.

2	whole skinless chicken breasts	2
2	lemons	2
¼ cup	unbleached flour	50 mL
½ tsp.	paprika	2 mL
¼ tsp.	salt	1 mL
¼ tsp.	freshly ground pepper	1 mL
½ cup	chicken stock	125 mL
1 tsp.	malt syrup	5 mL
1 Tbsp.	fresh rosemary, chopped, or 1 tsp. (5 mL) dried, crushed	15 mL

Halve chicken breasts, and place in a glass or stainless steel bowl.

Juice lemons, strain to remove seeds, and pour juice over chicken. Cover with plastic wrap, and refrigerate for a minimum of 4 hours and a maximum of 12. Remove chicken from the bowl, and discard juice.

Put flour, paprika, salt and pepper in a plastic bag, and shake to mix. Add chicken, one piece at a time, and shake until well coated.

Place chicken in a baking pan or an ovenproof casserole, and bake in a preheated 375°F (190°C) oven for 20 minutes. Remove from the oven, pour in the combined chicken stock, malt syrup and rosemary, and return to the oven. Bake for 15 minutes.

To make a sauce, remove chicken to a warm plate, put the baking pan with juices on the stovetop, and boil at high heat for about 4 minutes, stirring frequently, until the volume is reduced by half. Pour over chicken, and serve.

Serves 4.

ROAST MUSTARD LAMB

Lamb lovers will thank you for this juicy roast leg of lamb with a mustard crust.

4 lb.	leg of lamb	1.8 kg
12 Tbsp.	oil	150 mL
1 Tbsp.	soy sauce	15 mL
4 Tbsp.	mustard	50 mL
$\frac{1}{4}$ tsp.	garlic powder	1 mL
$\frac{1}{2}$ tsp.	rosemary	2 mL

Trim away most of the fat from the lamb, and place lamb in a shallow roasting pan. Mix together remaining ingredients, and spread over surface of lamb. Let stand at room temperature for about an hour, then roast at 325°F (160°C) for 20 to 30 minutes per pound or until an internal temperature of 175°F (80°C) is reached.

Serves 6.

ROASTING TO PERFECTION

Roasting is a technique of dry cooking in which the whole piece of meat is left uncovered throughout the entire cooking time. Ideally, it produces a dry, crisp surface and a moist, delicious interior that will melt in your mouth. Tender cuts are the best for roasting, and they should be cooked in an open roasting pan with the fat side to the top so that the meat bastes continually. The trick for all cooks is timing— knowing the precise moment to remove the roast from the oven when the meat is still pink and juicy. The cooking instructions and internal temperature given for Roast Mustard Lamb will produce a medium roast. For medium-rare, cook the roast in a preheated 325°F (160°C) oven for 20 to 25 minutes per pound (500 g) or until the internal temperature reaches 160°-165°F (71°-74°C).

Main Courses

CHICKEN POTPIE

Wild mushrooms lend interest to this otherwise traditional potpie.

5 Tbsp.	butter	65 mL
2	shallots, finely chopped	2
1	clove garlic, finely chopped	1
7 Tbsp.	flour	90 mL
1 cup	dry white wine	250 mL
3¾ cups	chicken stock	925 mL
1 Tbsp.	Worcestershire sauce	15 mL
2½ lb.	chicken breasts, cut into serving-sized pieces	1.1 kg
	Butter for sautéing	
1 cup	fresh mushrooms, thinly sliced	250 mL
½ cup	reconstituted dried porcini mushrooms	125 mL
½ cup	carrots, thinly sliced	125 mL
½ cup	celery, thinly sliced	125 mL
½ cup	red bell pepper, chopped	125 mL
½ cup	green pepper, chopped	125 mL
½ cup	parsley, finely chopped	125 mL
1 Tbsp.	tarragon, crumbled	15 mL
	Potpie Pastry (recipe follows)	

In a large pot, melt butter, and gently cook shallots and garlic until transparent. Add flour, and whisk over moderate heat until lightly browned. Add all liquids, whisking as you do. Bring to a light simmer, and allow to thicken.

Meanwhile, sauté chicken in butter, and add to the pot. Sauté fresh mushrooms, and add them, together with remaining vegetables and herbs. Stew for 15 minutes, then cool to room temperature or refrigerate overnight.

When ready to bake, preheat oven to 400°F (200°C). Roll out pastry in a circle large enough to drape 1 to 2 inches (2.5-5 cm) over 2-quart (2 L) soufflé dish, and cut a vent hole in the center of the dough. Place cooled filling in dish, leaving about 1 inch (2.5 cm) headspace. Place pie bird in the center, and drape pastry over the top, fitting the bird's head through the vent hole. Pat pastry down onto filling, and crimp edges. Bake for 1 hour or until the pastry is golden brown. Serve immediately.

Serves 6.

POTPIE PASTRY

This is an excellent potpie crust, easy to make and delicious. Many pastry cooks believe lard produces the most tender and flavorful crust, but for those who prefer to avoid this form of animal fat, identical quantities of either vegetable shortening or butter can be substituted.

2 cups	sifted flour	500 mL
¾ tsp.	salt	4 mL
8 Tbsp.	butter	100 mL
4 Tbsp.	lard	50 mL
3 Tbsp.	ice water	45 mL

This pastry can be made by hand with a pastry cutter or in a food processor. Combine flour and salt. Work in butter and lard until dough is the texture of cornmeal. Add water, form dough into a ball, wrap, and refrigerate for several hours.

SAVORY LAMB PIE

This ground-lamb pie is a tasty alternative to the traditional holiday leg of lamb.

2 Tbsp.	ouzo	25 mL
1½ lb.	ground lamb, uncooked	750 g
4 tsp.	olive oil	20 mL
1	large onion, chopped	1
1	clove garlic, minced	1
1	small apple, peeled, cored & grated	1
3 Tbsp.	currants	45 mL
2	eggs, lightly beaten	2
¾ cup	blanched almonds, chopped	175 mL
¾ cup	firmly packed parsley, finely chopped	175 mL
1 Tbsp.	dried mint	15 mL
	Salt & freshly ground pepper	
	Homemade Phyllo Dough (recipe follows)	
1	egg yolk, beaten with 2 Tbsp. (25 mL) milk, for brushing crust (opt.)	1

Sprinkle ouzo over lamb, cover, and refrigerate for 1 hour. Preheat oven to 350°F (180°C), and brush a 10- or 12-inch (3 L) round baking pan with 1 tsp. (5 mL) oil.

In a large skillet, heat remaining oil, and sauté onion until soft. Add lamb, and stir for a few minutes until it just begins to brown. Stir in garlic, apple and currants, and sauté until lamb is lightly browned. Drain off excess fat. Remove from skillet, and cool slightly.

Combine lamb mixture, eggs, almonds, herbs and salt and pepper in a large bowl, and mix well.

Follow general instructions for rolling and filling phyllo dough. Brush top of pie with egg-and-milk mixture, if desired, and bake for 50 to 60 minutes or until crust is golden brown.

Note: To substitute store-bought phyllo, you will need about 12 sheets of phyllo, ¼ cup (50 mL) olive oil and a 9-by-12-inch (3 L) baking pan. (Keep a damp cloth over the phyllo to prevent it from drying out.) Layer 7 phyllo sheets on the bottom of the pan, brushing each with oil. Spoon in filling, spread evenly, and cover with remaining phyllo, again brushing each sheet with oil. Roll edges inward to form a rim. Using a sharp knife, cut the pie into 12 pieces. Brush pie with egg-and-milk mixture, if desired, and bake as above.

Serves 4 to 6.

HOMEMADE PHYLLO DOUGH

This recipe requires little of the coaxing and stretching involved in making phyllo sheets for delicate sweets. Instead, the dough is quite malleable, and the result is a hearty breadlike texture that works well with any of the savory pies.

2½ cups	flour	625 mL
1 tsp.	(scant) salt	5 mL
2 tsp.	baking powder	10 mL
2 Tbsp.	vegetable shortening	25 mL
¾ cup	water	175 mL
1 Tbsp.	olive oil	15 mL

Combine 2 cups (500 mL) flour, salt and baking powder in a medium bowl. Cut in shortening until dough is mealy and coarse. Make a well in the center, and add water. Combine with a fork until a dough mass begins to form.

Use remaining flour, a little at a time, to dust the work surface. Knead the dough for about 10 minutes, incorporating flour, until it is soft and silky to the touch. Add more flour if necessary.

Before rolling out dough, have filling and greased 10- or 12-inch (3 L) round baking pan ready. Divide dough into 2 equal balls. Roll out first ball on a lightly floured surface to the thickness of a dime, about 13 inches (33 cm) in diameter. Carefully place in bottom and up sides of baking pan, and brush with oil. Spoon filling into dough, spreading evenly.

Roll out remaining dough, and place on top of filling. Trim excess dough to about 1 inch (2.5 cm), then gently roll it inward to form a rim around the side of the pan and twist slightly to create a decorative edge. Make several cuts in top of pie with a sharp knife. Bake as indicated in individual recipe.

LEEK QUICHE

This savory tart is tasty when served hot or at room temperature.

2 Tbsp.	butter	25 mL
3	medium leeks, trimmed, cleaned & chopped	3
2	cloves garlic, minced	2
3	large eggs, beaten	3
¾ cup	light cream	175 mL
½ tsp.	salt	2 mL
¼ tsp.	freshly ground pepper, plus extra for sprinkling on top	1 mL
	Pinch nutmeg	
	Pinch cayenne pepper	
	Baked 9-inch (23 cm) pie crust	
1 tsp.	Dijon mustard	5 mL
1 cup	grated Gruyère cheese	250 mL
3 Tbsp.	grated Parmesan cheese	45 mL

In a heavy skillet, melt butter over medium heat. Add leeks, and sauté for 10 minutes. (Add a little water if leeks begin to scorch.) Add garlic, and cook, stirring occasionally, for 10 to 15 minutes or until leeks are tender and lightly browned. Let cool.

In a medium-sized bowl, whisk together eggs, cream, salt, pepper, nutmeg and cayenne. Set aside.

Brush pastry crust with mustard. Sprinkle ½ cup (125 mL) Gruyère and 1 Tbsp. (15 mL) Parmesan over bottom of crust. Spread leek mixture over cheese, and top with 1 Tbsp. (15 mL) Parmesan and remaining Gruyère. Carefully pour egg mixture over leeks and cheese. Sprinkle with remaining Parmesan and freshly ground pepper.

Preheat oven to 375°F (190°C), and set the pan on a baking sheet in the middle of the oven. Bake for 35 to 40 minutes or until top is golden brown and custard is set. Let cool for 10 minutes before serving.

Serves 8.

TOURTIÈRE

Although there are endless variations on tourtière, this one, from Quebec, is a favorite.

Pastry

2 cups	flour	500 mL
$1\frac{1}{3}$ tsp.	baking powder	6 mL
$\frac{1}{2}$ tsp.	salt	2 mL
$5\frac{1}{3}$ oz.	lard, butter or vegetable shortening, cut into chunks	160 g
$\frac{1}{3}$ cup	boiling water	75 mL
1 tsp.	lemon juice	5 mL
1	large egg, beaten	1

Filling

2 lb.	pork butt, trimmed & finely chopped	1 kg
1	medium onion, peeled & finely chopped	1
1	clove garlic, crushed	1
$\frac{1}{4}$ cup	water	50 mL
$\frac{1}{4}$ cup	cognac or rye whiskey	50 mL
$\frac{1}{4}$ tsp.	celery salt	1 mL
$\frac{1}{4}$ tsp.	cloves	1 mL
	Salt & freshly ground pepper	
$\frac{1}{4}$ cup	dry breadcrumbs	50 mL

To make pastry, mix flour, baking powder and salt, then cut in two-thirds of the lard. Place remaining lard in boiling water that has been taken off the heat, and allow to melt. Then add lemon juice and egg. Add to dry ingredients. Knead briefly into a circle, wrap dough in plastic, and refrigerate for at least 4 hours.

To make filling, put all ingredients, except breadcrumbs, in a saucepan, and simmer until meat is tender, about 20 minutes. Stir in breadcrumbs, and cool.

Roll out half the dough on a floured surface, and place in bottom of a 9-inch (23 cm) pie pan; trim dough, leaving a $\frac{1}{2}$-inch (1 cm) overhang. Fill pan with pork filling, and smooth top. Roll out remaining dough, cut a vent hole in the center, and drape over filling. Roll edges under, and crimp decoratively. Bake at 350°F (180°C) for 35 minutes or until nicely browned. Let set for 5 minutes before serving. The tourtière freezes very well.

Serves 6.

WILD MUSHROOM TATIN

This upside-down shallow and very intense mushroom potpie is an excellent appetizer. The tart can be made with cultivated button mushrooms, but exotic varieties add a distinctive richness.

Pastry

¼ lb.	plus 2½ Tbsp. (35 mL) butter, softened	125 g
1½ cups	sifted flour	375 mL
¼ tsp.	salt	1 mL
3 Tbsp.	ice water	45 mL

Filling

½ cup	dried porcini mushrooms	125 mL
2 cups	boiling water	500 mL
1	clove garlic, minced	1
2	shallots, minced	2
6 Tbsp.	butter	75 mL
½ cup	heavy cream	125 mL
½ tsp.	salt	2 mL
3 Tbsp.	parsley, finely chopped	45 mL
1 tsp.	thyme, crumbled	5 mL
	Freshly ground pepper	
12 oz.	cultivated domestic mushrooms, sliced	375 g
1 lb.	fresh chanterelles, cleaned & cut into long wedges	500 g

This pastry can be made by hand with a pastry cutter or in a food processor.

To make pastry, work butter into flour and salt until it has the texture of cornmeal. Add ice water, and work in. Wrap dough in plastic wrap, and refrigerate for at least 4 hours—preferably overnight.

To make filling, soak porcini mushrooms in boiling water for 30 minutes. Drain, reserving stock and mushrooms. Meanwhile, sauté garlic and shallots in butter in a large skillet until transparent. Add cream, porcini stock and seasonings, and simmer until mixture is reduced to a creamy, somewhat thick consistency. (Remember that this sauce will continue to cook for 30 minutes in the oven, so it should not be too thick at this stage. Thin with a little water if necessary.)

In a separate frying pan, sauté cultivated and porcini mushrooms over high heat until lightly browned, then add to sauce. Lay raw chanterelles on top of this mixture. If using only cultivated mushrooms, slice and sauté them in butter with shallots and garlic and use chicken stock instead of wild-mushroom stock.

Roll out pastry, and lay over mushrooms, crimp edges, and bake at 450°F (230°C) for 30 minutes or until pastry is nicely browned. Remove from oven, invert onto a large flat plate, slice, and serve.

Serves 6.

SPANAKOPITTA
(Spinach Pie)

A delectable, savory treat, this spinach pie is also elegant enough to grace a holiday table.

2 Tbsp.	olive oil, plus ¼ cup (50 mL)	25 mL
½ lb.	scallions, trimmed & finely chopped	250 g
1	large leek, trimmed & coarsely chopped	1
1½ lb.	spinach, trimmed & chopped	750 g
½ cup	fresh parsley, chopped	125 mL
¼ cup	fresh dill, chopped	50 mL
1	egg, lightly beaten	1
¾ lb.	feta cheese, crumbled	375 g
2 Tbsp.	grated kefalotyri or Parmesan cheese	25 mL
¾ tsp.	nutmeg	4 mL
½ tsp.	cumin	2 mL
½ tsp.	salt	2 mL
¼ tsp.	freshly ground pepper	1 mL
12	phyllo sheets	12
¼ cup	melted butter	50 mL

Heat 2 Tbsp. (25 mL) oil in a heavy skillet over medium heat. Add scallions and leek, and sauté for 5 to 7 minutes or until softened. Gradually add spinach, and cook, stirring, until wilted, about 5 to 7 minutes. Transfer vegetables to a colander, drain completely, and cool.

In a large bowl, combine spinach mixture, parsley, dill, egg, remaining oil, cheese, nutmeg, cumin, salt and pepper. Mix thoroughly with a wooden spoon. Set aside.

Preheat oven to 375°F (190°C). Unroll phyllo sheets, and place on a flat surface. Cover with wax paper and a damp tea towel to prevent the sheets from drying out.

Brush a 10-inch (25 cm) pie plate lightly with a little butter. Lay 1 phyllo sheet on the counter, and brush lightly with butter. Lay it over the pie plate, letting corners hang over the edges. Repeat with 3 more phyllo sheets, placing each sheet at right angles to the previous one. Gently press the phyllo into the base of the pie plate. Tightly roll the overhanging dough up all around so that it rests on the rim of the pie plate. Spoon spinach filling into the shell.

Brush 1 phyllo sheet with butter, and roll it lengthwise into a ½-to-¾-inch-wide (1-2 cm) rope. Place it over the filling, forming a semicircle along the edge. Brush another phyllo sheet with butter, roll it up, and place it on the filling so that it completes the circle. Loop the remaining length of the roll toward the center to form the beginning of a spiral. Repeat with the 6 remaining phyllo sheets, brushing them with butter, rolling them up and continuing the spiral, leaving a 1-inch (2.5 cm) hole in the center to allow steam to escape. Brush top with remaining butter.

Bake for 20 to 30 minutes or until golden brown. Let cool for at least 10 minutes before serving.
Serves 8.

GROUNDNUT STEW

In many parts of Africa, stews of meat, fish or vegetables are enriched with peanut butter. Serve over millet for an authentic touch.

2½ cups	sweet potato, peeled & cubed	625 mL
2 cups	carrots, peeled & chopped	500 mL
1 Tbsp.	peanut oil	15 mL
1	large onion, chopped	1
2	cloves garlic, minced	2
1 Tbsp.	gingerroot, peeled & minced	15 mL
2 tsp.	ground coriander	10 mL
3	tomatoes, cored & chopped	3
2 cups	zucchini, cut into cubes	500 mL
2 cups	tomato juice	500 mL
½ cup	peanut butter	125 mL
	Salt & freshly ground pepper	

Steam or boil sweet potato and carrots for 5 to 7 minutes or until tender-crisp. Set aside, reserving ½ cup (125 mL) of the cooking liquid. In a large pot or a Dutch oven, heat oil over medium heat. Add onion, garlic and gingerroot, and sauté for 5 minutes. Add coriander, and sauté for 2 to 3 minutes. Add tomatoes, reserved cooking liquid and zucchini. Cook, uncovered, over low heat for about 10 minutes, or until zucchini is just tender. Stir in sweet potato, carrots, tomato juice and peanut butter. Simmer for 5 to 10 minutes or until heated through. Season with salt and pepper.

Serves 4.

ZUCCHINI SPOONBREAD

This makes a hearty but elegant meatless meal.

3 cups	milk	750 mL
1 cup	cornmeal, preferably stone-ground	250 mL
½ cup	grated Parmesan cheese	125 mL
1½ cups	grated zucchini, well drained	375 mL
2 tsp.	fresh marjoram, chopped or 1 tsp. (5 mL) dried	10 mL
1 tsp.	salt	5 mL
	Freshly ground pepper	
5 Tbsp.	unsalted butter	65 mL
3	eggs at room temperature, separated	3
	Pinch cream of tartar	

Pour milk into a large saucepan, and bring almost to a boil. Gradually stir in cornmeal with a wire whisk. Continue cooking for 2 to 3 minutes, until thickened. Remove from heat, and stir in cheese, zucchini, marjoram, salt, pepper, butter and egg yolks. Beat egg whites with cream of tartar until stiff, not dry. Fold into cornmeal mixture, and pour batter into a well-buttered casserole or soufflé dish. The batter should come within 1 inch (2.5 cm) of the top of the baking dish.

Bake at 350°F (180°C) for 30 to 40 minutes or until firm, browned and puffed. Serve immediately. (As the texture of spoonbread is denser and less fragile than that of a soufflé, its rise is not as dramatic nor its fall as significant.)

Serves 4 to 6.

Main Courses

HOLIDAY SQUASH

Filled with a light stuffing and topped with a dollop of fruity sauce, this squash is good enough to replace the traditional bird at the holiday table. Hubbard squash can be stuffed by cutting off 2 to 3 inches (5-8 cm) at one end, hollowing out the seed cavity, filling it with stuffing and plugging the hole with an apple. To serve, either scoop out the flesh and stuffing with a spoon or cut it into round slices. Cut smaller squashes, such as delicata, acorn and dumpling, in half before stuffing, and halve the quantity of stuffing. Any extra stuffing can be baked in a casserole dish, covered for 20 minutes and uncovered for 10 minutes longer.

1	Hubbard or sweetmeat squash	1
1 cup	onion, chopped	250 mL
1 cup	celery, chopped	250 mL
2 Tbsp.	oil	25 mL
1 tsp.	sage	5 mL
½ tsp.	thyme	2 mL
½ tsp.	basil	2 mL
½ tsp.	rosemary	2 mL
¼ cup	fresh parsley, chopped	50 mL
	Salt (opt.)	
	Freshly ground pepper	
¾ cup	stock or water, or more as needed	175 mL
3 cups	whole grain breadcrumbs	750 mL
¾ cup	toasted pecans, coarsely chopped	175 mL
1	egg, beaten (opt.)	1
	Apricot Sauce (recipe follows)	

Cut squash in half if it is small. If it is large, cut a hole at one end. Hollow out the seed cavity.

Sauté onion and celery in oil along with sage, thyme, basil, rosemary, parsley, salt (if water is used instead of stock) and pepper. When celery is crisp-tender, add stock, breadcrumbs and pecans. Add egg, if desired (it binds the stuffing and makes it richer-tasting). If stuffing seems dry, add a little more liquid.

Fill squash with stuffing, and replace the "lid" or, if you have made a round hole at one end, plug it with an apple.

Bake at 375°F (190°C) for 1 hour (or between 30 and 40 minutes if using smaller squash), until squash is tender when pierced with a fork. Serve with Apricot Sauce.

Makes 8 cups (2 L) stuffing.

APRICOT SAUCE

1 Tbsp.	butter	15 mL
⅓ cup	dried apricots, chopped	75 mL
2¼ cups	apple juice	550 mL
1 Tbsp.	arrowroot or cornstarch	15 mL

Bring butter, apricots and 2 cups (500 mL) apple juice to a boil in a small saucepan. Simmer for 20 minutes, then combine arrowroot with remaining apple juice, and stir into apricot mixture. Heat, stirring, until mixture comes to a boil again, then simmer for 10 minutes.

LEMON-PARSLEY STUFFED TROUT

The tangy lemon in this stuffing brings out the delicate flavor of the trout, and the croutons taste fresh and savory.

4	lemons	4
¾ cup	Italian parsley, plus extra for garnish	175 mL
7	slices firm-textured white bread, crusts removed	7
8 Tbsp.	unsalted butter	100 mL
2 Tbsp.	olive oil	25 mL
3	cloves garlic, crushed	3
	Salt and freshly ground pepper	
2 Tbsp.	fresh lemon juice	25 mL
4	brook trout (about ¾ lb./ 375 g each), cleaned & boned, head & tail left on	4
¼ cup	dry white wine	50 mL

Grate all the lemon zest. Chop parsley, and cut bread into ½-inch (1 cm) cubes. In a large skillet, heat 4 Tbsp. (50 mL) butter, and add bread cubes. Sauté over medium heat, tossing frequently, until crisp and golden. Remove croutons from skillet; set aside.

Add 1 Tbsp. (15 mL) butter and 1 Tbsp. (15 mL) oil to skillet, then add garlic and lemon zest, and toss until fragrant. Add croutons, parsley, salt and pepper and lemon juice.

Stuff each fish with a quarter of the stuffing, lay fish in a single layer in a greased shallow baking pan, and dot with remaining butter. Sprinkle with more salt and pepper. Pour wine and remaining oil around fish, and bake for 15 to 20 minutes at 400°F (200°C). Garnish with additional parsley. Serve immediately.

Serves 4.

FISH WITH YAMS & GINGER

Any white-fleshed fish is suitable for this spicy recipe, but whitefish and pike are especially recommended.

1½ lb.	fish	750 g
½ lb.	yams, peeled & diced	250 g
4	green onions, chopped	4
4	slices gingerroot, chopped	4
4	cloves garlic, chopped	4
2 Tbsp.	oil	25 mL
2 cups	water	500 mL
1 Tbsp.	sherry	15 mL
2 Tbsp.	hoisin sauce	25 mL
1 Tbsp.	Chinese chili sauce	15 mL
1 Tbsp.	vinegar	15 mL
1 Tbsp.	soy sauce	15 mL

Clean fish, then slash diagonally in three places on each side.

Sauté yams, onions, gingerroot and garlic in oil in a 9-by-13-inch (3.5 L) ovenproof dish. Place fish on top of vegetables. Combine remaining ingredients, and pour over fish. Cover, and bake at 250°F (120°C) for 20 minutes.

Serves 6.

CREAMY BAKED FISH

Easy to make and rich in taste, this fish recipe is sure to become a favorite.

1 lb.	fish fillet, preferably a thick, flavorful variety such as haddock, hake or perch	500 g
¼ cup	fresh lemon juice	50 mL
1 cup	Almost Sour Cream (recipe follows)	250 mL
1 Tbsp.	fresh chives, dill or tarragon, minced (opt.) Freshly ground pepper	15 mL

Place fish, skin side down, in a baking dish. Pour lemon juice over it.

Combine the Almost Sour Cream with chives, if desired, and spread on top of fish.

Cover, and bake in a 375°F (190°C) oven for 15 to 20 minutes (less time with thin fish). Uncover, and bake for 5 minutes longer. Grind pepper over the fillet, and serve.

Serves 4.

ALMOST SOUR CREAM

There are 25 calories in a tablespoon (15 mL) of sour cream, almost 95 percent of which comes from fat. As an alternative, this recipe contributes only 12 calories per serving, which is less than 25 percent fat (15 percent if you use 1 percent cottage cheese).

Almost Sour Cream will stay fresh in the refrigerator for up to 4 days. It can also be used in tuna salads instead of mayonnaise, tossed with vegetables, spooned onto baked potatoes and spiced up with garlic and onion powders, chives or parsley.

2 cups	low-fat cottage cheese	500 mL
¼ cup	low-fat yogurt	50 mL

Blend cottage cheese and yogurt in a food processor fitted with a metal blade until smooth and without lumps (a blender makes it too thin).

Serve immediately, or store in the refrigerator and use as needed.

KULBIAKA

Whether called by its Russian name, *kulbiaka*, or by the French *coulibiac*, this handsome dish is ideal for parties. All the preparation, except the final assembling and baking, can be done up to a day in advance.

$\frac{1}{3}$ cup	white rice, preferably basmati	75 mL
$\frac{1}{2}$ tsp.	salt	2 mL
$\frac{1}{4}$ cup	butter, plus melted butter for sauce	50 mL
3	whole cloves garlic, peeled	3
1	large onion, finely chopped	1
$\frac{1}{2}$ cup	fresh dill, finely snipped	125 mL
8 oz.	mushrooms, coarsely chopped	250 g
3	hard-cooked eggs	3
$1\frac{1}{2}$ lb.	skinless, boneless raw salmon	750 g
$\frac{1}{2}$	batch Egg Bread dough (page 182), after its overnight rising (include glaze) Salt & freshly ground pepper Fresh nutmeg	$\frac{1}{2}$

Put rice in a heavy tight-lidded pan with salt, $1\frac{1}{2}$ tsp. (7 mL) butter and garlic. Pour in $\frac{2}{3}$ cup (150 mL) boiling water, cover tightly, and cook over very low heat for 20 minutes or until all water is absorbed and rice is fully cooked.

Melt 2 Tbsp. (25 mL) butter in a wide, heavy skillet, and sauté onion over medium-low heat until it is softened and transparent but not colored. Remove onion with a slotted spoon, and add to cooked rice. Allow rice mixture to cool, remove garlic, and stir in dill. Set aside.

Put the unwashed skillet over medium-high heat, add mushrooms, and sauté until they are lightly browned and reduced in size. Keep heat high so that juice rises as steam; mushrooms should cook "dry," not stew in liquid. Add more butter if mushrooms start to stick or burn. Spread on a plate to cool.

At assembly time, finely chop eggs, and butter a baking sheet or line it with parchment paper. All filling ingredients, except salmon, should be at room temperature.

Roll the Egg Bread dough out on a lightly floured board to make a 12-by-18-inch (30 x 45 cm) rectangle. Thickness should taper from about $\frac{1}{4}$ inch (5 mm) at the center to quite thin at the edges. Arrange a 4-by-14-inch (10 x 35 cm) rectangle of chopped eggs in the center of the dough, and sprinkle lightly with salt and pepper. Add a layer of mushrooms, then arrange salmon over them. Having the fish layer $\frac{3}{4}$ inch (2 cm) thick is more important than having it exactly 4 by 14 inches (10 x 35 cm).

Spoon the rice mixture over the top, letting a bit come around the sides, pressing and molding with your hands so that it adheres as well as possible. Grate on a little nutmeg, and sprinkle with salt and pepper.

Lift the two sides of the dough, stretching gently, and overlap generously. Fold in the ends, pinch to the bottom, then pinch all around the overlap to make a secure seal.

Flip the roll onto the prepared baking sheet, seam side down, press gently on top, then cover loosely with plastic wrap, and let rise in a warm room for about 45 minutes or until puffy—it won't quite double. Paint generously with glaze. Cut a small vent hole for steam to escape, and line it with a foil funnel.

Heat oven to 425°F (220°C), then lower heat to 400°F (200°C), and bake for 15 minutes. Lower heat to 350°F (180°C), and bake for 30 minutes longer, then cut into slices about 1 inch (2.5 cm) wide, and serve at once. Offer melted butter as a sauce.

Serves 6 to 8 (about 12 slices).

TUNA SAUTÉ
WITH TOMATO SAUCE

Tuna steaks studded with garlic, seared in olive oil and served with a tomato-pepper sauce give this recipe a happy combination of flavors, which justifies the extra time it takes to prepare the sauce.

Tomato Sauce

4 Tbsp.	olive oil	50 mL
1	small onion, chopped	1
1	clove garlic, minced	1
1	red bell pepper, roasted until charred, then peeled, seeded & cut into 1-inch (2.5 cm) chunks	1
1	green pepper, roasted until charred, then peeled, seeded & cut into 1-inch (2.5 cm) chunks	1
1	small chili pepper, chopped, or $\frac{1}{4}$ tsp. (1 mL) cayenne pepper	1
2 cups	tomatoes, peeled & seeded	500 mL
2 tsp.	fresh basil, chopped, plus extra for garnish, or 1 tsp. (5 mL) dried	10 mL
1 tsp.	fresh oregano, chopped, or $\frac{1}{2}$ tsp. (2 mL) dried	5 mL
	Salt & freshly ground pepper	
4	6 oz. (175 g) tuna steaks, about $\frac{1}{2}$ inch (1 cm) thick	4
2	large cloves garlic, slivered	2
3 Tbsp.	olive oil	45 mL

To make tomato sauce, heat oil in a saucepan. Add onion, garlic, red and green peppers and chili pepper, and sauté for 3 to 5 minutes until onion is soft. Add tomatoes and dried herbs, if not using fresh, and cook over high heat until most of the liquid has evaporated, about 5 minutes. If using fresh herbs, add at this point, along with salt and pepper to taste. Set aside.

With a paring knife, make tiny slits in tuna steaks, and insert slivers of garlic. Heat oil in a skillet, and sauté steaks over high heat until browned on each side, about 6 minutes total. Make a slice in one of the steaks to test for doneness. (The tuna steaks can also be charcoal-grilled.) Heat tomato sauce, and serve tuna surrounded by sauce and sprinkled with fresh basil, if available.

Serves 4.

POLLACK MEUNIÈRE

Delightfully simple and quick, this dish is great for a last-minute meal.

4 Tbsp.	clarified butter	50 mL
2 Tbsp.	oil	25 mL
$\frac{3}{4}$ cup	flour	175 mL
	Salt & freshly ground pepper	
$1\frac{1}{2}$ lb.	pollack fillets	750 g
3 Tbsp.	fresh parsley, finely chopped	45 mL

Heat butter and oil in a large skillet until sizzling. Put flour and salt and pepper in a plastic bag, and add portion-sized pieces of fish. Shake to coat. Place fish in hot skillet, and cook for 2 to 5 minutes on each side, depending on the thickness of fillets. Sprinkle with parsley, and serve immediately.

Serves 4.

Fish & Seafood

RICE ADVICE

Although North Americans are eating more rice than ever before, this staple remains an underappreciated food in the West. Annually, North Americans consume less than 10 pounds (4.5 kg) of rice per person, while inhabitants of Asian countries eat as much as 1 pound (500 g) per day. Low in calories and free of cholesterol, brown, white, basmati, long- and short-grained varieties are all available to the contemporary cook. (Wild rice is a delicious, though misnamed, seed from water grass that is indigenous to the northern United States and the Great Lakes in Canada.) While long-grain white rice is still a North American favorite, delicately fractured grains of aromatic basmati rice are especially well suited to spicy dishes, such as Fish Curry.

FISH CURRY

Fast-cooking fish makes this spicy curry an easy rush-hour meal.

1½ lb.	sole fillets	750 g
3 Tbsp.	oil	45 mL
2	small onions, finely chopped	2
4 Tbsp.	Green Curry Paste (page 145)	50 mL
1½ tsp.	ground cumin	7 mL
1 tsp.	Szechuan pepper	5 mL
	Salt	
2	large tomatoes, chopped	2
	Lemon juice	
2 tsp.	garam masala (page 145)	10 mL

Cut fish into serving-sized pieces. Heat oil in a heavy pot, and sauté onions and curry paste until onions are translucent. Add cumin, Szechuan pepper, salt and tomatoes, and cook for 1 minute, stirring. Add lemon juice.

Place fish in the pot, spooning liquid over it. Cover, and simmer for 10 minutes. Sprinkle with garam masala, and serve over basmati rice.

Serves 6.

SAUTÉED SOLE WITH ROMAINE LETTUCE, PEAS & GRAPEFRUIT JUICE

Flounder or sole will melt in your mouth in this extraordinary citrus combination. Fresh peas add both crunch and color. Prepare the sauce first, and serve with the lightly sautéed fish.

1 cup	fish stock	250 mL
1 tsp.	shallots, finely minced	5 mL
¾ lb.	fresh peas	375 g
¼ lb.	Romaine lettuce, shredded	125 g
1 tsp.	cornstarch	5 mL
	Flour, salt, pepper & grated grapefruit zest	
4	large fillets of sole or flounder	4
4 Tbsp.	clarified butter	50 mL
1	grapefruit, preferably pink	1

In a saucepan, bring fish stock and shallots to a boil, and let stock reduce to ½ cup (125 mL). Add peas and lettuce, and cook for 1 minute. Mix cornstarch with a little water, then add to skillet. Cook 1 minute longer or until sauce thickens. Set aside.

Mix flour, salt, pepper and grapefruit zest, and put on a flat dish. Dip fish into mixture to coat lightly. Heat butter in a skillet until sizzling, then add fish, sauté for 2 minutes on each side, and remove to a warmed dish. Squeeze juice from half the grapefruit into the skillet, whisk until slightly thickened, then add sauce to skillet, mix gently until hot, taste for seasoning, and serve to the side of the fish.

Serves 4.

SOLE FLORENTINE

Nutmeg-seasoned spinach and cheese delicately blend together with the mild flavor of sole in this classic fish preparation.

1 lb.	spinach	500 g
¼ tsp.	sugar	1 mL
2 Tbsp.	butter	25 mL
2 Tbsp.	flour	25 mL
1 cup	milk	250 mL
	Pinch nutmeg	
½ cup	mushrooms, thinly sliced	125 mL
½ cup	Cheddar or Swiss cheese, grated	125 mL
2 Tbsp.	parsley, chopped	25 mL
	Salt & freshly ground pepper	
1 lb.	sole fillets	500 g

Wash spinach, and pack it into a saucepan. Sprinkle with sugar, cover, and cook over medium heat for 3 to 4 minutes. Turn spinach, cover, and cook for an additional 2 minutes. Drain, and spread on the bottom of a buttered 1½-quart (1.5 L) casserole.

Melt butter, stir in flour, and cook over low heat for 1 minute. Add milk, and stir to blend. Cook until slightly thickened, then add nutmeg, mushrooms, cheese, parsley and salt and pepper.

Spread fillets over spinach, then pour sauce over fish. Bake at 350°F (180°C) for 30 minutes.

Serves 4.

Spanakopitta

Main Courses, page 92

Lemon-Rosemary Chicken

Main Courses, page 85

SEA SCALLOP, SWEET CORN & SNAP PEA SAUTÉ

Corn adds sweetness to the gently flavored scallops, while the snap peas lend a fresh crunch to this seafood dish.

4 Tbsp.	clarified butter	50 mL
2 Tbsp.	oil	25 mL
1 Tbsp.	shallots, minced	15 mL
1	small hot red pepper, seeded & minced	1
2 lb.	sea scallops	1 kg
$\frac{1}{3}$ cup	chicken stock	75 mL
3 cups	corn kernels	750 mL
$\frac{1}{4}$ cup	scallions, sliced on the diagonal into pieces	50 mL
10	pea pods, cut in half on the diagonal	10
	Chives & pea pods for garnish	

Heat butter and oil until foaming, add shallots and hot pepper, and sauté for 1 minute. Add scallops, and sear quickly. Add chicken stock and vegetables. Cover, and cook for 2 to 3 minutes. Garnish with chives and pea pods.

Serves 4.

SHRIMP WITH BLACK MUSTARD SEEDS & CUMIN

The exotic flavors of shrimp, mustard and spices belie the ease of preparation of this stir-fry.

6 Tbsp.	butter	75 mL
3-4 Tbsp.	black mustard seeds	45-50 mL
1 Tbsp.	cumin	15 mL
1 tsp.	red pepper flakes	5 mL
2	cloves garlic, crushed	2
1 lb.	shrimp, shelled & deveined	500 g
1	bunch green onions, chopped	1
2	celery stalks, diced	2
$\frac{1}{2}$	green pepper, diced	$\frac{1}{2}$
$\frac{1}{2}$ lb.	mushrooms, sliced	250 g
$\frac{1}{2}$ lb.	salted cashews	250 g
	Freshly ground pepper	

Melt butter in a wok. Add mustard seeds, cumin, red pepper and garlic, and cook over high heat, stirring constantly, until mustard seeds begin to pop—about 2 minutes. Add shrimp, green onions, celery and green pepper. Stir-fry over medium-high heat for 5 minutes or until shrimp turn pink. Add mushrooms, cashews and pepper to taste. Cook for 2 more minutes. Serve over rice.

Serves 2.

SAUTÉED SHRIMP WITH ROSEMARY, THYME & MUSHROOMS

Plump, pink shrimp and aromatic fresh herbs make a dramatic dinnertime combination. The mushrooms add a contrasting texture, depth and flavor.

6 Tbsp.	clarified butter	75 mL
3	cloves garlic, minced	3
$\frac{1}{2}$ lb.	mushrooms, sliced	250 g
2 lb.	large, pink shrimp, shelled & deveined	1 kg
1 tsp.	fresh thyme or lemon thyme or $\frac{1}{2}$ tsp. (2 mL) dried	5 mL
1 tsp.	fresh rosemary, crushed, or $\frac{1}{2}$ tsp. (2 mL) dried	5 mL
$\frac{1}{4}$ cup	scallions, cut into ringlets	50 mL
$\frac{1}{2}$ cup	clam juice	125 mL
$\frac{1}{4}$ cup	dry white wine	50 mL
3-5	sprigs each rosemary & thyme, flowering if possible.	3-5

Put 3 Tbsp. (45 mL) butter in a skillet, add garlic and mushrooms, and sauté over high heat until mushrooms are lightly browned and liquid has disappeared. Remove to a bowl. Add remaining butter, heat until sizzling, then add shrimp; sauté for 3 minutes, shaking and stirring constantly. Add herbs, scallions, reserved mushrooms and clam juice, and cook for 2 minutes. Add sprigs of rosemary and thyme, toss lightly, and serve.

Serves 4.

BLACKENING SPICE

In a small dry skillet, toast $\frac{1}{4}$ tsp. (1 mL) each coriander seeds, cumin seeds and red pepper flakes over medium-high heat, shaking pan back and forth to prevent scorching, until spices release their fragrance. In a food chopper or processor, grind spice mixture with 2 Tbsp. (25 mL) paprika, 2 tsp. (10 mL) chili powder, 1 tsp. (5 mL) thyme, $\frac{1}{2}$ tsp. (2 mL) salt and $\frac{1}{4}$ tsp (1 mL) black peppercorns.

CAJUN GUMBO

The richly flavored gumbos of Louisiana's Acadians were more than simple stews—they were party food. When Cajuns gathered for a celebration, all would contribute ingredients for a *gros gumbo*—a little chicken, a piece of ham, crawfish. To make a leaner version, this recipe departs from tradition but without leaving the flavor behind. Serve with rice.

1 Tbsp.	vegetable oil	15 mL
¾ lb.	andouille or other firm spicy sausage, cut into pieces	375 g
½ lb.	skinless, boneless chicken breast, cut into bite-sized pieces	250 g
2	medium onions, chopped	2
1	small green pepper, seeded & chopped	1
1	celery stalk, chopped	1
3	cloves garlic, finely chopped	3
2 cups	chicken stock	500 mL
2 Tbsp.	flour	25 mL
1	can (28 oz./796 mL) plum tomatoes; reserve juice	1
3 Tbsp.	blackening spice (facing page)	45 mL
¾ lb.	ham steak, cut into large cubes	375 g
1 cup	frozen okra pods, very thickly sliced	250 mL
4	green onions	4
12	large uncooked shrimp, peeled & deveined	12
¼ cup	fresh parsley, finely chopped	50 mL

In a Dutch oven or a large saucepan, heat oil. Add sausage, and cook over medium heat for 5 minutes, turning often, or until firm and lightly browned. Transfer to a plate, and set aside. Add chicken to pan, and cook, turning frequently, for about 1 minute or until opaque. Stir in onions, green pepper, celery and garlic. Add 1 Tbsp. (15 mL) chicken stock, and cook, covered, over medium-low heat for 3 to 4 minutes or until onions are transparent. Increase heat to medium-high. Sprinkle with flour, and cook, stirring constantly, for 2 minutes. Blend in remaining chicken stock and juice from tomatoes.

Stir in blackening spice, and return sausage to pan. Add ham. Cover, and simmer gently for 25 minutes. Add tomatoes and okra. Cover, and simmer for 10 minutes. Trim away all but 1 inch (2.5 cm) of dark green from onions. Add onions, shrimp and parsley. Cover, and simmer for 3 to 5 minutes or until shrimp are opaque.

Serves 6.

QUICK-COOKING TOMATO SAUCE

This sauce is best used right away, but it can be made up to two days ahead, refrigerated, then reheated a few minutes before serving. If you prepare sauce in advance, do not add the basil until you reheat.

2 lb.	fresh, ripe tomatoes, peeled, seeded & chopped	1 kg
1	large clove garlic, minced	1
2-3 Tbsp.	olive oil	25-45 mL
	Fresh basil (about 12 leaves), finely chopped	
	Salt & freshly ground pepper	

Lightly drain tomatoes if they seem watery. In a wide, shallow non-aluminum pan, gently stew garlic in oil until soft. Add tomatoes, basil and salt and pepper to taste. Bring to a boil, and cook briskly, uncovered, for 10 to 15 minutes, stirring occasionally and crushing the tomatoes with a wooden spoon. The sauce should be just slightly thickened. Serve with vermicelli, spaghettini or other thin pasta.

Makes about 2 cups (500 mL).

UNCOOKED TOMATO SAUCE

Fresh, simple sauces go with thin pasta shapes. If the tomatoes are very juicy, add a few more than are called for and drain off some of the liquid.

1	small onion	1
1	medium clove garlic	1
2 lb.	fresh, ripe tomatoes, peeled, seeded & coarsely chopped	1 kg
2-4 Tbsp.	olive oil	25-50 mL
1-3 tsp.	balsamic vinegar or lemon juice (opt.)	5-15 mL
	Salt & freshly ground pepper	
	Fresh basil for garnish	

Mince onion and garlic together. Stir into tomatoes along with 2-3 Tbsp. (25-45 mL) oil. Season to taste with more oil, vinegar, if desired, and salt and pepper. Let stand, unrefrigerated, for 1 to 4 hours. Serve with angel-hair pasta, and sprinkle a few torn basil leaves over each portion.

Makes about 3 cups (750 mL) thin sauce.

SUGO FINTO
(Faux Meat Sauce)

Translators gnash their teeth over *sugo*, which can mean anything from "sap" to "pithy idea." Applied to sauces, it usually indicates something infused with rich meat juices. The point of *finto* (false, mock) is to get a fine meaty flavor without the expense of using fresh meat.

2 lb.	fresh, ripe tomatoes, peeled, seeded & coarsely chopped, or one can (28 oz./796 mL)	1 kg
1	medium carrot	1
1	medium onion	1
1	medium celery stalk	1
1 Tbsp.	olive oil, butter or lard	15 mL
2 oz.	pancetta, prosciutto fat or salt pork	50 g
1	large clove garlic	1
	Small handful fresh parsley	
1-1½ cups	water, white wine or reserved tomato juice	250-375 mL
	Large pinch oregano (opt.)	
	Salt & freshly ground pepper	

Let tomatoes drain in a colander over a bowl while you prepare the basis of the sauce. Finely chop carrot, onion and celery together (or coarsely puree in a food processor). Heat oil in a wide, shallow non-aluminum pan, and gently sauté the vegetables, stirring occasionally, until fragrant. Meanwhile, mince pancetta with garlic and parsley until they are almost a paste (or process to a coarse paste in a food processor).

Add pancetta mixture to vegetables. Cook slowly, uncovered, stirring frequently. After a few minutes, as the fat begins to render out of the meat, add a few tablespoons water, and let it boil away. Gradually add remaining water, a few tablespoons at a time, soaking for 10 to 15 minutes longer or until the liquid has been absorbed and the vegetables are a soft paste. The aim is to let the flavors infuse while the ingredients lightly braise without scorching.

Add tomatoes and, if desired, oregano. Simmer, uncovered, stirring occasionally and crushing tomatoes with a wooden spoon, for 20 to 30 minutes or until the sauce is of a good consistency. Season with salt and pepper to taste.

Makes about 2½ cups (625 mL).

PASTA CON MOLLICA DI PANE
(Pasta With Toasted Breadcrumbs)

As well as providing a contrast in textures, the breadcrumbs absorb the sauce and help it cling to the strands of pasta. The anchovies are mandatory: even people who claim to dislike them will taste nothing "fishy" in this sauce.

1	small clove garlic, minced	1
¼ cup	olive oil, plus a few drops	50 mL
4 oz.	anchovies, rinsed	114 mL
1½ cups	plum tomatoes, chopped	375 mL
⅓ cup	fresh parsley, minced	75 mL
½ tsp.	oregano	2 mL
	Freshly ground pepper	
½ cup	whole wheat breadcrumbs	125 mL
¾ lb.	spaghetti	375 g

In a skillet, sauté garlic in ¼ cup (50 mL) oil until golden. Add anchovies, and mash into a paste with a spoon. Cook briefly. If using canned tomatoes, drain them. Add tomatoes and parsley to the skillet. Simmer for 2 to 3 minutes. Season with oregano and pepper.

In a separate skillet, sauté breadcrumbs in a few drops of oil until crisp and golden. Set aside.

Cook pasta in a large pot of boiling salted water until tender but still slightly firm. Drain. Toss with sauce and breadcrumbs, and serve immediately. Serves 4.

'FIGHTING-MAD'
SAUCE FOR PENNE

The nomenclature of Italian sauces often puzzles North Americans. It is usual to mention the name of the pasta and then add "with" or "in the style of" some identifying element in the sauce or its place of origin. A well-known Roman dish is *penne* (quills) *all'arrabbiata* (fighting-mad style), made with a quick-cooking tomato sauce laced with hot peppers. The degree of hotness can be varied to taste, and this sauce is meant to be mildly spicy.

3 Tbsp.	olive oil or a mixture of olive oil & butter	45 mL
3	large cloves garlic, peeled & quartered or lightly crushed	3
2 lb.	fresh, ripe tomatoes, peeled, seeded & chopped, or one can (28 oz./796 mL), undrained	1 kg
2-3	small, dried hot red peppers, crushed & seeded, or ½ tsp. (2 mL) red pepper flakes	2-3
	A few fresh basil leaves, torn, plus extra for garnish	
	Salt & freshly ground pepper	
2-4 Tbsp.	freshly grated Romano cheese (preferably imported Italian *pecorino romano*) or imported Parmesan cheese, plus extra for garnish	25-50 mL

In a large, wide non-aluminum skillet, heat oil until not quite smoking. Quickly brown garlic, and remove with a slotted spoon. Add tomatoes, peppers and basil. Season lightly with salt and pepper. Bring to a boil, and simmer, uncovered, for 15 to 20 minutes, stirring frequently and crushing the tomatoes with a wooden spoon. The sauce should be just slightly thickened, still runny enough to slurp nicely into the hollows of the pasta.

Just before serving, toss the sauce and the pasta together with cheese. Garnish with more basil, and pass extra cheese at the table.

Makes 2 to 3 cups (500-750 mL).

BASIL PESTO

Serve pesto over hot, buttered spaghetti, or add a couple of spoonfuls to a vegetable soup to enrich the flavor. Pesto can easily be frozen and thawed for use.

2 cups	fresh basil	500 mL
2	cloves garlic	2
½ tsp.	salt	2 mL
⅓–½ cup	olive oil	75–125 mL
¼ cup	grated Parmesan cheese	50 mL
3 Tbsp.	pine nuts	45 mL

Place basil, garlic, salt and ⅓ cup (75 mL) oil in a blender or a food processor. Process to a smooth paste, adding more oil if necessary. Add cheese and pine nuts, and blend for a few more seconds, leaving the pine nuts in tiny chunks to provide some texture.
Makes 1 cup (250 mL).

RED-PEPPER PESTO

A sweet alternative to basil-based pesto.

2	red bell peppers	2
3	large cloves garlic, peeled	3
½ cup	pine nuts, toasted	125 mL
¼ cup	olive oil	50 mL
¼ cup	freshly grated Parmesan cheese	50 mL
¼ cup	fresh cilantro or parsley, chopped	50 mL
	Salt & freshly ground pepper	

Place peppers over a gas burner, and roast, turning frequently, until blackened and blistered all over, about 10 minutes (or broil peppers 4 inches/10 cm from the heat, turning frequently, for about 15 minutes). Put peppers in a paper bag, and set aside for 15 minutes. Peel, and discard seeds and membrane; rinse under cold water.

In a food processor or a blender, mince garlic. Add roasted peppers and pine nuts; process until smooth. With motor running, drizzle in oil through feed tube. Transfer mixture to a small bowl, and stir in cheese and cilantro. Season with salt and pepper. (Can be stored in the refrigerator for up to 2 days or in the freezer for a month.)
Makes about 1 cup (250 mL).

PEROGIES WITH POTATO-CHEESE FILLING

Serve with sautéed onions and sour cream or yogurt. Meat, fruit and other vegetable fillings are equally tasty. For a variation using mushrooms and cheese, see facing page.

Dough

3 cups	flour, plus extra for kneading	750 mL
1½ tsp.	salt	7 mL
1	large egg	1
4 tsp.	vegetable oil	20 mL

Filling

2	medium potatoes, peeled & cut into pieces	2
1 Tbsp.	butter	15 mL
1	onion, chopped	1
1¼ cups	grated sharp Cheddar cheese	300 mL
4-6 Tbsp.	sour cream or yogurt	50-75 mL
1 Tbsp.	parsley, chopped	15 mL
	Salt & freshly ground pepper	

To make dough, stir together flour and salt in a large bowl. In a small bowl, whisk together egg, oil and ¾ cup (175 mL) water. Stir egg mixture into flour to make a soft but not sticky dough. If dough does not hold together in a ball, add more water 1 tsp. (5 mL) at a time, being careful not to make dough sticky. Turn dough onto a lightly floured surface, and knead briefly about 10 times, until dough is smooth. Cover with a mixing bowl or plastic wrap, and let rest for 30 to 40 minutes.

To make filling, boil potatoes for 7 to 9 minutes or until tender. Drain, and let cool. In a small skillet, melt butter. Add onion, and cook over medium heat for 4 to 6 minutes or until onion is tender and lightly browned. Set aside. Place potatoes in a large bowl, and mash until smooth. Add onion, cheese and enough sour cream to give a soft but not moist puree. Add parsley, and season with salt and pepper to taste.

Working with a quarter of the dough at a time, roll out on a lightly floured surface as thin as possible (about 1/16 inch/1.5 mm thick). Using a 3-inch (8 cm) round cutter, cut dough into circles. Place a heaping teaspoon of filling in the center of each circle, and lightly brush edges with water. Fold in half, pinch edges together to seal, and set aside on a floured surface, making sure perogies do not touch. Cover with plastic wrap to prevent drying while working with the remaining dough.

(The perogies can be prepared ahead and stored, covered with plastic wrap, for up to 8 hours in the refrigerator or a month in the freezer. Once frozen, they can be layered in an airtight container. Do not thaw before cooking.)

In a large pot of gently boiling salted water, cook perogies in batches, stirring to prevent them from sticking, for 2 to 3 minutes or until tender. With a slotted spoon, remove to a warm serving platter, and keep warm while cooking remaining perogies.

Makes 48 perogies.

MUSHROOM FILLING FOR PEROGIES

2 Tbsp.	butter	25 mL
1	onion, chopped	1
4 cups	finely chopped mushrooms	1 L
¼ lb.	farmer cheese	125 g
4-5 tsp.	fresh dill, chopped, or 1 tsp. (5 mL) dried	20-25 mL
2 tsp.	fresh lemon juice	10 mL
	Salt & freshly ground pepper	

In a large skillet, melt butter. Add onion, and cook over medium heat for 3 minutes or until onion begins to soften. Add mushrooms, and continue cooking, stirring occasionally, for 8 to 10 minutes or until moisture has evaporated. Transfer to a large bowl, and let cool to room temperature.

Add farmer cheese, dill and lemon juice. Mix well. Season with salt and pepper to taste.

SPAETZLE

Instead of parsley, try chives or scallion greens, caraway seeds sautéed in butter, poppy seeds or fresh dill.

3 cups	flour	750 mL
1 tsp.	salt	5 mL
¼ tsp.	baking powder	1 mL
¼ tsp.	nutmeg	1 mL
4	large eggs, lightly beaten	4
1 cup	milk	250 mL
2 Tbsp.	butter	25 mL
2 Tbsp.	fresh parsley, chopped	25 mL
	Salt & freshly ground pepper	

In a large bowl, stir together flour, salt, baking powder and nutmeg. Stir in eggs, and gradually add enough milk to make a smooth but not stiff dough.

Force mixture through a large-holed colander (or a spaetzle maker) into a big pot of boiling salted water. Boil for 4 to 5 minutes or until spaetzle rises to the surface. Drain, and transfer to a warm serving bowl. Toss with butter and parsley, and season with salt and pepper to taste.

Serves 4 to 6.

WHOLE WHEAT PIZZA CRUST

This recipe produces a relatively light crust. Its lovely texture and nutty flavor work especially well with slightly heavy toppings.

1¾ tsp.	active dry yeast	9 mL
1 cup	plus 2 Tbsp. (25 mL) warm water (105°F/40°C)	250 mL
	Pinch sugar or 1 tsp. (5 mL) honey	
4½ Tbsp.	olive oil	60 mL
¾ cup	whole wheat flour	175 mL
2½ cups	unbleached flour	625 mL
1 tsp.	sea salt	5 mL

Stir yeast, water and sugar together, and let sit for 5 minutes or until foamy. Stir in oil, and add flour, 1 cup (250 mL) at a time, and salt. Mix until all the lumps are gone. You can do this by hand, in a heavy-duty mixer with a dough hook or in a food processor. If using a mixer or a food processor, put the flour and salt in the work bowl, and add the liquid ingredients while the motor is running.

Knead for 8 to 10 minutes, until the dough is satiny and elastic (this can be done in the work bowl, but try kneading by hand for the sheer pleasure of it).

Place the dough in an oiled bowl, turn to coat, and cover tightly with plastic wrap. For the White Pizza Crust (facing page), let rise for 45 minutes to 1 hour; for the Semolina (facing page) and Whole Wheat Pizza Crusts, let rise for 2 hours or until doubled in bulk—this will help lighten these crusts a little bit.

Roll or press dough lightly into a flattened ball. Pick up dough, and stretch it with your fists, from underneath, until you achieve the desired size and thinness. Place on a cookie sheet or a pizza peel that has been sprinkled generously with cornmeal. At this point, push the edge of the crust outward with your fingertips to give it a final stretch, and pinch the edge lightly (there should be almost no visual distinction between the center and the edge of the dough). Cover with a kitchen towel for the second rise of 30 minutes. Shake occasionally to keep it from sticking to the work surface.

When ready to bake, add toppings, leaving about 1 inch (2.5 cm) of dough edge uncovered. Transfer the pizza to a preheated pizza stone or tiles, and bake in a 500°F (260°C) oven for 10 minutes or until done. Watch the pizza while it is baking because, at this temperature, it could burn quickly.

These recipes will make one 15-to-16-inch (38-40 cm) pizza or five or six individual ones.

The dough can be frozen at any stage during the process: simply wrap in aluminum foil, and label as to whether it has risen once or twice. Defrost in the refrigerator for at least 8 hours, and pick up where you left off.

WHITE PIZZA CRUST

Heavenly and foolproof, this dough is easy to work with and quick to rise, and it produces a beautiful puffy edge. If you stretch it really thin, you'll get a 15-inch (38 cm) pizza and some extra dough. You can also divide it into two or four pieces for individual sizes.

$1\frac{3}{4}$ tsp.	active dry yeast	9 mL
$1\frac{1}{3}$ cups	warm water (105°F/40°C)	325 mL
	Pinch sugar or 1 tsp. (5 mL) honey	
$\frac{1}{4}$ cup	olive oil	50 mL
$3\frac{3}{4}$ cups	unbleached flour	925 mL
$1\frac{1}{2}$ tsp.	sea salt	7 mL

To make crust, follow instructions given for Whole Wheat Pizza Crust.

SEMOLINA PIZZA CRUST

This crust is more crackerlike and is, some insist, authentically Italian. The dough requires a longer rising time, is very easy to roll and has a delicious flavor. The edge is narrow and crunchy, rather than puffy.

2	packages active dry yeast	2
1 cup	plus 4 Tbsp. (50 mL) warm water (105°F/40°C)	250 mL
	Pinch sugar or 2 tsp. (10 mL) honey	
6 Tbsp.	olive oil	75 mL
2 cups	semolina flour	500 mL
$1\frac{1}{2}$ cups	unbleached flour	375 mL
2 tsp.	sea salt	10 mL

To make crust, follow instructions given for Whole Wheat Pizza Crust.

PLUM TOMATO, SCALLION & PARMESAN PIZZA

This pizza reflects the best flavor of the Mediterranean. It is easy to prepare, either for dinner or as an elegant appetizer.

	Pizza dough	
	Olive oil	
10-12	plum tomatoes, thinly sliced, salted & dried for at least 1 hour	10-12
3	scallions, sliced into thin ringlets	3
$1\frac{1}{2}$ cups	grated Parmesan cheese	375 mL

Brush shaped risen dough with oil. Arrange tomato slices in a circular overlapping pattern, and sprinkle with scallions, then cheese. Bake in a preheated 500°F (260°C) oven for 10 minutes or until done.

SMOKED HAM, ASPARAGUS TIPS & WHITE CHEDDAR PIZZA

If you mound the asparagus generously, this pizza is as beautiful as it is light and delicious. The smoked ham accents the fresh taste of asparagus.

	Pizza dough	
	Olive oil	
$\frac{1}{4}$ lb.	smoked ham, sliced paper-thin	125 g
6 cups	asparagus tips & stalks, washed, cut into pieces & steamed for 5 minutes	1.5 L
2 cups	grated white Cheddar cheese	500 mL

Brush shaped risen dough with oil. Lay down a single thin layer of ham, top with mounds of asparagus, and sprinkle with cheese. Bake in a preheated 500°F (260°C) oven for 10 minutes or until done.

Pasta & Pizza

CAULIFLOWER, BÉCHAMEL & GOUDA PIZZA

This unusual pizza is delicate, and its soft texture and mild flavor are highlighted by the tang of aged Gouda.

1	large cauliflower	1
4 Tbsp.	unsalted butter	50 mL
4 Tbsp.	flour	50 mL
2 Tbsp.	shallots, minced	25 mL
	Salt	
2 cups	milk	500 mL
	Pizza dough	
	Olive oil	
2½ cups	grated aged Gouda cheese	625 mL

Trim cauliflower into flowerets, and steam for 5 to 8 minutes or until al dente. Set aside. Make a béchamel sauce with butter, flour, shallots, salt and milk.

Brush shaped risen dough with oil, spread with béchamel sauce, lay cauliflower on top in a circular pattern, and sprinkle with cheese. Bake in a preheated 500°F (260°C) oven for 10 minutes or until done.

RATATOUILLE PIZZA WITH RED PEPPERS, PARMESAN & MOZZARELLA

This pizza is reminiscent of classical Neapolitan pizza. The added flavor comes from using a version of ratatouille instead of tomato sauce.

2	large eggplants	2
2 Tbsp.	salt	25 mL
¼ cup	olive oil	50 mL
2	medium yellow onions, chopped	2
2	cloves garlic, pressed	2
3	medium zucchini, diced	3
2	red bell peppers, roasted & peeled	2
8	ripe plum tomatoes, blanched, peeled & diced, or one can (28 oz./796 mL) drained & diced	8
2 tsp.	fresh thyme, chopped, or 1 tsp. (5 mL) dried, crumbled	10 mL
1 Tbsp.	red wine vinegar	15 mL
1 cup	grated Parmesan cheese	250 mL
1½ cups	grated mozzarella cheese	375 mL
	Pizza dough	

Dice eggplants, and sprinkle with salt. Toss, and let sit in a colander for 1 hour (this helps remove any bitterness), then rinse.

Put oil in a pot, and add onions and garlic, then eggplant, zucchini and red peppers sequentially. Sauté each for 5 to 10 minutes before adding the next one. Finally, add tomatoes, thyme and vinegar, and let cook until the vegetables are soft, the liquid is mostly cooked off and the flavor is mellow, about 30 minutes. Taste for seasoning, and add whatever is necessary.

Put the mixture, in batches, into the work bowl of a food processor, and pulse until mixture has a medium-fine texture, like a chunky sauce. Spread onto the shaped risen dough, sprinkle with Parmesan, then mozzarella, and bake in a 500°F (260°C) oven for 10 minutes or until done.

RICOTTA, ZUCCHINI & TOMATO PIZZA

This is a meal in itself—full-bodied, rich and satisfying. It takes some extra time to prepare but is well worth the effort. It is excellent with the Semolina Pizza Crust (page 113).

1½ cups	ricotta cheese	375 mL
2	eggs	2
¼ cup	parsley, chopped	50 mL
½ tsp.	salt, plus extra for tomatoes	2 mL
3	plum tomatoes	3
1 cup	breadcrumbs	250 mL
1 cup	grated Parmesan cheese	250 mL
1	clove garlic, minced	1
2 tsp.	basil	10 mL
1 tsp.	oregano	5 mL
2	medium zucchini	2
3	eggs, beaten	3
	Olive oil	
	Pizza dough	
2 cups	grated mozzarella cheese	500 mL

Mix ricotta with eggs, parsley and salt, and set aside. Slice, salt and air-dry tomatoes for at least 1 hour. Put breadcrumbs, Parmesan, garlic, basil and oregano in a plastic bag, and shake to mix well.

Slice zucchini into ¼-inch (5 mm) wheels, dip in eggs, place in the bag of breadcrumbs, and shake to cover. Fry in a hot skillet with oil, and drain on paper towels.

Spread ricotta mixture on the shaped risen dough, then arrange zucchini and tomatoes over the ricotta mixture, alternating them in a circular pattern.

Scatter mozzarella evenly over the top, and bake in a 500°F (260°C) oven for 10 minutes or until done.

BROCCOLI, CHERRY TOMATO, PARSLEY PESTO & WHITE CHEDDAR PIZZA

The Cheddar melts to the crust, exposing the broccoli and cherry tomatoes. The parsley pesto with tarragon sauce is a herbal delight.

Pesto		
2	cloves garlic	2
2 cups	parsley	500 mL
¼ cup	fresh tarragon	50 mL
⅓ cup	olive oil	75 mL
⅓ cup	grated Parmesan cheese	75 mL
¼ cup	walnuts, lightly toasted	50 mL
	Salt	
	Pizza dough	
4	heads broccoli, steamed until al dente	4
4	cherry tomatoes, halved	4
1 cup	grated white Cheddar cheese	250 mL

Put pesto ingredients in a blender jar or the work bowl of a food processor, and blend until smooth. Spread pesto on the shaped risen dough; lay broccoli in a circle on top. Arrange cherry tomatoes in the center. Sprinkle with cheese, and bake in a preheated 500°F (260°C) oven for 10 minutes or until done.

Barbecue

CHICKEN WINGS WITH BARBECUE SAUCE

Ideal on chicken wings, this barbecue sauce can be used with equally tasty results on chicken pieces or grilled pork chops. Serve the wings with a tangy blue-cheese dip to spice them up even more. Simply combine blue cheese to taste with sour cream and/or yogurt in a blender or a food processor, and blend until almost smooth.

20	chicken wings	20
1½ cups	brown sugar	375 mL
2 Tbsp.	apple cider vinegar	25 mL
4 Tbsp.	soy sauce	50 mL
2 Tbsp.	oyster sauce	25 mL
2 Tbsp.	black bean sauce	25 mL
1 cup	tomato sauce	250 mL
2	cloves garlic, chopped	2
	Juice of 1 lemon	
	Freshly ground pepper	

Cook chicken wings in boiling water to cover for 15 minutes. Drain, reserving stock for another use.

Meanwhile, combine remaining ingredients in a heavy saucepan, and cook for 15 minutes, stirring frequently.

Dip wings in sauce, then place on grill 3 to 4 inches (8-10 cm) from white ashes (hot coals), and cook for 5 to 10 minutes per side, basting frequently with sauce.

Serves 4 to 6.

LAMB KABOBS

Assemble the meat and vegetable kabobs on separate skewers. Although created for lamb, this recipe is also delicious with chicken, beef or pork.

Marinade
1 cup	red wine	250 mL
¼ cup	red wine vinegar	50 mL
½ cup	olive oil	125 mL
2 tsp.	thyme	10 mL
6	peppercorns	6
2	bay leaves	2
4	cloves garlic	4
1 tsp.	salt	5 mL
1	onion, minced	1
	Parsley	

Kabobs
4-5 lb.	lean lamb, cubed	1.8-2.2 kg
2	large green peppers	2
1 lb.	large mushrooms	500 g
3	onions	3
1 pint	cherry tomatoes	500 mL
	Bamboo skewers, soaked	
	in cold water for 1 hour	

Combine marinade ingredients, and mix well. Pour over meat in a glass or porcelain bowl. Cover, and refrigerate for 24 hours. Drain, and reserve marinade.

When ready to assemble kabobs, cut vegetables into large cubes and thread a combination of them on half the skewers and the meat on the remainder. Brush vegetables with a little marinade, if you like.

Place meat kabobs on the grill approximately 4 inches (10 cm) from the white ashes (hot coals). Cook, turning frequently and basting with reserved marinade each time you turn, for 10 minutes or until meat is brown on the outside but still pink in the middle. Place vegetable kabobs on the grill, and cook them in the same manner for 5 minutes.

Serves 8 to 10.

Barbecue

BARBECUE MARINADE

Suitable for beef and poultry, this marinade can be used to season a variety of meat dishes, from kabobs to boneless chicken breasts, before they are grilled, broiled or baked. One to two hours before cooking, place meat in a shallow pan, and cover with marinade.

$1\frac{1}{2}$ cups	red wine	375 mL
$\frac{1}{2}$ cup	olive oil	125 mL
3	cloves garlic, diced	3
1	large onion, diced	1
2	bay leaves	2
2 tsp.	coarsely ground pepper	10 mL
1 tsp.	salt	5 mL
1 tsp.	thyme	5 mL
1 tsp.	basil	5 mL
1 tsp.	marjoram	5 mL
1 tsp.	oregano	5 mL

Combine all ingredients. Keeps in the refrigerator for several weeks.
Makes 2 cups (500 mL).

GRILL-ROASTED LOIN OF PORK

A covered grill can be used as an oven to roast meats to perfection. Here, a rosemary-garlic-cider marinade and apple glaze enhance the flavor and juiciness of lean, tender pork. The marinade is also good with lamb, chicken or turkey breast.

3 lb.	boneless pork loin roast	1.5 kg

Marinade

3	cloves garlic, crushed	3
2 tsp.	dried rosemary or 2 Tbsp. (25 mL) fresh, chopped	10 mL
2 tsp.	dry mustard	10 mL
$\frac{1}{4}$ cup	olive oil	50 mL
$\frac{1}{2}$ cup	cider or apple juice	125 mL
$\frac{1}{4}$ cup	cider vinegar	50 mL
	Salt & freshly ground pepper	

Glaze

$\frac{1}{4}$ cup	apple jelly, melted	50 mL

Dry surface of roast with paper towels. Place in a shallow nonreactive dish.

Chop garlic and rosemary together until very fine. Transfer to a small bowl, and stir in mustard and 1 Tbsp. (15 mL) oil. Rub paste all over meat. Combine remaining oil with cider and vinegar. Pour over meat, and refrigerate for 4 to 8 hours, turning meat occasionally. Remove from refrigerator 30 minutes before cooking. Transfer marinade to a small saucepan, bring to a boil, then set aside.

Place meat on a greased cooking grate. Sprinkle with salt and pepper. Close lid, and grill using indirect method (medium setting on a gas grill or medium-hot coals), turning and basting occasionally with reserved marinade for about $1\frac{1}{2}$ hours or until meat thermometer reads 160°F (70°C). Don't overcook. Brush with glaze several times during the last 20 minutes of cooking.

When meat is done, remove from the grill, place on a carving board, and cover loosely with foil. Let stand for 10 minutes before slicing.

Serves about 6.

Barbecue

BARBECUED SPARERIBS

Nothing pleases picnic guests like a mess of traditional barbecued ribs. Serve with cold potato salad, and end the meal with a refreshing no-fuss watermelon for dessert.

15 lb.	pork spareribs	6.75 kg
4 Tbsp.	oil	50 mL
4	large cloves garlic, minced	4
2	large onions, finely chopped	2
1 Tbsp.	gingerroot, finely minced	15 mL
2 Tbsp.	curry powder	25 mL
½ cup	toasted coconut	125 mL
½ cup	apple cider	125 mL
1	can (5½ oz./156 mL) tomato paste	1
2	bay leaves	2
⅔ cup	peanut butter	150 mL
½ tsp.	salt	2 mL
¼ cup	soy sauce	50 mL
	Juice of 1 lemon	
	Hot pepper sauce	
	Worcestershire sauce	
½ cup	chili sauce	125 mL
1 cup	beer	250 mL

Cover ribs with water in a large pot. Bring to a boil, and cook for 15 to 20 minutes or until ribs are cooked through. Remove ribs from pot, and reserve stock (you should have about 2 cups/500 mL).

Heat oil in a heavy skillet, and sauté garlic, onions and gingerroot until onions are translucent. Add curry powder, and continue to cook over high heat, stirring, for 5 minutes. Add reserved stock, coconut, cider, tomato paste and bay leaves. Bring to a boil, and cook for 10 minutes.

Stir in peanut butter, salt, soy sauce, lemon juice, hot pepper sauce, Worcestershire, chili sauce and beer. Cook for 10 minutes, then remove from heat.

Place ribs on the grill 4 inches (10 cm) from hot coals, and baste with sauce. Turn, and baste other side. Cook, turning and basting frequently, for 20 to 30 minutes or until crisp and browned.

Serves 10 to 12.

BARBECUED STUFFED SALMON

The outdoor smoky taste of barbecued salmon is a delicious alternative to traditional grill fare. Surprisingly easy to prepare, a whole grilled fish leaves you time to visit with guests.

	Oil	
1	whole salmon, cleaned, but with head & tail left on	1
	Salt	
1 cup	pine nuts	250 mL
1	bunch parsley, chopped	1
4	carrots, peeled & sliced	4
2	zucchini, sliced	2
4	celery stalks, chopped	4
3	onions, sliced into rings	3
½ lb.	butter, melted	250 g
	Freshly ground pepper	
	Thyme	
4	lemons	4

Grease a large piece of aluminum foil with oil, and place salmon on it. Sprinkle the cavity with salt. Combine pine nuts, parsley and vegetables in a large bowl. Stir in butter, and mix well, adding pepper and thyme to taste. Place stuffing in the cavity. Mound any extra stuffing around the salmon. Rub oil over the scales, then squeeze the juice of 2 lemons over all. Wrap salmon gently but securely in foil.

Place on grill approximately 6 inches (15 cm) from medium-hot coals, and cook, turning occasionally, for approximately 30 minutes. Check frequently, as cooking time will vary greatly depending on the heat of the coals. When salmon flakes easily but is still moist, it is done. Serve immediately, garnished with lemon wedges, or chill and then serve.

Serves 10 as part of a buffet or 4 as a main course.

Perogies

Main Courses, page 110

Buckwheat Blini

Brunches & Light Lunches, page 17

Barbecue

GRILLED SEAFOOD SALAD

For an update of the "wilted lettuce" classic, use a mix of watercress, radicchio, romaine and escarole.

¾ lb.	fresh shrimp (about 18 medium-large)	375 g
½ lb.	fresh scallops, halved if large	250 g
2 Tbsp.	lime juice	25 mL
2 Tbsp.	tarragon or white wine vinegar	25 mL
2 Tbsp.	shallots or mild onion, finely chopped	25 mL
2	cloves garlic, finely chopped	2
1 tsp.	Dijon mustard	5 mL
⅔ cup	olive oil, preferably extra-virgin	150 mL
	Salt & freshly ground pepper	
¼ cup	parsley, finely chopped	50 mL
12 cups	mixed salad greens	3 L

Peel and devein shrimp, leaving tails on. Combine with scallops in a bowl. In another bowl, whisk together lime juice, vinegar, shallots, garlic and mustard. Gradually whisk in oil, and season with salt and pepper. Pour over seafood, and marinate in refrigerator for 15 to 30 minutes (no longer, or seafood will become soft).

Drain seafood well, reserving marinade. Curve each shrimp into a C-shape, and skewer through both ends. Thread scallops onto separate skewers. (The recipe can be made ahead to this point; refrigerate seafood and marinade separately up to 4 hours.)

Heat reserved marinade to boiling. Add parsley. Remove ¼ cup (50 mL) marinade for basting, and set the remainder at the edge of the grill to keep warm.

Grill seafood over medium heat, brushing with marinade until firm to the touch and opaque in the center, about 2 minutes per side for shrimp, 3 to 4 minutes per side for scallops. Don't overcook.

Meanwhile, toss salad greens with just enough of the warm marinade to coat lightly. Remove shrimp and scallops from skewers, and scatter on top of greens. Drizzle with additional marinade, if needed.

Serves 6.

GRILLED VEGETABLES WITH PESTO

Take advantage of garden-fresh basil and parsley with this quick and simple recipe for cooking vegetables on the barbecue.

Pesto

2 cups	fresh basil	500 mL
2	cloves garlic	2
½ cup	fresh parsley	125 mL
½ tsp.	salt	2 mL
½ cup	olive oil	125 mL
¼ cup	grated Parmesan cheese	50 mL
4 Tbsp.	pine nuts	50 mL

Vegetables

4	medium eggplants	4
	Salt	
4	medium zucchini	4
4	large tomatoes	4
	Oil	

To make pesto, place basil, garlic, parsley, salt and ⅓ cup (75 mL) oil in a blender or a food processor. Process, adding oil, if necessary, to make a smooth paste. Add cheese and pine nuts, and blend for a few seconds more. Cover, and set aside.

Wash eggplants, and cut into thick slices. Place in a colander, and sprinkle liberally with salt. Leave for 30 minutes. Wash and thickly slice zucchini and tomatoes.

Place sliced eggplant on the grill 3 inches (8 cm) from medium coals, and brush with oil. Grill for 2 to 3 minutes, then turn. Add zucchini, brush with oil, and cook for 1 minute, then turn. Add tomato, brush with oil, and cook for 30 seconds, then turn. When all vegetables have been grilled on both sides, remove to a serving dish and top each slice with a heaping spoonful of pesto.

Serves 8 to 10 as a side dish.

SUMMER GARDEN GRILL

This recipe allows you to choose a variety of seasonal vegetables from your garden or market. Grilling each vegetable on separate skewers allows for variations in cooking times.

Marinade

¾ cup	olive oil	175 mL
2 Tbsp.	lemon juice	25 mL
2 Tbsp.	parsley, finely chopped	25 mL
2 Tbsp.	chives or scallions, finely chopped	25 mL
2	cloves garlic, crushed	2
½ tsp.	salt	2 mL
	Dash finely ground pepper	

Vegetables

12	very small onions, peeled, or 3 medium onions, peeled & quartered	12
12	very small new potatoes	12
1	large red bell pepper, cored & cut into pieces	1
1	large yellow bell pepper, cored & cut into pieces	1
12	mushrooms	12
1	small zucchini, ends trimmed & sliced into ovals ½ inch (1 cm) thick	1

In a small bowl, combine oil, lemon juice, parsley, chives, garlic, salt and pepper. Set aside.

Wash and trim vegetables. Parboil onions and potatoes until slightly tender, about 5 to 8 minutes. Place vegetables in a large nonreactive bowl.

Pour marinade over vegetables. Turn to coat thoroughly Set aside for up to 2 hours.

Reserving marinade, thread vegetables onto skewers (one kind per skewer). Place the skewered vegetables on the grill. Using direct method (medium setting on a gas grill or medium-hot coals), cook vegetables for 7 to 15 minutes, turning often and basting with marinade, or until each kind is fork-tender. As soon as vegetables are cooked, push them off the skewers into a large shallow pan at the edge of the grill (or on a warming grate if you have one). Cover with foil until ready to serve.

Serves 6.

Chapter 5

SIDE DISHES

he plaintive call for an extra pan of stuffing from some Johnny-come-lately to the holiday feast is a common cry. Reminded that sometimes it's the fixin's—the whipped potatoes, vegetable casserole or stuffing—which are the favorite part of a meal, we salute side dishes.

Renewed interest in healthy eating and the influx of exotic vegetables have boosted the popularity of produce, which remains the most rapidly expanding frontier in food stores. *Harrowsmith Country Life* readers who grow their own vegetables are ritual fans of the simple freshness that is available with each growing season. Whether it's pencil-thin asparagus lightly steamed and garnished with lemon during the first week in June or simmered vine-ripened tomatoes seasoned with herbs in August, food lovers have an extra reason to embrace the coming of summer.

Those who don't garden can optimize their love of vegetables by buying in season and close to home.

While Tuscany Stewed Tomatoes and Spiced Cauliflower & Potatoes are sure to please, we gratefully tip our hats to their grain-based side-dish cousins, such as Bulgur With Celery & Sage, Garlicky Couscous With Roasted Peppers or spoonbread made with cornmeal and green onions. With chameleonlike ease, these low-fat alternatives subtly complement a wide range of flavors, from roasted poultry to poached fish and grilled meat.

Unlimited in variety and versatile in taste, exciting side dishes need not wait for a holiday bird. Whether you use them to enliven your menu or serve some of the more hearty offerings for the main event, you will no doubt be inspired by the recipes presented on the following pages.

Side Dishes

SQUASH WITH WILD-RICE STUFFING

This mixture is so pleasing, you can serve it as a side dish or even chilled as a salad.

½ cup	wild rice	125 mL
1¼ cups	chicken or vegetable stock or water	300 mL
2	cloves garlic, chopped	2
½ Tbsp.	shallots, minced	8 mL
1	small leek, minced	1
	Olive oil	
1	celery stalk with leaves, minced	1
½ tsp.	grated orange zest	2 mL
1	orange, peeled & segmented (membranes removed)	1
¼ cup	pecans, toasted & chopped	50 mL
	Salt & freshly ground pepper	
½ Tbsp.	sherry	8 mL
1	egg white, lightly beaten	1
2	squashes, halved, seeded & steamed or baked to soften	2

Cook wild rice in stock until all liquid is absorbed, about 50 minutes. (Some varieties of rice come partially cooked and need less liquid, so if your rice came in a box, add as much liquid as the directions suggest.)

Sauté garlic, shallots and leek in enough oil to lightly coat the bottom of a pan. Add celery, and sauté for a few more minutes.

Combine cooked rice, sautéed vegetables, orange zest, orange, pecans, salt and pepper, sherry and egg white.

Spoon stuffing into squashes, and place in a baking pan so that they are not touching. Add about ¼ inch (5 mm) water to the pan. Bake in a preheated 375°F (190°C) oven for 30 minutes.

Serves 4.

PAPPA AL POMODORO
(Tuscany Stewed Tomatoes)

Plumped up with tomato juice, oil and seasonings, the bread thickens the stew and softens its acidity. Canned tomatoes make this a fine midwinter side dish.

¼ cup	extra-virgin olive oil	50 mL
3	large cloves garlic, minced	3
3 cups	stale Italian bread, including crusts, cut into cubes	750 mL
1	can (28 oz./796 mL) Italian tomatoes, drained (reserve juice) & coarsely chopped, or 3 cups (750 mL) fresh	1
5	fresh basil leaves, cut into strips or ½ tsp. (2 mL) dried	5
1½ cups	chicken stock	375 mL
¼ tsp.	salt	1 mL
	Freshly ground pepper	

Heat oil in a large saucepan over medium heat. Add garlic and bread, and cook, stirring occasionally, for about 3 minutes or until bread is well coated and beginning to brown. Mix in tomatoes and ½ cup (125 mL) reserved juice, basil, chicken stock, salt and pepper. Bring to a boil, and simmer, covered, for 40 minutes, stirring occasionally.

Serves 4.

Side Dishes

STUFFED POTATOES

Although it takes a little more time to prepare than a sandwich, a stuffed potato is a favorite of children and tastes great at room temperature served with yogurt.

4	potatoes, baked, split & scooped out (reserve skins)	4
¼ cup	cottage cheese	50 mL
¼ cup	grated Cheddar cheese	50 mL
7	strips crisp bacon, crumbled	7
3	celery stalks, finely diced	3
2	green onions, finely diced	2
1 tsp.	Dijon mustard	5 mL
	Salt & freshly ground pepper	
3 Tbsp.	plain yogurt	45 mL

Mash scooped-out potato, and combine with remaining ingredients. Mix well. Stuff gently into skins.
  Serves 4.

ROSEMARY POTATOES

Potato lovers go crazy for these savory slices, and no cook can ever make too many. The recipe can be followed quite loosely, and the seasoning can be adapted to any palate.

12	medium potatoes, peeled & cut into ¼-inch (5 mm) slices	12
½ cup	oil	125 mL
½ cup	melted butter	125 mL
3 Tbsp.	rosemary	45 mL
1 Tbsp.	ground cumin	15 mL
	Salt & freshly ground pepper	

Boil potato slices until almost cooked. Drain, and allow to cool slightly. Pour oil into a 9-by-13-inch (3 L) baking pan. Place potatoes in pan, then pour butter over potatoes, coating them as thoroughly as possible. Sprinkle with rosemary, cumin and salt and pepper.
  Bake at 375°F (190°C) for 45 to 60 minutes, turning potatoes several times so that they crisp and brown evenly. Remove from oil, and drain briefly before serving.
  Serves 8.

Side Dishes

SPICED CAULIFLOWER & POTATOES

This spicy recipe from *The Harrowsmith Cookbook, Volume III*, is a tasty preparation of vegetables that will complement a curry dinner.

1	cauliflower	1
6	potatoes, peeled	6
5 Tbsp.	olive oil, plus extra if needed	65 mL
1 tsp.	fennel seeds	5 mL
1 tsp.	cumin seeds	5 mL
$\frac{1}{4}$ tsp.	mustard seeds	1 mL
$\frac{1}{4}$ tsp.	fenugreek	1 mL
1	dried red chili pepper, crushed	1
1 tsp.	salt	5 mL
1 tsp.	cumin	5 mL
1 tsp.	coriander	5 mL
2 tsp.	turmeric	10 mL
	Freshly ground pepper	
1 tsp.	garam masala	5 mL

Break cauliflower into florets, and dice potatoes. Heat oil in a large, heavy frying pan until oil is smoking. Add fennel, cumin and mustard seeds and fenugreek, and cook, shaking pan, until seeds begin to pop. Add chili pepper, then stir in cauliflower and potatoes.

Reduce heat to medium, and add salt, cumin, coriander, turmeric and pepper. Sauté for 10 minutes, stirring and adding more oil if needed. Stir in 3 Tbsp. (45 mL) water. Cook, covered, over low heat for 15 minutes. Stir. Add water (just a bit) if needed, and cook for 20 minutes more or until vegetables are tender. Stir in garam masala.

Serves 6.

ETHIOPIAN VEGETABLES

Fiery-hot Ethiopian cuisine starts with an intense and complex base of garlic, gingerroot and onion, then adds other vegetables and seasonings. The flavors of the many spices meld and mellow as they simmer slowly with sweet, starchy vegetables. Add extra cayenne if you find this recipe needs more spice.

$\frac{1}{2}$	small yellow onion	$\frac{1}{2}$
2	cloves garlic, minced	2
1 tsp.	gingerroot, grated	5 mL
2 tsp.	vegetable oil	10 mL
1	large potato, peeled & cubed, or new potatoes, unpeeled (about $\frac{1}{4}$ lb./125 g)	1
1	carrot, cut into rounds	1
1 lb.	spinach, washed (discard coarse stems)	500 g
	Pinch cinnamon	
	Pinch cardamom	
$\frac{1}{4}$ tsp.	salt	1 mL
	Pinch cayenne pepper	
	Dash hot pepper sauce	

Sauté onion, garlic and gingerroot in oil in a thick-bottomed pot. Cook slowly until onion turns translucent.

Add potato and carrot, and pour in water to half cover the vegetables. Stir in remaining ingredients.

Simmer, covered, until potatoes and carrots start to fall apart. Stir occasionally, adding water, as needed, to cook the vegetables.

Serves 3.

Side Dishes

SANDY'S GINGERED SQUASH

This makes a light dish to serve alongside any dark green vegetable.

3 cups	cooked, mashed winter squash	750 mL
1½ tsp.	butter	7 mL
	Pinch salt	
	Juice of 1 lemon	
2 Tbsp.	honey	25 mL
2 Tbsp.	gingerroot, peeled & minced	25 mL

Mix all ingredients except gingerroot, adjusting the amount of lemon and honey, as required. Place gingerroot in a garlic press, express juice into squash, and stir.

Serves 4 to 6.

EGGPLANT WITH BLACK BEANS

The oiliness of the eggplant in this dish is traditional in Szechuan cooking but takes a little getting used to.

2 cups	oil	500 mL
1 lb.	eggplant, peeled & cubed	500 g
2	green onions, chopped	2
1	slice gingerroot, diced	1
1	clove garlic, diced	1
1 Tbsp.	soy sauce	15 mL
1 Tbsp.	sherry	15 mL
2 Tbsp.	Chinese chili sauce	25 mL
2 Tbsp.	fermented black beans	25 mL

Heat oil, then deep-fry eggplant for 3 to 4 minutes. Remove eggplant from oil, using a slotted spoon. Drain well, and set aside.

Pour off all but 1 Tbsp. (15 mL) oil, then stir-fry onions, gingerroot and garlic. Add soy sauce, sherry, chili sauce and beans, then eggplant. Heat through.

Serves 4.

SAUTÉED BEET GREENS

Butter, garlic and a little salt and pepper are all that sautéed greens require to join the ranks of vitamin-rich dark leafy greens (like spinach) which are welcome on the dinner table.

8 cups	beet greens	2 L
6 Tbsp.	butter	75 mL
2 Tbsp.	oil	25 mL
2	cloves garlic, crushed	2

Clean beet greens well, cutting off the tough stems and tearing the leaves if very large. Drain thoroughly.

Heat butter and oil in a heavy skillet. Sauté garlic until golden, then add beet greens. Stir to coat with oil mixture, then cover skillet, and reduce heat to medium. Allow greens to steam for 3 minutes, remove lid, and continue to sauté until greens are bright green and reduced in volume but still crunchy. Serve immediately.

Serves 4.

CREAMED BEETS

Borscht lovers will relish the flavor of this rich and creamy side dish.

8	beets	8
4 Tbsp.	butter	50 mL
1 Tbsp.	vinegar	15 mL
	Salt & freshly ground pepper	
1 cup	heavy cream	250 mL
3 Tbsp.	chives, chopped	45 mL
2 Tbsp.	sour cream	25 mL
2 Tbsp.	lemon juice	25 mL
	Dill for garnish	

Cook, peel and cube beets, and keep warm. Melt butter, and stir in all remaining ingredients except dill. Cook until slightly thickened. Pour over beets, and toss lightly. Garnish with dill.

Serves 6.

Side Dishes

KASHA WITH SOUR CREAM, MUSHROOMS, ONIONS & HERBS

Flavorful enough to be a main dish, this is also a fine accompaniment for grilled or roasted meat.

1	egg, lightly beaten	1
1 cup	coarse or whole kasha (buckwheat groats)	250 mL
1¾ cups	boiling chicken stock	425 mL
1½ tsp.	fresh thyme or ¾ tsp. (4 mL) dried	7 mL
½ tsp.	salt	2 mL
3 Tbsp.	butter	45 mL
1	large onion, finely chopped	1
6 cups	fresh mushrooms, diced, preferably meaty wild ones like ceps or shiitake	1.5 L
1 cup	sour cream	250 mL
½ cup	parsley, minced	125 mL

Mix egg and kasha together, and place in a medium-sized heavy-bottomed saucepan. Cook, stirring, over medium heat until the mixture begins to dry out, about 3 minutes. Stir in chicken stock, thyme and salt. Cover, and turn heat to low. Simmer until groats are tender and liquid is absorbed, about 12 minutes.

Meanwhile, make the sauce. In a skillet, melt butter over medium-high heat, add onion and mushrooms, reduce heat to low, and cook, stirring often, until mushrooms are fairly dry. Add sour cream, and stir until heated, but do not boil. Stir parsley into cooked kasha, and top with sauce.

Serves 6.

LEEK, SHIITAKE & KASHA PILAF

Coating the kasha with egg is essential to keep it fluffy, but for an even quicker side dish, omit the leeks and shiitake.

1	large egg	1
1 cup	whole kasha (buckwheat groats)	250 mL
2 cups	stock or water	500 mL
1 tsp.	thyme	5 mL
¼ tsp.	cayenne pepper	1 mL
1½ tsp.	olive oil	7 mL
2	small leeks, white parts only, washed & thinly sliced	2
12	shiitake mushrooms, stems removed & caps thinly sliced	12
1 Tbsp.	tamari sauce	15 mL
	Salt & freshly ground pepper	

Break egg into a medium bowl, and beat lightly. Stir in kasha, and mix until the grains are evenly coated. Set a deep, heavy skillet or a Dutch oven over high heat, and add kasha. Cook, stirring with a wooden spoon, for 2 to 3 minutes or until the grains are dry and separate.

In another pot, bring beef stock to a boil. Remove kasha from heat, and stir in boiling stock, thyme and cayenne. Cover, place over low heat, and simmer for 20 to 25 minutes or until liquid is absorbed and kasha is tender.

Meanwhile, heat oil in a small nonstick skillet over medium-high heat, and sauté leeks and mushrooms with tamari sauce until tender, about 5 minutes. Fluff kasha with a fork. Stir in leek mixture. Season with salt and pepper, and serve hot.

Serves 4.

Side Dishes

GARLICKY COUSCOUS WITH ROASTED PEPPERS

Couscous is the quick-change artist of the kitchen: it can take on any flavor—fast. Crushed garlic does the work here, a boon to anyone who dreads mincing the stuff.

1	small red bell pepper or a 6-oz. (160 mL) jar roasted red peppers or pimientos, drained & diced	1
1¼ cups	water	300 mL
1 tsp.	olive oil	5 mL
½ tsp.	salt	2 mL
2	large cloves garlic, peeled & lightly crushed	2
1 cup	couscous	250 mL
	Freshly ground pepper	

If using a fresh red pepper, roast it over the flame of a gas burner or broil it, turning often, for about 10 minutes or until blackened and blistered. Place in a paper bag, and set aside for 15 minutes. Slip the skin off the flesh, remove the stalk and seeds, and rinse. Dice, and set aside.

In a medium saucepan, combine water, oil, salt and garlic, and bring to a boil. Stir in couscous, and remove from heat. Cover, and let stand for 5 minutes. Fluff the grains with a fork. Remove garlic cloves, and stir in diced peppers. Season with pepper, and serve hot.

Serves 4.

FAST & HOT COUSCOUS

This spicy side dish, one of the easiest imaginable, is good with veal, chicken or fish. The hot sauce can be adjusted to taste.

1¼ cups	chicken stock or water	300 mL
1 Tbsp.	unsalted butter	15 mL
½ tsp.	hot pepper sauce	2 mL
¼ tsp.	salt	1 mL
1½ cups	couscous	375 mL
1 Tbsp.	fresh parsley, chopped, preferably flat-leaved	15 mL
	Freshly ground pepper	

In a heavy saucepan with a tight-fitting lid, combine chicken stock, butter, hot pepper sauce and salt; bring to a boil. Stir in couscous, and remove from heat. Cover, and let stand for 5 minutes. Uncover, and fluff the grains with a fork to separate. Stir in parsley. Season with pepper, and serve hot.

Serves 4.

Side Dishes

BULGUR WITH CELERY & SAGE

Bulgur cooks up quickly and simply with fresh ingredients that have all the savory satisfaction of a good poultry dressing.

2 tsp.	olive oil	10 mL
1 cup	medium-grain bulgur	250 mL
1	small onion, chopped	1
2	celery stalks, chopped	2
2	cloves garlic, minced	2
½ tsp.	each sage, thyme & marjoram	2 mL
1¾ cups	beef stock or water	425 mL
1	bay leaf	1
1 Tbsp.	fresh parsley, chopped	15 mL
	Salt & freshly ground pepper	

Heat oil in a heavy medium saucepan over medium heat. Add bulgur, onion, celery, garlic and herbs, and sauté for 5 to 8 minutes or until the vegetables are softened.

Stir in beef stock and bay leaf. Bring to a boil, reduce heat to low, cover, and simmer for about 15 minutes or until liquid is absorbed and bulgur is tender but still chewy. Remove bay leaf, stir in parsley, and season with salt and pepper.

Serves 4.

ORZO PRIMAVERA

Orzo, with its mild flavor, can be easily dressed up with green peas, red peppers and lemon.

1 cup	orzo	250 mL
1 tsp.	salt	5 mL
1 cup	frozen baby peas, thawed	250 mL
1	small red bell pepper, seeded & diced	1
1 Tbsp.	fresh dill, chopped	15 mL
1-2 Tbsp.	fresh lemon juice	15-25 mL
1 tsp.	olive oil	5 mL
	Salt & freshly ground pepper	

Bring a large pot of water to a rolling boil. Stir in orzo and salt, and return to a boil. Cook, stirring occasionally to prevent orzo from sticking, for 6 to 10 minutes or until the grains are tender but firm.

Drain, and transfer to a serving bowl. Add peas, red pepper, dill, 1 Tbsp. (15 mL) lemon juice and oil. Mix well, taste, and adjust seasonings, adding more lemon juice, if desired. Season with salt and pepper, and serve hot.

Serves 4.

Side Dishes

YESTERDAY'S BREAD

Day-old bread has never tasted so delicious as when it is baked together with a few eggs, some leftover vegetables and a handful of fresh herbs. Spoonbreads and stuffings can form a mouth-watering partnership with a whole fish, a roast or a hollowed-out pepper or onion. Loaded with corn, peppers, cheese and zucchini, they will stand alone as a versatile side dish or as a main course. Quick and simple to prepare, spoonbreads and stuffings are a perfect alternative to potatoes and rice for workday family meals.

BULGUR-CHICKPEA PILAF

Bulgur can be eaten after just a 10-minute soak in boiling water, but additional cooking with seasonings makes it more interesting. This easy pilaf, with hints of the Middle East and Asia, has double the carbohydrate punch, thanks to the chickpeas.

1 cup	medium-grain bulgur	250 mL
1 tsp.	sesame oil	5 mL
½ tsp.	vegetable oil	2 mL
1	medium onion, chopped	1
1	clove garlic, minced	1
1 tsp.	ground cumin	5 mL
1	can (10½ oz./297 mL) chickpeas, drained	1
1 cup	beef stock or water	250 mL
	Salt & freshly ground pepper	

Place bulgur in a medium bowl, and cover with 1 cup (250 mL) boiling water. Let stand for 10 minutes to soften.

Meanwhile, heat oils in a deep, heavy skillet or a Dutch oven over medium heat. Add onion, garlic and cumin, and sauté for about 5 minutes or until onion is soft but not brown. Stir in chickpeas. Add bulgur and beef stock, and mix well. Bring to a boil, reduce heat to low, cover, and simmer for about 10 minutes or until liquid is absorbed. If bulgur seems too wet, uncover the pan and cook over medium heat until liquid is absorbed. Fluff with a fork, season with salt and pepper, and serve hot.

Serves 4.

Side Dishes

GREEN ONION SPOONBREAD

Delicate and light, this basic spoonbread is an excellent companion to sautéed vegetables or a roast of any kind.

3 cups	milk	750 mL
1 cup	cornmeal, preferably stone-ground	250 mL
3 Tbsp.	green onion, chopped	45 mL
1½ tsp.	salt	7 mL
	Freshly ground pepper	
6 Tbsp.	unsalted butter	75 mL
4	large eggs at room temperature, separated	4
	Pinch cream of tartar	

Pour milk into a large saucepan, and bring almost to a boil. Gradually stir in cornmeal with a wire whisk. Continue cooking for 2 to 3 minutes, until thickened. Remove from heat, and stir in onion, salt, pepper, butter and egg yolks. Beat egg whites with cream of tartar until stiff, not dry. Fold into cornmeal mixture, and pour batter into a well-buttered casserole or soufflé dish. The batter should come within 1 inch (2.5 cm) of the top of the dish.

Bake at 350°F (180°C) for 30 to 40 minutes or until firm, browned and puffed. Serve immediately. (As the texture of spoonbread is denser and less fragile than that of a soufflé, its rise is not as dramatic nor its fall as significant.)

Serves 4 to 6.

BETTY'S MEXICAN SPOONBREAD

A spicy-hot combination that accentuates the flavor of the corn.

3 cups	milk	750 mL
1 cup	cornmeal, preferably stone-ground	250 mL
1 cup	corn kernels	250 mL
1½ tsp.	salt	7 mL
	Freshly ground pepper	
½ tsp.	cayenne pepper	2 mL
2 Tbsp.	fresh coriander leaves, finely chopped	25 mL
2 Tbsp.	jalapeño peppers, finely chopped	25 mL
6 Tbsp.	unsalted butter	75 mL
4	eggs at room temperature, separated	4
	Pinch cream of tartar	

Follow basic directions for Green Onion Spoonbread.
Serves 4 to 6.

Side Dishes

TRADITIONAL HERBED BREAD DRESSING FOR TURKEY

High-quality bread, fresh herbs and butter make this the best dressing around.

12 cups	cubed bread	3 L
6 Tbsp.	butter	75 mL
2	onions, finely chopped	2
3	celery stalks with leaves, finely chopped	3
3 Tbsp.	fresh sage, chopped	45 mL
4 tsp.	fresh thyme, chopped	20 mL
1 tsp.	fresh rosemary, chopped	5 mL
1½ cups	vegetable, turkey or chicken stock	375 mL
3	green onions, trimmed & chopped	3
	Salt & freshly ground pepper	

Preheat oven to 325°F (160°C). Spread bread cubes on two baking sheets in a single layer, and toast lightly in the oven for 5 to 10 minutes. Set aside in a large mixing bowl.

Melt butter in a large skillet over medium heat. Add onions, celery and herbs; sauté until onions are translucent, about 5 minutes. Add sautéed vegetables to bread cubes. Add stock and green onions, and toss until well mixed. Season with salt and pepper to taste.

Use to stuff turkey, or spoon into a greased 9-by-13-inch (3 L) baking dish. Cover, and bake for 30 minutes, uncovering for the last 15 minutes so that the top gets a nice crispy crust.

Makes about 10 cups (2.5 L).

THREE-BREAD STUFFING FOR TURKEY

Bland white-bread stuffing cannot hold a candle to this mix of whole wheat, rye and sourdough. The result is light and moist, much like a spoonbread or a savory pudding. The bird will release abundant juices, so if you like your stuffing on the dry side, decrease the liquid by ½ cup (125 mL). Pumpernickel bread may be used in place of rye, or for a sweeter stuffing, substitute raisin bread.

2 cups	whole wheat bread cubes	500 mL
1 cup	sourdough bread cubes	250 mL
1 cup	rye bread cubes	250 mL
1 cup	onion, chopped	250 mL
1 cup	celery, chopped	250 mL
1 cup	mushrooms, chopped	250 mL
1 Tbsp.	butter	15 mL
¼ cup	fresh parsley, chopped	50 mL
½ tsp.	paprika	2 mL
1 tsp.	sage	5 mL
¾ tsp.	marjoram	4 mL
1 cup	walnut pieces	250 mL
1 cup	chicken stock	250 mL
	Salt & freshly ground pepper	

On a baking sheet, lightly toast bread cubes in an oven preheated to 350°F (180°C), turning occasionally. In a skillet, sauté onion, celery and mushrooms in butter. Add seasonings, and sauté for about 5 minutes. In a large bowl, combine bread cubes, vegetables, walnuts and chicken stock. Season with salt and pepper. Extra stuffing can be placed in a covered casserole dish and baked at 350°F (180°C) for 20 to 30 minutes.

Makes enough stuffing for a 15-pound (6.75 kg) turkey.

WILD-RICE DRESSING

Wild rice is a superb alternative to traditional dressing. Often served as a side dish, this dressing is so good, it can stand by itself as a main course.

½ cup	wild rice	125 mL
1 Tbsp.	olive oil	15 mL
6 oz.	turkey sausage	175 g
3	celery stalks with leaves, finely chopped	3
1	onion, finely chopped	1
1	red bell pepper, seeded & finely chopped	1
1½ cups	long-grain brown rice	375 mL
3 cups	turkey or chicken stock	750 mL
1 cup	golden raisins	250 mL
3	medium-tart apples, cored & chopped	3
1 cup	toasted pecans, coarsely chopped	250 mL
1 Tbsp.	fresh thyme, chopped	15 mL
	Salt & freshly ground pepper	

Rinse wild rice, and place in a medium-sized saucepan, then cover with 2 cups (500 mL) water, and bring to a boil. Cover, reduce heat to low, and simmer for about 45 minutes or until most of the grains have burst open. Remove from heat, drain off any excess water, and set aside.

Meanwhile, heat oil in a large skillet over medium-high heat. Add sausage, and cook until browned, about 3 minutes, breaking up meat with a spoon as it cooks. Add celery, onion and red pepper; sauté for 2 minutes or until onion is translucent. Add brown rice, and sauté for 2 more minutes or until rice is lightly toasted. Add stock, and bring to a boil. Reduce heat to low, cover, and simmer for about 40 minutes or until liquid is absorbed.

While the brown-rice mixture is simmering, cover raisins with water in a small saucepan, and bring to a boil. Reduce heat to low, and simmer for 5 minutes. Drain raisins, and set aside.

Add apples, pecans, thyme, wild rice and raisins to the cooked brown-rice mixture. Season with salt and pepper to taste.

Use to stuff turkey, or spoon into a greased 9-by-13-inch (3 L) baking dish. Cover, and bake for 30 minutes at 325°F (160°C), uncovering for the last 15 minutes.

Makes about 10 cups (2.5 L).

RED PEPPER, TOMATO & BASIL STUFFING

This dish requires special ingredients and approximately 30 minutes of preparation. The result is an aromatic molded stuffing appealing to the eye and truly delicious.

$\frac{1}{2}$ cup	currants	125 mL
$\frac{1}{2}$ cup	sherry vinegar	125 mL
6	red bell peppers	6
1 cup	extra-virgin olive oil	250 mL
1	large onion, chopped	1
2	cloves garlic, crushed	2
12	large tomatoes, blanched, peeled & chopped, or 3 cups (750 mL) canned Italian tomatoes, drained & crushed	12
$\frac{1}{2}$ tsp.	salt	2 mL
	Coarsely ground pepper	
$\frac{1}{4}$ cup	fresh basil, finely chopped, or 2 Tbsp. (25 mL) dried	50 mL
4 cups	firm-textured white bread pieces (use crusts from bread squares below)	1 L
3	eggs, lightly beaten	3
10-12	square slices of firm-textured white bread, crusts removed	10-12
	Tomato rose for garnish (opt.)	

Soften currants by soaking in vinegar for 10 minutes. Roast red peppers until completely charred, then place in a paper bag to steam for 10 minutes. Peel and core peppers, then chop in a food processor.

In a large skillet, heat $\frac{1}{2}$ cup (125 mL) oil, and add onion, garlic, vinegar-currant mixture and red peppers. Cook for 15 to 20 minutes, stirring constantly. Add tomatoes, salt, pepper and basil, and simmer until liquid is the consistency of a thin sauce, approximately 20 minutes. Remove skillet from heat, and add bread pieces and eggs. Toss lightly.

Cut five of the bread slices in half. Cut remaining bread slices diagonally into quarters, making triangles. Dip one side of each piece of bread into remaining $\frac{1}{2}$ cup (125 mL) oil. Place triangles, oiled side down, on bottom of a 7-inch (2 L) springform pan, fitting them together like a mosaic. Line sides of pan with rectangles.

Spoon pepper-tomato mixture into pan, packing lightly with the back of the spoon. Bake at 350°F (180°C) for 30 minutes or until bread is lightly browned and crisped. Remove from oven, allow to set for 5 to 10 minutes, invert pan, unmold, and serve immediately. Garnish with tomato rose, if desired.

Serves 4 to 6.

Side Dishes

CRANBERRY-SAGE STUFFING

Red, tart and fruity, this stuffing is excellent with poultry and pork.

6 Tbsp.	unsalted butter	75 mL
1 cup	onion, chopped	250 mL
1 cup	celery with leaves, chopped	250 mL
2 cups	cranberries, chopped (easier to do when fruit is frozen)	500 mL
4 cups	firm-textured white bread cubes	1 L
1 cup	chicken stock	250 mL
2 tsp.	fresh sage, chopped, or 1 tsp. (5 mL) dried	10 mL
	Grated zest of 1 orange	
2 Tbsp.	brown sugar	25 mL
2	eggs, lightly beaten	2
¼ tsp.	salt	1 mL
	Freshly ground pepper	

In a large skillet, heat butter, add each of the ingredients, one at a time, and toss lightly. Scrape mixture into an oiled soufflé dish or casserole, and bake at 350°F (180°C) for 25 minutes or until lightly browned.

Serves 6 to 8.

OYSTER STUFFING

A delicious and rich side-dish stuffing that makes a meal in itself.

30	oysters, shucked	30
	Flour seasoned with salt & freshly ground pepper	
2	eggs, lightly beaten with 1 Tbsp. (15 mL) oil and ½ tsp. (2 mL) hot pepper sauce	2
1 cup	fine breadcrumbs	250 mL
4 Tbsp.	butter	50 mL
1 cup	onion, chopped	250 mL
¼ cup	oil	50 mL
1 cup	celery, chopped	250 mL
4 cups	coarse breadcrumbs, dried	1 L
2 cups	chicken stock	500 mL
½ cup	parsley, chopped	125 mL
1 tsp.	celery seeds	5 mL
2 tsp.	sage	10 mL
3½ tsp.	fresh rosemary, chopped, or 2 Tbsp. (25 mL) dried	17 mL
2	eggs, lightly beaten	2
	Salt & freshly ground pepper	

Dip oysters into seasoned flour, then egg mixture, then breadcrumbs, and let stand for 10 minutes. Melt butter, and fry oysters until lightly browned, about 1 minute on each side. Drain on paper towels.

Sauté onion in oil until browned. Add celery, and cook for 5 minutes. Add remaining ingredients, except oysters, and toss. Gently fold fried oysters into stuffing. Place stuffing in a soufflé dish or a casserole, and bake at 350°F (180°C) for 20 to 30 minutes or until nicely browned on top.

Serves 6 to 8.

Spiced Cauliflower & Potatoes

Side Dishes, page 126

Barbari Bread

Baking, page 178

Chapter 6

SAUCES, SEASONINGS & PRESERVES

hough something of a lost art during the latter decades of the 20th century, putting up preserves remains a ritual dear to the hearts of many *Harrowsmith Country Life* readers, whose own gardens abound with tomatoes, cucumbers, peppers and fruit that can be savored throughout the year. In the dead of winter, when it's time to crack open a jar of Cranberry-Citrus Chutney to brighten a homemade chicken stew or a vibrant green Basil Jelly to put out the fire of a smoldering lamb curry, we hear no expressions of regret for the effort devoted during the harvest season.

Before your kitchen overflows with the season's abundance, however, we recommend that you obtain a complete canning guide at a local bookstore or library. Invaluable sources of information, such guides offer tips on everything from the best equipment to use to optional processing and packing methods for preserves and lively discussions on the merits of low- versus high-sugar recipes.

While diners will embrace with gusto sassy fruit compotes and chutneys as complements to the exotic flavors of their home-cooked stir-frys, curries and roasts, our recipes also include some of the pleasurable basics that, whether as the result of routine or the convenience of commercial brands, have become too predictable: gravy for a holiday bird, for instance; a variety of mustards; homemade mayonnaise; and recipes for fresh curry powder and paste.

Whether it's spread on a sandwich or placed in a dollop beside a main-course dish, a condiment made at home from the finest ingredients picked fresh from the garden and canned at the peak of their flavor is a most worthy accent to the rest of the meal.

Sauces

MAYONNAISE

No commercial product even approximates the taste and texture of homemade mayonnaise. And, when you make your own, you can ensure that it contains only pure ingredients. The following recipe is for a basic mayonnaise. Add various seasonings in small quantities to complement the dish being prepared.

The amount of garlic used here produces a mild mayonnaise, but more can be added. Any kind of lightly flavored oil is good for making mayonnaise. Try half olive and half sunflower.

1	clove garlic	1
1 tsp.	dry mustard	5 mL
	Salt & freshly ground pepper	
2	eggs	2
6 Tbsp.	wine vinegar or lemon juice	75 mL
2 cups	oil	500 mL

Place garlic, mustard, salt and pepper, eggs, vinegar and ½ cup (125 mL) oil in a blender or a food processor. Blend to combine. With machine still running, add the remaining oil in a slow, steady stream. Blend until the oil is thoroughly mixed in and the mayonnaise is thick and creamy. Store in the refrigerator, where it will keep for up to 1 week.

Makes about 3 cups (750 mL).

GARLIC MAYONNAISE

This mayonnaise not only is the basis for a salad dressing but also spices up a sandwich and makes a good vegetable dip. Keep it refrigerated at all times.

1	egg	1
1	clove garlic	1
	Salt & freshly ground pepper	
1 tsp.	dry mustard	5 mL
3 Tbsp.	red wine vinegar or lemon juice	45 mL
1 cup	oil	250 mL

Place egg, garlic, salt and pepper, mustard, vinegar and ½ cup (125 mL) oil in a blender, and blend until well mixed. With blender running, slowly trickle in remaining oil, and process until mayonnaise is thick and creamy. Keeps well in the refrigerator for up to 2 weeks.

Makes about 1½ cups (375 mL).

DIJON MUSTARD

Stand back when adding the hot liquid to the mustard powder, because the fumes can burn your eyes.

½ cup	brown mustard seeds	125 mL
½ cup	water	125 mL
1 Tbsp.	chervil	15 mL
1 tsp.	thyme	5 mL
1 tsp.	tarragon	5 mL
1 tsp.	salt	5 mL
1 Tbsp.	lemon juice	15 mL

Pulverize mustard seeds in a blender, then push through a strainer.

Bring water, chervil, thyme and tarragon to a boil, reduce heat, and simmer for 5 minutes.

Strain into mustard powder. Add salt and lemon juice. Let sit, refrigerated, for 2 weeks before using.

Makes about 1 cup (250 mL).

Sauces

MUSTARD DRESSING

This is a rich, creamy dressing, particularly tasty over a green salad.

¼ cup	mayonnaise	50 mL
½ cup	yogurt	125 mL
2-4 Tbsp.	Dijon mustard	25-50 mL
2 Tbsp.	white wine vinegar	25 mL
4 Tbsp.	parsley, chopped	50 mL
	Cayenne pepper	
	Salt & freshly ground pepper	

Combine all ingredients, and mix well.
  Makes about ¾ cup (175 mL).

POMMERY MUSTARD

A coarsely textured mustard that is a classic as a garnish, glaze or tasty addition to a sauce.

½ cup	brown mustard seeds	125 mL
½ cup	yellow mustard seeds	125 mL
¾ cup	water	175 mL
2 tsp.	salt	10 mL
	Green peppercorns	
	Other herbs, as desired	
	Honey (opt.)	
2-4 Tbsp.	white wine vinegar	25-50 mL

Blend half of the seeds to a powder. Mash remaining seeds in a mortar and pestle, or blend only until coarsely ground, and add to powder. Set aside.
  Bring water to a boil, reduce heat, and simmer for 5 minutes. Add remaining ingredients, then strain into mustard powder. Let sit, refrigerated, for at least 2 weeks before using.
  Makes about 1 cup (250 mL).

TWO-MUSTARD DRESSING

A thick low-fat dressing with just the right balance of flavors.

2 cups	buttermilk	500 mL
2 Tbsp.	Dijon mustard	25 mL
3 Tbsp.	Pommery mustard	45 mL
1 Tbsp.	frozen apple juice concentrate	15 mL

Combine all ingredients in a glass jar, cover, and shake well.
  Makes about 2¼ cups (550 mL).

MUSTARD SAUCE

Delicious with smoked fish, cold chicken or other cold meats, this sauce keeps in the refrigerator for several weeks. Garnish with fresh dill when available.

6 Tbsp.	Dijon mustard	75 mL
1 tsp.	dry mustard	5 mL
4 Tbsp.	sugar	50 mL
3 Tbsp.	red wine vinegar	45 mL
½ cup	oil	125 mL
½ cup	dill, finely chopped	125 mL

Combine mustards, sugar and vinegar. Add oil very slowly, beating constantly until sauce is thick. (A food processor makes this much easier.) Stir in dill.
  Makes about 1 cup (250 mL).

HERBED YOGURT DIP

With fewer calories than dips made from sour cream or cream cheese, yogurt dips can be created to suit all tastes. Add a ripe avocado and some chili powder for instant guacamole. A bit of curry powder, cumin and coriander adds an Indian flavor.

2 cups	thick plain yogurt	500 mL
1-2	cloves garlic	1-2
1 Tbsp.	dill weed	15 mL
½ tsp.	dry mustard	2 mL
3 Tbsp.	lemon or lime juice	45 mL
	Salt & freshly ground pepper	

Place all ingredients in a blender, and process until smooth. Refrigerate.

Makes about 2 cups (500 mL).

YOGURT-DILL SALAD DRESSING

Light, creamy and not too tart, this dressing is a basic for all leafy green salads.

½	large cucumber, peeled & seeded	½
1 Tbsp.	olive oil	15 mL
1 Tbsp.	fresh dill, minced & tightly packed	15 mL
½ tsp.	oregano	2 mL
¼ tsp.	garlic, finely minced	1 mL
¼ tsp.	salt	1 mL
	Pinch freshly ground pepper	
2 tsp.	lemon juice	10 mL
1½ tsp.	honey	7 mL
¾ cup	yogurt	175 mL

Combine all ingredients except yogurt in a blender or a food processor, then stir into yogurt.

Makes about 1 cup (250 mL).

TRADITIONAL GIBLET GRAVY FOR TURKEY

The flavor of this classic holiday gravy is enriched by the cooked giblets.

	Turkey giblets & neck	
3 cups	turkey or chicken stock	750 mL
1	celery stalk with leaves, chopped	1
1	onion, quartered	1
	Pan drippings	
¼ cup	flour	50 mL
	Salt & freshly ground pepper	

While the turkey is roasting, place giblets and neck (reserve liver for another use) in a medium-sized saucepan. Add stock, and bring to a boil. Reduce heat to low, skim off any foam, and add celery and onion. Simmer for about 1 hour. Remove giblets and neck, and reserve. Strain the stock, discarding the vegetables, and set aside. Finely chop the giblets and neck meat, and set aside.

When the turkey is roasted, strain the drippings from the roasting pan into a clear-glass 4-cup (1 L) measure. Skim off the fat that rises to the top, reserving ¼ cup (50 mL) and discarding the rest. A 12-lb. (5.5 kg) bird will yield about 2 cups (500 mL) defatted drippings. Add enough giblet stock to make 4 cups (1 L).

Heat the reserved fat in a medium-sized saucepan over medium heat. Stir in flour, and cook, stirring constantly, for 2 minutes. Whisk in the stock mixture. Cook, stirring constantly, until gravy thickens. Add the reserved chopped meat, and simmer for about 5 minutes. Season with salt and pepper to taste.

Makes 4 cups (1 L).

PEANUT BUTTER

Everybody's favorite, homemade peanut butter is pure and effortless to prepare. Make it smooth or crunchy, or for a sweeter peanut butter, add a little honey.

3½ cups	*dry-roasted, unsalted peanuts*	*875 mL*
1-2 Tbsp.	*peanut oil*	*15-25 mL*
½ tsp.	*salt (opt.)*	*2 mL*

Place peanuts and 1 Tbsp. (15 mL) oil in a blender or a food processor. Process on low speed in blender or pulse in food processor until nuts are coarsely ground. Increase blender speed to high or process continuously until smooth, scraping down the sides twice. Add more oil for a creamier peanut butter, and season with salt, if desired.

Can be stored in the refrigerator, well covered, for up to 10 days.

Makes 2 cups (500 mL).

GADO GADO

Serve this spicy Indonesian peanut sauce with steamed vegetables (potatoes, green beans, carrots, broccoli) or hard-boiled eggs and bean sprouts on a bed of rice.

½ cup	peanut butter	125 mL
2 Tbsp.	fresh lime juice	25 mL
2 tsp.	soy sauce	10 mL
1 tsp.	honey	5 mL
1 tsp.	cider vinegar	5 mL
1	clove garlic, minced	1
1 tsp.	gingerroot, peeled & minced	5 mL
½ tsp.	red pepper flakes	2 mL

In a saucepan, combine all ingredients with ½ cup (125 mL) water. Bring to a simmer over medium heat, whisking constantly. Remove from heat. Sauce will thicken as it cools. Serve warm or at room temperature. The sauce can be stored, covered, in the refrigerator for up to 1 week.

Makes 1¼ cups (300 mL).

Seasonings

CURRY POWDER

The quickest way to shell cardamom pods is to crush them with a rolling pin, then separate the seeds from the pods. Roasting eliminates the powdery taste common to commercial curry powders.

$\frac{1}{2}$ cup	coriander seeds	125 mL
5 Tbsp.	black peppercorns	65 mL
1 Tbsp.	whole cloves	15 mL
2 Tbsp.	cumin seeds	25 mL
2 Tbsp.	green cardamom seeds	25 mL
1 Tbsp.	fenugreek seeds	15 mL
$\frac{1}{2}$ cup	turmeric	125 mL
1 Tbsp.	mace	15 mL
1 Tbsp.	cinnamon	15 mL
$1\frac{1}{2}$ tsp.	ground ginger	7 mL
$\frac{1}{2}$ tsp.	cayenne pepper	2 mL

Grind seeds coarsely. Place all spices in a heavy skillet or a roasting pan. Roast until spices have darkened and begun to give off an aroma, stirring often. This will take approximately 5 minutes on top of the stove or 20 minutes in a 375°F (190°C) oven.

Cool, then place in a jar with a tight-fitting lid.
Makes about $1\frac{1}{2}$ cups (375 mL).

MADRAS-STYLE CURRY PASTE

When making a curry dish with curry paste, use about 1 Tbsp. (15 mL) paste for each pound (500 g) of meat, fish or poultry, or use to replace garlic, ginger and spices in any recipe.

1 cup	ground coriander	250 mL
$\frac{1}{2}$ cup	ground cumin	125 mL
1 Tbsp.	freshly ground pepper	15 mL
1 Tbsp.	Szechuan pepper	15 mL
1 Tbsp.	black mustard seeds	15 mL
1 Tbsp.	turmeric	15 mL
1 Tbsp.	salt	15 mL
4	cloves garlic	4
1	piece gingerroot (about 3 inches/8 cm long)	1
1-$1\frac{1}{2}$ cups	cider vinegar	250-375 mL
$\frac{3}{4}$ cup	oil	175 mL

Combine spices and salt. Crush garlic, peel and grate gingerroot, and add to spice mixture. Add vinegar to make a smooth paste.

Heat oil in a heavy frying pan. Place spice mixture in pan, reduce heat, and cook, stirring constantly, until spices are cooked and oil separates out—3 to 5 minutes.

Cool, then bottle.
Makes about $1\frac{3}{4}$ cups (425 mL).

Seasonings

GREEN CURRY PASTE

This paste provides color and an aromatic flavor in any spiced dish.

1 tsp.	fenugreek seeds	5 mL
1 cup	mint leaves	250 mL
1 cup	coriander leaves	250 mL
½ cup	cider vinegar	125 mL
6	cloves garlic	6
3 Tbsp.	grated gingerroot	45 mL
2 tsp.	salt	10 mL
2 tsp.	turmeric	10 mL
½ tsp.	cloves	2 mL
1 tsp.	cardamom	5 mL
½ cup	sunflower oil	125 mL
¼ cup	sesame oil	50 mL

Soak fenugreek seeds in water overnight. Place seeds in a blender or a food processor with mint, coriander, vinegar, garlic and gingerroot. Blend until completely smooth. Add salt and remaining spices.

Heat oils, add spice mixture, bring to a boil, then turn off heat. Cool, and bottle.

Makes about 2 cups (500 mL).

GARAM MASALA

There are many varieties of garam masala. This recipe is spicy, but for a more fragrant effect, eliminate the peppercorns and cumin. Garam masala should be added to a dish just before serving, since heat destroys its delicate flavor.

5 Tbsp.	coriander seeds	65 mL
3 Tbsp.	cumin seeds	45 mL
4 tsp.	black peppercorns	20 mL
1 Tbsp.	green cardamom seeds	15 mL
3	cinnamon sticks	3
1 tsp.	whole cloves	5 mL
1	nutmeg, grated	1

In a small, heavy frying pan, roast, one at a time, the coriander, cumin, peppercorns, cardamom, cinnamon and cloves—approximately 3 to 5 minutes each. Place on a plate to cool thoroughly, then grind, using a mortar and pestle or an electric blender. Mix in nutmeg. Bottle.

Makes about 1 cup (250 mL).

SPICED PLUM JELLY

The beautiful red color and spicy sweetness make this the perfect companion to chicken and turkey.

6 lb.	'Red Beauty' plums, pitted but not peeled	2.7 kg
20	allspice berries	20
$1\frac{3}{4}$ cups	cold water	425 mL
1	box Sure-Jell Light pectin	1
5 cups	sugar	1.25 L

Chop plums finely, and place in a large pot with all-spice and water. Cover, and simmer for 10 minutes, stirring occasionally. Ladle into a dampened jelly bag suspended over a bowl, and let drip, undisturbed, for 2 to 4 hours or until it yields $6\frac{3}{4}$ cups (1.7 L) liquid.

Mix the Sure-Jell Light with $\frac{1}{4}$ cup (50 mL) sugar, and gradually stir into the fruit juice. Return mixture to pot, which should be only a third full at this point to allow room for a full boil. Bring to a rolling boil over high heat, and immediately add remaining sugar. Boil hard for 1 minute, then ladle into sterilized jelly jars, and cover with a double layer of melted paraffin or seal with two-piece lids. Let jelly stand to cool.

LEMON-LIME JELLY WITH ROSEMARY

Rosemary, lemon and lime are a wonderful combination. Spoon this jelly next to roast chicken or turkey, and enjoy the strong citrus-herbal taste.

6	limes	6
2	lemons	2
4 cups	cold water	1 L
20	rosemary sprigs	20
$7\frac{1}{2}$ cups	sugar	1.9 L
3 oz.	pouch plus 3 Tbsp. (45 mL) liquid pectin	75 g
1 tsp.	unsalted butter	5 mL

Extract the juice from all but 1 lime and 1 lemon. Chop up the remaining lemon and lime, and add to a pot with the juice, water and 4 rosemary sprigs. Bring liquid to a boil, then simmer for 15 minutes.

Pour into a dampened jelly bag suspended over a bowl, and let drip, undisturbed, for 2 hours or until it yields $4\frac{3}{4}$ cups (1.2 L) juice. Return juice to the pot, and add sugar and pectin. Bring to a rolling boil, add butter, and let boil for 1 minute, stirring constantly.

Meanwhile, place 2 rosemary sprigs in each of 8 half-pint (250 mL) sterilized jars; ladle the hot jelly into the jars. Cover with a double layer of melted paraffin, or seal with two-piece lids, and let sit for 24 hours to gel.

ORANGE & GREEN-PEPPERCORN JELLY

This light and somewhat loose citrus jelly is infused with the soft bite of green peppercorns. It is a wonderful accompaniment to roast duck.

5	oranges (extract & save juice & cut up skins)	5
1	lemon (extract & save juice & cut up skin)	1
1½ cups	cold water	375 mL
½ cup	Pomona's pectin solution (read instructions in package)	125 mL
2 tsp.	calcium solution (read instructions in package)	10 mL
¼ cup	green peppercorns	50 mL

Dampen a jelly bag, and suspend over a bowl. Put the orange and lemon skins in a pot, and add water. Boil for 5 minutes, then pour this and the extracted juices into the jelly bag. Let drip, undisturbed, for 2 hours or until it yields 2 cups (500 mL) liquid.

Put liquid, pectin, calcium solution and green peppercorns in a pot, and boil for 1 minute. Ladle into sterilized jars, tighten two-piece lids, invert for 15 minutes, then turn upright.

BASIL JELLY

Preserve the taste of fresh garden basil for the whole winter. This sparkling jelly is great with turkey and lamb and works wonders with a mundane chicken breast. The natural color of this jelly is an earthy greenish brown, which, like mint jelly, can be transformed into a glittering emerald green by adding green food coloring.

2 cups	fresh basil leaves, firmly packed	500 mL
2¾ cups	cold water	675 mL
3 Tbsp.	fresh lemon juice, strained	45 mL
3½ cups	sugar	875 mL
3 oz.	package plus 2 Tbsp. (25 mL) liquid pectin	75 g
1	drop green food coloring (opt.)	1

To make a basil infusion, put basil and water in a pot and bring to a full boil. Lower to a simmer, cover, and let mixture steep for 15 minutes. Ladle into a dampened jelly bag suspended over a bowl, and let drip, undisturbed, for 2 hours or until it yields 2 cups (500 mL) liquid. If there is not enough, pour a little boiling water through the bag.

Return basil infusion to the pot, add lemon juice and sugar, and bring to a full boil. Add pectin and food coloring, if desired, and boil, stirring constantly, for 1 minute. Skim off froth, and pour into sterilized jars. Cover with a double layer of melted paraffin, or seal with two-piece lids, and let stand for 24 hours.

SOUR CHERRY COMPOTE

Tart cherries are a fine companion to duck and goose. The color is lively, the kirsch (cherry brandy) adds depth to the flavor, and allspice gives an unexpected spiciness.

8 cups	sour cherries, pitted	2 L
4 Tbsp.	fresh lemon juice, strained	50 mL
2 cups	cold water	500 mL
¾ cup	sugar	175 mL
20	allspice berries in a cheesecloth bag	20
1 cup	Pomona's pectin solution (read instructions in package)	250 mL
4 tsp.	calcium solution (read instructions in package)	20 mL
1 cup	kirsch	250 mL

Bring cherries, lemon juice, water, sugar and allspice to a simmer. Add pectin and calcium solution, and boil hard for 1 minute. Add kirsch, and spoon mixture into sterilized jars. Process for 10 minutes, or seal with a double layer of melted paraffin. This compote is excellent right away, but it also keeps well.

PLUM COULIS

This coulis is an excellent condiment with all poultry. It can also be brushed on the bird during the last few minutes of roasting or on pork tenderloin before grilling.

2 cups	chicken stock	500 mL
1 cup	fruity white wine	250 mL
1½ lb.	ripe red or purple plums, pitted & finely chopped	750 g
1 Tbsp.	sugar	15 mL
½ tsp.	lemon juice	2 mL
	Salt & freshly ground pepper	

Simmer chicken stock and wine until reduced to ¾ cup (175 mL). Add remaining ingredients, and simmer, uncovered, for 5 minutes. Preserving is not recommended.

PEACH CHUTNEY

Perfumed with peaches and apricots, this chutney has a bite of vinegar and red pepper. It improves with age and, although excellent with poultry, is also good with barbecued hamburgers.

5 lb.	peaches, peeled, stoned & cut into chunks	2.2 kg
4 oz.	dried apricots, diced	115 g
1 cup	onions, minced	250 mL
½ cup	currants	125 mL
½ cup	crystallized ginger, chopped	125 mL
2 Tbsp.	mustard seeds in a cheesecloth bag	25 mL
3 cups	brown sugar	750 mL
2 tsp.	hot red pepper flakes	10 mL
2 tsp.	salt	10 mL
½ cup	water	125 mL
3½ cups	apple cider vinegar	875 mL

Combine everything in a large noncorrosive pot, and simmer, stirring occasionally, for 1½ hours or until chutney is thick and syrupy. Remove mustard seeds.

Transfer chutney to a bowl; let cool. Cover, and chill overnight or for up to 2 weeks. Or, if desired, spoon chutney into sterilized jars, cover, and process jars for 10 minutes, or seal with two layers of melted paraffin. For optimal flavor, store chutney in a cool, dark place for at least 4 weeks to allow the flavors to marry.

RHUBARB CHUTNEY

Tamarind concentrate and fenugreek can be found in Indian groceries and some health-food stores. This chutney is delicious served right away, but the flavors mellow with time.

4 cups	rhubarb, cut into pieces	1 L
3 cups	light brown sugar, firmly packed	750 mL
2½ cups	cider vinegar	625 mL
2	onions, chopped	2
1 cup	crystallized ginger, finely chopped	250 mL
½ cup	raisins	125 mL
6	serrano chilies, seeded & finely chopped	6
1 Tbsp.	mustard seeds	15 mL
1 Tbsp.	tamarind concentrate	15 mL
1 tsp.	fenugreek	5 mL
1 tsp.	mixed pickling spices	5 mL
½ tsp.	salt	2 mL

Combine all ingredients in a large, heavy saucepan. Cover, and bring to a boil over medium heat. Uncover, reduce heat, and simmer, stirring occasionally, for about 1½ hours or until thickened.

Pack hot chutney into hot, sterilized half-pint (250 mL) or pint (500 mL) jars, leaving ½-inch (1 cm) headspace. Adjust caps, and process in a hot-water bath for 10 minutes.

Makes 2 pints (1 L).

149

CRANBERRY-CITRUS CHUTNEY

This recipe is particularly good with turkey or goose. It is an aromatic chutney, and cranberry and citrus make it refreshing.

¾ cup	apple cider vinegar	175 mL
2 cups	light brown sugar	500 mL
1¼ tsp.	curry powder	6 mL
¾ tsp.	ginger	4 mL
½ tsp.	cloves	2 mL
½ tsp.	allspice	2 mL
¾ tsp.	cinnamon	4 mL
2¼ cups	cold water	550 mL
3	lemons, zest grated, pith discarded & fruit chopped	3
3	oranges, zest grated, pith discarded & fruit chopped	3
1	'Granny Smith' apple, peeled & chopped	1
¾ cup	seedless golden raisins	175 mL
¾ cup	dried apricots, chopped	175 mL
9 cups	cranberries	2.25 L
¾ cup	walnuts, chopped	175 mL

Combine vinegar, sugar, spices and water, and boil until sugar is dissolved. Add lemon and orange fruit and zest and apple, and simmer for 10 minutes. Add raisins, apricots and 4½ cups (1.1 L) cranberries. Simmer, stirring occasionally, for 40 minutes or until the mixture thickens.

Add 2½ cups (625 mL) cranberries, and simmer, stirring, for 10 minutes. Add remaining cranberries and walnuts, and simmer for 15 minutes.

Transfer chutney to a bowl, let cool, cover, and chill overnight or for up to 2 weeks. Alternatively, spoon chutney into sterilized jars, and process for 10 minutes, or cover with a double layer of melted paraffin. This chutney is also excellent when served immediately.

GARDENER'S SALSA

This salsa is rather mild. For a hotter version, use more chili peppers and proportionately fewer green peppers. For nachos, cover corn chips with grated cheese and salsa, then broil for about 10 minutes. Or make a Mexican "torte" by layering salsa, tortillas, refried beans (or ground beef) and cheese in a pie plate. Bake for about 25 minutes, and serve hot.

12 lb.	*ripe tomatoes, quartered*	*5.5 kg*
2 cups	*white vinegar*	*500 mL*
1 cup	*hot chili pepper, finely diced*	*250 mL*
1 cup	*green pepper, finely diced*	*250 mL*
3	*onions, finely diced*	*3*
1 Tbsp.	*salt*	*15 mL*

In an enameled or stainless steel saucepan, combine tomatoes with vinegar. Cover, and cook, stirring occasionally, until tomatoes are very soft, about 45 minutes. Puree briefly in batches in a blender or a food processor; tomatoes should be slightly chunky.

Return pureed tomatoes to the saucepan, and add peppers and onions. Simmer until salsa thickens, about 1 hour. Add salt to taste.

Ladle hot salsa into clean, hot pint (500 mL) sterilized jars, leaving ½-inch (1 cm) headspace. Seal. Process in a hot-water bath for 15 minutes. Let cool, undisturbed, for 12 hours. Check seals. Store in a cool, dry place.

Makes about 8 pints (4 L).

QUICK CROCK PICKLES

These crisp, tart pickles, which use vinegar in the brine, are less prone to spoilage than are traditional salt-cured pickles. Pickling novices will find this an astonishingly simple recipe.

8 cups	water	2 L
1 cup	distilled white vinegar	250 mL
¼ cup	pickling salt	50 mL
4 lb.	pickling cucumbers	1.8 kg
6	dill heads or 12 young dill shoots	6
8	cloves garlic, peeled	8

In a sterilized 1-gallon (4 L) or larger container, combine water with vinegar and salt. Mix well until salt has dissolved. Slice $\frac{1}{16}$ inch (1.5 mm) off the blossom end of each cucumber. Add dill, garlic and cucumbers, in that order, to the brine solution. Make sure the pickles are completely submerged in the brine.

Cover the container with a clean, heavy bath towel, and set where the temperature will remain at about 68°F (20°C). Check the container daily, and remove any scum that forms on the surface (after first rinsing your skimming tool with boiling water).

The pickles will be ready in about 2 days, although full flavor will not be reached for another 4 to 6 weeks. If your kitchen is reasonably cool, you can leave these pickles out for up to 2 weeks. After that, they should be refrigerated to prevent spoiling. The flavor of the dill and garlic will continue to develop. The pickles will keep for up to 3 months in the refrigerator.

Makes about 1 gallon (4 L).

FREEZER DILLS

No apologies are needed for these incredible dill pickles, which are crisp and flavorful, despite the little time it takes to make them.

4 cups	cucumbers, thinly sliced	1 L
1 Tbsp.	pickling salt	15 mL
1 cup	distilled white vinegar	250 mL
⅓ cup	sugar	75 mL
½ cup	fresh dill, chopped	125 mL
4	cloves garlic, peeled & thinly sliced	4

In a large ceramic, glass or stainless steel bowl, combine cucumbers and salt. Cover with cold water, and let stand at room temperature for 3 hours.

Meanwhile, combine vinegar and sugar in a small saucepan, and stir over medium heat just until sugar has completely dissolved. Let cool.

Drain cucumbers in a colander; rinse well under cold water, and drain thoroughly. Combine cucumbers, vinegar solution, dill and garlic. Pack into a freezer container, leaving at least 1-inch (2.5 cm) headspace. Close tightly, and freeze.

Defrost in the refrigerator for about 8 hours before serving. Thawed pickles can be stored in the refrigerator, covered, for up to 1 week.

Makes about 3 cups (750 mL).

FREEZER ORIENTAL LIME PICKLES

These refreshing pickles are great not only with Thai or Vietnamese dishes but with foods of any culture. *Nuoc mam*, a Vietnamese fish sauce, is available wherever Asian foods are sold.

4 cups	cucumbers, thinly sliced	1 L
1 Tbsp.	pickling salt	15 mL
$\frac{2}{3}$ cup	distilled white vinegar	150 mL
$\frac{1}{3}$ cup	sugar	75 mL
$\frac{1}{3}$ cup	fresh lime juice	75 mL
$\frac{1}{4}$ cup	fish sauce (*nuoc mam*)	50 mL
1	red bell pepper, seeded & minced	1
1 Tbsp.	fresh hot pepper, such as cayenne, serrano or jalapeño, minced	15 mL
1 Tbsp.	gingerroot, minced	15 mL

In a large ceramic, glass or stainless steel bowl, combine cucumbers and salt. Cover with cold water, and let stand at room temperature for 3 hours.

Meanwhile, combine vinegar and sugar in a small saucepan, and stir over medium heat just until sugar has dissolved. Let cool.

Drain cucumbers in a colander; rinse well under cold water, and drain thoroughly. Combine cucumbers, vinegar solution, lime juice, fish sauce, red pepper, hot pepper and gingerroot. Pack into a freezer container, leaving at least 1-inch (2.5 cm.) headspace. Close tightly, and freeze.

Defrost in the refrigerator for about 8 hours before serving. Thawed pickles can be stored in the refrigerator, covered, for up to 1 week.

Makes about 3 cups (750 mL).

FREEZER BREAD & BUTTER PICKLES

A quick, easy version of a favorite classic, these pretty pickles are a zesty accompaniment to stews and roasts, delicious with bread and cheese and perfect on a burger.

3 cups	cucumbers, thinly sliced	750 mL
1	medium onion, thinly sliced	1
1 Tbsp.	pickling salt	15 mL
1 cup	distilled white vinegar	250 mL
$\frac{1}{2}$ cup	sugar	125 mL
1 tsp.	turmeric	5 mL
1 tsp.	celery seeds	5 mL
1 tsp.	mustard seeds	5 mL
$\frac{1}{4}$ tsp.	freshly ground pepper	1 mL

In a large ceramic, glass or stainless steel bowl, combine cucumbers, onion and salt. Cover with cold water, and let stand at room temperature for 3 hours.

Meanwhile, combine vinegar and sugar in a small saucepan, and stir over medium heat just until sugar has dissolved. Let cool.

Drain cucumber-onion mixture in a colander; rinse well under cold water, and drain thoroughly. Combine cucumber-onion mixture, vinegar solution and spices. Pour into a freezer container, leaving at least 1-inch (2.5 cm) headspace. Close tightly, and freeze.

Defrost in the refrigerator for about 8 hours before serving. Thawed pickles can be stored in the refrigerator, covered, for up to 1 week.

Makes about 1 quart (1 L).

HALF-SOUR DILL PICKLES

Be sure to use a container that holds at least 1 gallon (4 L), and measure the water and salt accurately. After that, the recipe can tolerate a great deal of variation. Use more or less dill or garlic, according to your taste.

5 Tbsp.	pickling salt	65 mL
4 lb.	pickling cucumbers	1.8 kg
8	cloves garlic, peeled	8
6	dill heads or 12 young dill shoots	6

In a large saucepan, combine salt and 10 cups (2.5 L) water, and bring to a boil. Let cool to room temperature. Wash cucumbers well, and slice $\frac{1}{16}$ inch (1.5 mm) off the blossom end of each cucumber. Pack cucumbers, garlic and dill into a sterilized 1-gallon (4 L) or larger container. Pour in the brine solution, making sure that the pickles are completely submerged in the brine.

Cover the container with a clean, heavy bath towel, and set where the temperature will remain at about 68°F (20°C). Check the container daily, and remove any scum that forms on the surface (after first rinsing your skimming tool with boiling water).

Taste the pickles after 5 days. Refrigerate when they taste just right to you. After 2 weeks, the pickles will be good and sour and should be refrigerated by then to prevent them from spoiling. The pickles will keep for up to 3 months in the refrigerator.

Makes about 1 gallon (4 L).

PICKLED BEETS

Once made, these sassy beets are a treat to take down from the shelf to accompany anything from a grilled cheese sandwich to a luncheon quiche.

12 cups	sliced cooked beets	3 L
12 cups	cider vinegar	3 L
6 cups	honey	1.5 L
2 cups	beet cooking liquid	500 mL
3 Tbsp.	cloves	45 mL
3 Tbsp.	allspice	45 mL
10	cinnamon sticks	10
8	peppercorns	8
2 tsp.	salt	10 mL

Pack beets into clean pint (500 mL) jars. Combine vinegar, honey and cooking liquid, and bring to a boil. Combine spices in a cheesecloth bag, and add to boiling liquid. Simmer for 20 minutes, then remove spice bag, and pour liquid over beets. Seal, and process in a hot-water bath for 20 minutes.

Makes about 4 pints (2 L).

MUSTARD PICKLE

These pickled cucumbers are for mustard lovers only.

4	cucumbers	4
1 Tbsp.	salt	15 mL
½ cup	sugar	125 mL
2 cups	cider vinegar	500 mL
1 cup	water	250 mL
2 Tbsp.	yellow mustard seeds	25 mL
1 Tbsp.	peppercorns	15 mL
1 tsp.	juniper berries (opt.)	5 mL

Peel cucumbers, slice in half lengthwise, then into ½-inch (1 cm) pieces. Sprinkle salt over cucumbers, and let sit overnight in a strainer. Press to eliminate extra water from cucumbers.

Dissolve sugar in vinegar and water. Add remaining ingredients, and mix well. Pour over cucumbers, and store in a cool, dark place.

Makes about 1 quart (1 L).

WATER-BATH PRIMER

If you are new to canning, arm yourself with Putting Food By *by Ruth Hertzberg, Beatrice Vaughan and Janet Greene (Stephen Green Press, 3rd ed., 1982). Don't recycle food jars for jam making; instead, buy canning jars and lids at a supermarket or a hardware store for a better seal. For low-sugar jams, choose half-pint (250 mL) jars. You will also need a large stockpot or a hot-water bath as your canner.*

1. Wash jars and lids with hot, soapy water, rinse well, and sterilize in boiling water. Leave lids in water until you are ready to use them.

2. Make jam or pickles.

3. Pour fruit or vegetables into sterilized jars, leaving ¼-inch (5 mm) headspace.

4. Wipe jar rim with clean cloth. Place lid on jar, and secure with a metal screw band, hand-tightening into place.

5. Set jars on rack in preheated canner. Water should be hot, not boiling. Add more hot water, if necessary, to cover tops of jars by 2 inches (5 cm). Cover pot, turn heat to high, and allow water to reach full boil. Process for 10 minutes, keeping water at a moderate boil throughout processing.

6. Remove jars from canner, and let sit, undisturbed, for 12 hours.

7. As jars cool, you may hear a popping sound, which indicates that the jar has sealed (the center of a sealed lid will be slightly depressed). Gently remove screw bands, and test any questionable seals by lifting the jar by its lid. Unsealed jars should be stored in the refrigerator and used quickly.

8. Store sealed jars in a cool, dry place.

Fruit Compote

Brunches & Light Lunches, page 14

The World's Best Butter Tart

Desserts & Sweets, page 216

OLD-FASHIONED LOW-SUGAR STRAWBERRY JAM

You can use more or less sugar to taste. More sugar will thicken the syrup and reduce the cooking time; less sugar will increase the cooking time.

8 cups	strawberries, crushed (about 6 pints/3 L whole berries)	2 L
2 cups	sugar	500 mL
2 Tbsp.	lemon juice	25 mL

Combine all ingredients in a large nonreactive kettle. Bring to a boil over medium-high heat. Reduce heat to medium, and continue to boil, stirring frequently, until mixture thickens, about 40 minutes. The jam is ready when a teaspoonful holds its shape when dropped onto a chilled plate.

Remove jam from heat. Skim off foam. Carefully ladle hot jam into prepared jars, and process in a hot-water bath.

Makes about 6 half-pint (250 mL) jars.

MICROWAVE LOW-SUGAR STRAWBERRY JAM

Use a large container with high sides to avoid spillage while cooking.

4 cups	strawberries, crushed (about 3 pints/1.5 L whole berries)	1 L
1 cup	sugar	250 mL
2 Tbsp.	lemon juice	25 mL

Combine all ingredients in a tall 3-quart (3 L) glass microwave-safe container. Microwave on high for 5 minutes. Stir, then microwave again for 5 minutes. Continue microwaving for 30 to 35 minutes, stirring at 5-minute intervals, until jam thickens and a teaspoonful holds its shape when dropped onto a chilled plate.

Skim off foam. Ladle hot jam into prepared jars, and process in a hot-water bath.

Makes 2 to 3 half-pint (250 mL) jars.

LOW-SUGAR STRAWBERRY JAM WITH APPLES

By adding tart apples, a natural source of pectin, you can significantly reduce the cooking time.

2	apples, preferably tart, such as 'Granny Smith'	2
8 cups	strawberries, crushed (about 6 pints/3 L whole berries)	2 L
2 cups	sugar	500 mL
2 Tbsp.	lemon juice	25 mL

Core apples, but do not peel. Puree apples in a food processor, and combine with other ingredients in a large nonreactive kettle. Bring to a boil over medium-high heat. Reduce heat to medium, and continue to boil, stirring frequently, until mixture thickens, 15 to 25 minutes. The jam is ready when a teaspoonful holds its shape when dropped onto a chilled plate.

Remove jam from heat. Skim off foam. Ladle hot jam into prepared jars, and process in a hot-water bath.

Makes about 6 half-pint (250 mL) jars.

SURE-JELL LIGHT FREEZER JAM

While touted as "light," this brightly colored jam is as high in sugar as many traditional recipes. Its fresh-strawberry flavor is full and sweet, but the texture is a bit rubbery. This recipe is adapted from the instructions included with the Sure-Jell Light pectin.

4 cups	strawberries, crushed (about 3 pints/1.5 L whole berries)	1 L
3¼ cups	sugar	800 mL
1	package pectin	1

Place strawberries in a large bowl. In a small bowl, mix ¼ cup (50 mL) sugar with pectin. Add pectin-sugar mixture to strawberries, and stir vigorously. Let stand for 30 minutes, stirring occasionally. Gradually stir the remaining sugar into the strawberry mixture. Stir until sugar has dissolved.

Ladle jam into sterilized half-pint (250 mL) jars, leaving ½-inch (1 cm) headspace. Wipe jar rims. Seal jars, and let stand at room temperature for 24 hours. Place in freezer. Store in refrigerator after opening.

Makes 6 half-pint (250 mL) jars.

POMONA'S UNIVERSAL PECTIN FREEZER JAM

The tasters liked the flavor and bright color of this jam. "Tastes like fresh strawberries" was the overwhelming consensus. This recipe is adapted from the instructions included with the Pomona pectin (mono-calcium phosphate, for making calcium solution is included in the package of pectin).

4 cups	strawberries, crushed (about 3 pints/1.5 L whole berries)	1 L
¾ cup	water	175 mL
3 tsp.	pectin	15 mL
1 cup	sugar	250 mL
4 tsp.	calcium solution	20 mL

Place strawberries in a large bowl. In a small pan, bring water to a boil. Pour water into a blender or a food processor, and add pectin. Blend for 1 to 2 minutes or until pectin is dissolved. Add hot pectin mixture to strawberries, and stir vigorously for 1 minute. Add sugar, and stir well. Add calcium solution, and stir well.

Ladle jam into sterilized half-pint (250 mL) jars, leaving ½-inch (1 cm) headspace. Wipe jar rims. Seal jars, and place in freezer immediately. Store jam in refrigerator after opening.

Makes 6 half-pint (250 mL) jars.

SUNSHINE STRAWBERRY JAM

There's something magical about solar cooking, and it's a fine alternative to steaming up the kitchen on a hot July day. If the jam hasn't gelled in 2 days, finish it off in a 200°F (95°C) oven.

8 cups	strawberries, crushed (about 6 pints/3 L whole berries)	2 L
2 cups	sugar	500 mL
2 Tbsp.	lemon juice	25 mL

In a large bowl, combine all ingredients, stirring until sugar is dissolved. Transfer mixture to a large, shallow container. Cover with a mesh screen, and place outdoors in full sun for 2 consecutive days. Stir occasionally. (Take inside at night.) The jam is ready when a teaspoonful holds its shape when dropped onto a chilled plate.

Ladle jam into prepared jars, and process in a hot-water bath.

Makes 12 half-pint (250 mL) jars.

MAKING IT GEL

Low in natural pectin, strawberries pose a challenge to cooks who want to make firm-textured, low-sugar preserves. Tart apples, blackberries and sour plums all have a high level of natural pectin that is activated during boiling; when pectin reacts with sugar and acid in the recipe, the result is a firm preserve. Like cherries, grapes, peaches and pears, strawberries develop the best texture with the help of additional pectin, obtained from a commercial variety or from another high-pectin fruit.

Most recipes that use commercial pectin, though, call for lots of sugar. Cooks can avoid the pectin dilemma altogether by cooking the fruit until it reaches 220°F (105°C), the temperature at which sugar syrup thickens. A few tart apples added along the way provide gelling power, and sugar added to taste produces a no-fuss fruity result.

DUNDEE MARMALADE

This is one of the most popular marmalades around and makes a perfect midwinter taste pickup. Seville oranges come on the North American market in early January, and there is really no substitute.

2 lb.	Seville oranges	1 kg
2	lemons	2
4 lb.	sugar	1.8 kg

Wash oranges and lemons, and place, whole, into preserving kettle. Add 8 cups (2 L) water, cover, bring to a boil, and simmer for 1½ hours or until the fruit can be pierced easily. Remove fruit from pan, and cool. Slice coarsely, removing any seeds. Add seeds to juice in pan, boil for 10 minutes, then strain. Add fruit to juice, bring to a boil, then add sugar. Cook over medium-low heat, stirring, until sugar is dissolved, then boil rapidly, without stirring, for 30 minutes or until a temperature of 220°F (105°C) is reached. Pour into hot, sterilized jars, and seal.

Makes about 4 pounds (1.8 kg).

RHUBARB & FIG JAM

This recipe uses powdered pectin for a quick jam that preserves the fruity flavor of rhubarb.

6 cups	rhubarb, cut into pieces	1.5 L
¼ cup	fresh lemon juice	50 mL
1 cup	dried figs, finely chopped	250 mL
2 tsp.	grated lemon zest	10 mL
1	package (1¾ oz./50 g) powdered pectin (see *Note* below)	1
4 cups	sugar	1 L

Note: Powdered pectin is not interchangeable with liquid pectin.

In a large, heavy saucepan, combine rhubarb, lemon juice and ½ cup (125 mL) water. Bring to a boil. Reduce heat to low, cover, and simmer for 10 to 12 minutes or until rhubarb is soft. Stir in figs and lemon zest; simmer for 3 to 5 minutes. Add pectin, and bring to a full, rolling boil over high heat, stirring constantly. Add sugar, and return to a full boil for 1 minute, stirring constantly. Remove from heat, and skim off any foam.

Pour into hot, sterilized half-pint (250 mL) or pint (500 mL) jars, leaving ¼-inch (5 mm) headspace. Adjust caps, and process in a hot-water bath.

Makes 3 pints (1.5 L).

Chapter 7

BAKING

ust as the old-style country-fair competitions for the best fresh-fruit pies drew enthusiasts from all over the county, the *Harrowsmith Country Life* "Pantrys" featuring baking have always enjoyed a devoted following. While filling the air with intoxicating aromas, a baker also achieves a little bit of magic—something on the order of the magician pulling a rabbit out of a hat. After all, a roast chicken, though a succulent alternative to a cold bird, remains, nonetheless, a bird. But all forms of baking, which rely on the same few simple ingredients—butter, sugar, flour, eggs—are miraculously transformed into an endless variety of cookies, breads, cakes, pies and muffins.

Such fantastic and fanciful rewards from these humble ingredients also suggest that while baking is one part alchemy, it is another part discipline. Imagination and improvisation, which are at home in

other styles of cooking, are out of place in baking. The fine line between rise and fall, heavy and light, sweet and saccharine, is easily and forever crossed with an oversize pan, too many strokes of a wooden spoon or a misjudged ingredient.

Respect for the few methodologies in a given recipe is all one needs, however, to enjoy the unlimited potential of baked treats. Our quick breads and muffins make great morning starters and tasty sidekicks to soup or salad; homemade cookies have not yet been dethroned by supermarket impostors; easy-to-make flatbreads will ease timid bakers into the alternatives to yeast loaves; and our more elaborate cookies and fruitcakes will generate festive cheer during the holiday season. While home baking may not be your passport to first prize at the county fair, it will always earn rave reviews from those closer to home.

Biscuits, Muffins & Quick Breads

BAKING-POWDER BISCUITS

Although ¾ cup (175 mL) milk or sour milk can be substituted for the yogurt in this recipe, yogurt adds to the richness and lightness of the biscuits.

2 cups	flour	500 mL
1 Tbsp.	baking powder	15 mL
1 tsp.	sugar	5 mL
½ tsp.	baking soda	2 mL
7 Tbsp.	butter	90 mL
½ cup	yogurt	125 mL
⅓ cup	milk	75 mL

Sift together flour, baking powder, sugar and baking soda. Cut in butter until crumbly. Combine yogurt and milk, and stir into flour mixture. Mix until smooth, then knead gently for 1 minute.

Roll out dough ½ inch (1 cm) thick, cut into 2-inch (5 cm) circles, and bake on ungreased cookie sheets for 10 minutes at 425°F (220°C).

Makes 18 to 20 biscuits.

CHEROKEE SQUASH DROP BISCUITS

These biscuits are so moist, they can be served without butter. Good for dinner or breakfast.

¾ cup	cooked, mashed winter squash	175 mL
¾ cup	cooked, mashed apple	175 mL
3 Tbsp.	brown sugar	45 mL
¼ cup	oil	50 mL
1	egg, beaten	1
	Finely grated zest of 1 lemon	
1¾ cups	whole wheat flour	425 mL
2 tsp.	baking powder	10 mL
1 tsp.	cinnamon	5 mL
1 tsp.	salt	5 mL

Preheat oven to 400°F (200°C). Combine squash, apple, sugar, oil, egg and lemon zest. (If squash and apple are freshly cooked, let them cool somewhat before adding egg.)

Sift together flour, baking powder, cinnamon and salt. Combine with liquid ingredients, using as few strokes as possible (overmixing will toughen biscuits). Drop by spoonfuls onto a greased baking sheet. Bake for 10 to 12 minutes, until golden brown at edges.

Makes 12 to 15 biscuits.

Biscuits, Muffins & Quick Breads

ORANGE-CURRANT SCONES

Offer these scones as a special breakfast treat, and everyone will be up and out of bed in no time. The scones can be made and baked in about 30 minutes.

2 cups	flour	500 mL
1 Tbsp.	sugar, plus extra to sprinkle on top	15 mL
1 Tbsp.	baking powder	15 mL
½ tsp.	salt	2 mL
¼ cup	cold butter	50 mL
¼ cup	orange juice	50 mL
¼ cup	heavy cream	50 mL
2	eggs	2
	Grated zest of 1 orange	
½ cup	currants	125 mL

Sift together flour, sugar, baking powder and salt. Cut in butter until mixture resembles coarse meal. Make a well in the center, and add orange juice, cream, 1 egg, lightly beaten, and orange zest. Stir until dry ingredients are moistened. Add currants, and stir to distribute—mixture will be crumbly.

Press into a ball, then turn onto a floured board, and knead until dough holds together. Roll into a rectangle, and cut into 10 triangles by cutting dough into squares, then cutting in half diagonally. Place triangles ½ inch (1 cm) apart on ungreased cookie sheet. Brush with remaining egg, lightly beaten, and sprinkle with sugar. Bake at 400°F (200°C) for 15 minutes or until golden brown.

Makes 10 scones.

SUNPRINT BRAN MUFFINS

This muffin has several great qualities: it is delicious and high in fiber, and the batter will keep in the refrigerator for up to 6 weeks.

3 cups	bran flakes or bran bud cereal	750 mL
1 cup	boiling water	250 mL
1 cup	oil	250 mL
2	eggs	2
1½ cups	light brown sugar	375 mL
2 cups	buttermilk	500 mL
2½ tsp.	baking soda	12 mL
1 tsp.	salt	5 mL
2½ cups	flour	625 mL

Soak 1½ cups (375 mL) bran in water. Meanwhile, combine and mix all other ingredients. Add soaked bran, and mix. Spoon batter into greased muffin tins. Bake at 400°F (200°C) for 20 minutes.

Makes about 24 muffins.

Biscuits, Muffins & Quick Breads

BLUEBERRY MUFFINS

These have a surprise cluster of berries in the center, which makes them more intense than other blueberry muffins and a delightful breakfast treat.

1½ cups	fresh blueberries	375 mL
2 Tbsp.	white sugar	25 mL
	Grated zest of 1 lemon	
½ cup	unsalted butter	125 mL
¾ cup	light brown sugar	175 mL
2	eggs	2
1 cup	milk	250 mL
4 tsp.	baking powder	20 mL
½ tsp.	salt	2 mL
2 cups	flour	500 mL

Mix 1 cup (250 mL) blueberries, white sugar and lemon zest in a small bowl, and set aside. Meanwhile, cream butter and brown sugar until fluffy, then add eggs, one at a time, then milk. Add remaining ½ cup (125 mL) blueberries and dry ingredients all at once, and gently fold into batter. Fill greased muffin tin halfway with batter, add 1 Tbsp. (15 mL) blueberry-lemon mixture to each muffin, and top with more batter. Bake at 400°F (200°C) for 20 minutes or until done. If blueberries stick to the pan, muffins will be difficult to remove; try to distribute the batter accordingly.

Makes about 12 muffins.

MULTIGRAIN MUFFINS

Fresh-from-the-oven muffins for breakfast are a simple, delicious way to start the day when you have this ready-to-bake mixture in the refrigerator.

1 cup	wheat bran flakes	250 mL
½ cup	regular rolled oats	125 mL
½ cup	sesame seeds	125 mL
4 tsp.	grated orange zest	20 mL
1 cup	boiling water	250 mL
1 cup	milk	250 mL
½ cup	orange juice	125 mL
½ cup	vegetable oil	125 mL
⅓ cup	liquid honey	75 mL
4 tsp.	vanilla extract	20 mL
¼ cup	dark brown sugar, firmly packed	50 mL
2	large eggs	2
3 cups	flour	750 mL
1 Tbsp.	baking soda	15 mL
1 tsp.	salt	5 mL
¾ cup	dates, chopped	175 mL
½ cup	apple, coarsely chopped	125 mL

In a large bowl, combine bran flakes, rolled oats, sesame seeds and orange zest. Stir in boiling water, and let stand for 10 minutes. In a mixing bowl, blend together milk, orange juice, oil, honey, vanilla and sugar; whisk in eggs. Stir into bran mixture.

In a separate bowl, combine flour, baking soda and salt. Toss dates and apple pieces in flour mixture. Stir into bran mixture just until dry ingredients are moistened. Cover, and refrigerate for at least 12 hours or up to 2 weeks. (Batter will thicken upon standing.)

Preheat oven to 375°F (190°C). Lightly grease muffin tins, or line with paper baking cups. Without stirring, spoon in batter, filling cups almost completely. Bake for 20 minutes or until muffins have risen and are firm to the touch. Refrigerate remaining batter.

Makes 18 muffins.

MAPLE WALNUT MUFFINS

Flavorful and crisp at the edges, this is a truly subtle and marvelous muffin.

1¾ cups	flour	425 mL
2½ tsp.	baking powder	12 mL
¼ tsp.	salt	1 mL
1 cup	maple syrup	250 mL
¼ cup	unsalted butter, melted	50 mL
1	egg	1
¼ cup	milk	50 mL
½ cup	walnuts, chopped	125 mL

Combine flour, baking powder and salt in a large mixing bowl. Beat together liquid ingredients, and add, with walnuts, to dry ingredients all at once. Fold mixture gently but thoroughly. Fill greased muffin tin, and bake at 400°F (200°C) for 15 to 20 minutes or until done.

Makes about 10 muffins.

OATMEAL-APPLE MUFFINS

The nutty oats and fragrant vanilla enhance these breakfast muffins.

¼ cup	unsalted butter, melted	50 mL
¾ cup	milk	175 mL
2 tsp.	vanilla extract	10 mL
2	eggs	2
¾ cup	dark brown sugar	175 mL
1 cup	old-fashioned oats	250 mL
1½ cups	flour	375 mL
2½ tsp.	baking powder	12 mL
½ tsp.	salt	2 mL
1	apple, grated	1

Combine liquid ingredients. Add dry ingredients and apple all at once, and gently fold into batter. Fill greased muffin tin, and bake at 400°F (200°C) for 20 minutes or until done.

Makes about 12 muffins.

MASTERING THE MUFFIN

The key to a light muffin is restraint. Mixing muffins—this action can really be more like folding—requires a delicate touch and should last no more than 15 to 20 seconds. Lumpiness in the batter is standard, but an insufficiently mixed batch can yield a soapy, bitter-tasting muffin. Muffin batter should still be coarse in texture, although free of hidden dry spots; it should never be stirred so much that it becomes a smooth, thick liquid. Such overworking activates the flour's gluten, and the end result can be tough muffins riddled with air pockets.

Biscuits, Muffins & Quick Breads

ORANGE & CHOCOLATE MUFFINS

The classic combination of tangy orange and bitter-sweet chocolate make this muffin a fast favorite with fresh hot coffee, tea or cocoa.

½ cup	unsalted butter	125 mL
1 cup	sugar	250 mL
	Grated zest of 2 oranges	
2	large eggs	2
½ cup	sour cream	125 mL
½ cup	orange juice, freshly squeezed	125 mL
1 tsp.	baking powder	5 mL
½ tsp.	baking soda	2 mL
2 cups	flour	500 mL
3 oz.	bittersweet chocolate, chopped into small pieces (preferably a fine eating chocolate)	75 g

Beat butter and sugar together until fluffy. Continue beating while you add orange zest and 1 egg at a time, then sour cream and orange juice. Mix all dry ingredients and chocolate together, then fold lightly into batter. Fold only until blended, then fill greased muffin tin. Bake at 400°F (200°C) for 20 minutes or until done.

Makes about 10 muffins.

GINGER, LEMON & WALNUT MUFFINS

This unusual muffin is especially good with fish or Chinese food; it is also suitable for afternoon tea. Serve at room temperature for a full and balanced flavor.

	Grated zest of 2 lemons	
2 Tbsp.	gingerroot, peeled & chopped	25 mL
1 cup	sugar	250 mL
½ cup	unsalted butter	125 mL
2	eggs	2
1 cup	sour cream or yogurt	250 mL
½ cup	walnuts, chopped	125 mL
½ tsp.	ground ginger	2 mL
1 tsp.	baking soda	5 mL
2 cups	flour	500 mL

Put lemon zest, gingerroot and sugar in a food processor bowl; process until all large pieces are broken down. Add to butter, and beat with an electric mixer until fluffy. While beating, add eggs and sour cream. Add walnuts and dry ingredients all at once, and fold gently into batter. Bake in greased muffin tin at 400°F (200°C) for 20 minutes or until done.

Makes approximately 12 muffins.

Biscuits, Muffins & Quick Breads

APPLE-CARROT-RAISIN MUFFINS

These easy-to-make and healthful muffins contain lots of carrots and apples and use very little oil.

1 cup	flour	250 mL
1 cup	oat bran	250 mL
2 tsp.	baking soda	10 mL
1 tsp.	baking powder	5 mL
½ tsp.	salt	2 mL
2 tsp.	cinnamon	10 mL
1 cup	brown sugar	250 mL
1½ cups	carrots, finely shredded	375 mL
2	large, tart apples, peeled, cored & shredded	2
1 cup	pecans, chopped	250 mL
½ cup	raisins (opt.)	125 mL
¼ cup	vegetable oil	50 mL
½ cup	skim milk	125 mL
2	eggs, lightly beaten, or use egg substitute or 4 egg whites	2
1 tsp.	vanilla extract	5 mL

Combine flour, oat bran, baking soda, baking powder, salt and cinnamon in a large bowl. Stir in sugar. Add carrots, apples, pecans and raisins, if desired, and mix together.

Make a well in the center of the mixture, and add oil, milk, eggs and vanilla. Stir until just moistened. Use a ¼-cup (50 mL) measure to scoop batter into greased muffin tins. Bake at 375°F (190°C) for 18 to 20 minutes or until nicely browned.

Makes 18 muffins.

CARROT-COCONUT MUFFINS

Chock-full of fruit, nuts and fiber, this coarse-textured muffin is dense and especially nutritious.

2 cups	flour	500 mL
1 cup	sugar	250 mL
2 tsp.	baking soda	10 mL
2 tsp.	cinnamon	10 mL
¼ tsp.	salt	1 mL
2 cups	grated carrots	500 mL
½ cup	currants	125 mL
½ cup	walnuts or pecans, chopped	125 mL
½ cup	shredded coconut	125 mL
1	apple, peeled, cored & grated	1
3	eggs	3
1 cup	oil	250 mL
1 tsp.	vanilla extract	5 mL

Combine dry ingredients in a large mixing bowl. Add carrots, currants, walnuts, coconut and apple, and stir to mix. Beat eggs, oil and vanilla, and combine with dry ingredients. Fold thoroughly. Fill greased muffin tin, and bake at 400°F (200°C) for 20 minutes or until done.

Makes about 12 muffins.

Biscuits, Muffins & Quick Breads

SUNSHINE MUFFINS

Substitute poppy seeds for the sunflower seeds and grated apple for the carrots in these delicious muffins that can be tailor-made for different tastes.

2 cups	whole wheat flour	500 mL
1 cup	sugar	250 mL
2 tsp.	baking soda	10 mL
1 Tbsp.	cinnamon	15 mL
2 cups	grated carrots	500 mL
⅓ cup	dried apricots, chopped	75 mL
⅓ cup	sunflower seeds	75 mL
⅓ cup	chocolate chips	75 mL
⅓ cup	shredded coconut	75 mL
1	banana, mashed	1
3	eggs	3
1 cup	oil	250 mL
2 tsp.	vanilla extract	10 mL

Combine flour, sugar, baking soda and cinnamon, and mix well. Stir in carrots, apricots, sunflower seeds, chocolate chips, coconut and banana.

Beat together eggs, oil and vanilla. Stir into flour mixture until just moistened. Spoon into greased muffin tins, and bake at 375°F (190°C) for 15 to 20 minutes.

Makes about 24 muffins.

PROTEIN MUFFINS

This recipe makes simple, basic muffins. Dried fruits, poppy seeds, grated carrots or mashed bananas can be added. If adding carrots or bananas, reduce the amount of milk very slightly. Prepared as the recipe indicates, these muffins serve as an excellent accompaniment to a spicy meal or as the base of a cheese or peanut butter sandwich.

1 cup	whole wheat flour	250 mL
½ cup	soy flour	125 mL
½ cup	engevita yeast	125 mL
1 Tbsp.	baking powder	15 mL
1	egg	1
1 cup	sour milk (see *Note*)	250 mL
3 Tbsp.	oil	45 mL
3 Tbsp.	maple syrup	45 mL

Note: To sour milk, add 1 Tbsp. (15 mL) vinegar or lemon juice to 1 cup (250 mL) milk.

Combine dry ingredients. Beat together egg, milk, oil and maple syrup. Pour into dry ingredients all at once, stirring just to moisten.

Spoon into greased muffin tin, and bake at 400°F (200°C) for 20 to 25 minutes.

Makes 12 muffins.

Biscuits, Muffins & Quick Breads

CHEDDAR & HONEY-MUSTARD MUFFINS

This savory muffin is tangy with mustard and a sprinkling of black pepper, sweet with honey and rich with Cheddar cheese. It can accompany almost any soup and is excellent with eggs at brunch.

2 cups	flour	500 mL
1 Tbsp.	baking powder	15 mL
¼ tsp.	salt	1 mL
	Freshly ground pepper	
1 cup	grated sharp Cheddar cheese	250 mL
1	egg	1
3 Tbsp.	honey mustard	45 mL
2 Tbsp.	honey	25 mL
1¼ cups	milk	300 mL
¼ cup	butter, melted	50 mL

Combine dry ingredients in a large mixing bowl. Whisk together the remaining ingredients, and fold them, gently but thoroughly, into dry ingredients. Fill greased muffin tin, and bake at 400°F (200°C) for 20 minutes or until done.

Makes about 12 muffins.

HERBED COTTAGE-CHEESE MUFFINS

Try these with your favorite tomato soup or as a special treat with smoked ham, sandwich-style. They have a smooth, crisp surface and a moist interior.

2 cups	flour	500 mL
1 Tbsp.	sugar	15 mL
2½ tsp.	baking powder	12 mL
2 Tbsp.	dill	25 mL
½ tsp.	salt	2 mL
	Freshly ground pepper	
1	egg	1
1 cup	cottage cheese	250 mL
¾ cup	milk	175 mL
4 Tbsp.	butter, melted	50 mL
1 Tbsp.	shallots, finely chopped	15 mL

Combine dry ingredients in a large mixing bowl. Whisk egg, cottage cheese, milk, butter and shallots together. Add to dry ingredients, and fold gently but thoroughly. Fill greased muffin tin, and bake at 400°F (200°C) for 20 minutes or until done.

Makes about 12 muffins.

169

Biscuits, Muffins & Quick Breads

PUMPKIN-PECAN MUFFINS

Moist and cakelike, these muffins have a melt-in-your-mouth quality. Serve with soup and salad or as a breakfast or brunch treat.

½ cup	unsalted butter	125 mL
¾ cup	dark brown sugar	175 mL
4 Tbsp.	maple syrup	50 mL
1¼ cups	cooked pumpkin, mashed	300 mL
2	eggs	2
1 cup	heavy cream	250 mL
4 tsp.	baking powder	20 mL
1 tsp.	fresh nutmeg, grated	5 mL
1 tsp.	cinnamon	5 mL
½ tsp.	salt	2 mL
1 tsp.	vanilla extract	5 mL
2½ cups	flour	625 mL
½ cup	toasted pecans, chopped	125 mL

Beat butter and sugar, add maple syrup, pumpkin, eggs and cream, and continue beating. Add remaining ingredients all at once, and gently fold together. Fill greased muffin tin, and bake at 400°F (200°C) for 20 minutes or until done.

Makes about 10 muffins.

CORN MUFFINS

These corn muffins are especially good with chili or spicy soups and stews.

1¼ cups	flour	300 mL
¾ cup	yellow cornmeal, preferably stone-ground	175 mL
3 tsp.	baking powder	15 mL
½ tsp.	salt	2 mL
¼ cup	sugar	50 mL
½ tsp.	baking soda	2 mL
1 cup	sour cream	250 mL
1	egg	1
½ cup	buttermilk	125 mL

Put dry ingredients, except baking soda, in a large mixing bowl. Mix baking soda with sour cream until it bubbles a little, then add to dry ingredients with egg, and fold in gently but thoroughly. Add up to ½ cup (125 mL) buttermilk if batter seems too thick. Fill greased muffin tin, and bake at 350°F (180°C) for 20 to 25 minutes or until done.

Makes about 12 muffins.

Biscuits, Muffins & Quick Breads

BUCKWHEAT PRIMER

Depending on the quantity of hulls it contains, buckwheat flour is sold as "light" or "dark." Commercial buckwheat flour contains a medium amount of hull, making its taste distinctive but not overpowering. (If you buy your flour at a health-food store that grinds fresh flour, be sure it is ground from the unroasted groats.)

Because buckwheat flour contains no gluten (the elastic protein that enables bread to rise), it must be mixed with plenty of wheat flour when making yeast breads. A ratio of no more than one part buckwheat flour to four parts wheat flour will help prevent a leaden-textured result. Since pancakes, quick breads and muffins contain a higher proportion of baking powder and eggs, which serve as leavening agents, they can carry more buckwheat. The sandy quality that is characteristic of buckwheat flour disappears when it is mixed with liquid and baked into breads and muffins, while buckwheat cookies and pie crusts retain the grainy texture. Unlike wheat flour, buckwheat flour has little natural sugar to enhance browning, so baked goods made exclusively with buckwheat flour come out of the oven with a grayish rather than a golden color. Any natural sweetener—sugar, honey or maple syrup—will restore the toasty glow.

BUCKWHEAT, SESAME & CORN MUFFINS

These crunchy muffins are so moist and rich-tasting, they don't need to be buttered. Grease the muffin tin with butter, however, to get a crunchy coating. Serve warm.

4 Tbsp.	sesame seeds	50 mL
¾ cup	buckwheat flour	175 mL
¼ cup	white flour	50 mL
⅔ cup	cornmeal, preferably stone-ground	150 mL
½ tsp.	salt	2 mL
1 tsp.	baking soda	5 mL
2	eggs, well beaten	2
1 Tbsp.	buckwheat honey or other dark, full-flavored honey	15 mL
2 Tbsp.	sesame oil	25 mL
1½ cups	buttermilk	375 mL

Preheat oven to 450°F (230°C). Butter the muffin tin—generously, if you want a crisp crust—and sprinkle with sesame seeds. Combine flours, cornmeal, salt and baking soda in a large, shallow bowl, stirring with a whisk until well mixed.

Beat eggs with honey until honey dissolves, then beat in oil and buttermilk. Make a well in the center of the dry ingredients, and add liquid all at once, stirring just until moistened and combined. Do not overmix.

Fill muffin tin about ⅔ full, pinching out any major lumps in the batter as they appear. Bake for 15 to 20 minutes or until muffins are well risen and browned.

Makes 12 muffins.

ORANGE-CRANBERRY BREAD

A festive loaf, this citrus-scented bread makes a wonderful snack.

¾ cup	cranberries, chopped	175 mL
½ cup	raisins, chopped	125 mL
1 Tbsp.	grated orange zest	15 mL
1¼ cups	orange juice	300 mL
¼ cup	honey	50 mL
¼ cup	butter or oil	50 mL
1½ cups	whole wheat pastry flour	375 mL
½ cup	whole wheat bread flour	125 mL
2½ tsp.	baking powder	12 mL
½ tsp.	baking soda	2 mL
½ tsp.	salt	2 mL
½ cup	toasted wheat germ	125 mL
½ cup	lightly toasted walnuts, chopped	125 mL

Preheat oven to 375°F (190°C). Grease an 8-by-4-inch (1.5 L) loaf pan. In a saucepan, combine cranberries, raisins, orange zest, juice and honey. Bring to a boil, stir in butter, and remove from heat. Allow to cool while measuring and combining the other ingredients.

Sift together flours, baking powder, baking soda and salt, and stir in wheat germ. When liquid mixture has cooled to lukewarm, stir in dry ingredients and fold in walnuts, reserving 3 Tbsp. (45 mL) for topping.

Spread batter in loaf pan. Sprinkle remaining walnuts on top, and press down lightly with your hand or the back of a spoon.

Bake for 50 to 60 minutes or until done. Test with a clean knife or a toothpick, but if you should pierce a cranberry, the testing device will come out wet, so try in more than one spot to be sure.

Let the loaf rest in its pan on a wire rack for 10 minutes, then turn it out on the rack to cool for at least half an hour more before slicing.

Makes 1 loaf.

CHEDDAR HERB BREAD

This savory herb bread is crisp and brown on the outside and moist inside. Crumble rather than grate the Cheddar so that the pockets of melted cheese will be large and gooey.

4 cups	unbleached white flour or 2½ cups (625 mL) white flour & 1½ cups (375 mL) whole wheat pastry flour	1 L
¼ cup	sugar	50 mL
2 Tbsp.	baking powder	25 mL
2 tsp.	salt	10 mL
1½ tsp.	thyme	7 mL
½ tsp.	celery seeds	2 mL
	Pinch freshly ground pepper	
	Pinch allspice	
3 cups	sharp Cheddar cheese, coarsely crumbled	750 mL
½ cup	whole scallions, chopped & lightly packed	125 mL
1	egg	1
1¾ cups	skim milk	425 mL

Preheat oven to 375°F (190°C). In a large bowl, combine and mix flour, sugar, baking powder, salt and seasonings. Add cheese and scallions, and toss to coat. In a separate bowl, beat egg with milk, and pour into dry ingredients. Mix until just blended; batter will be stiff. Spoon into two greased 9-by-5-inch (2 L) loaf pans, and let rest for 10 minutes. Bake for 45 minutes or until a toothpick inserted in the center of the loaf comes out clean.

Makes 2 loaves.

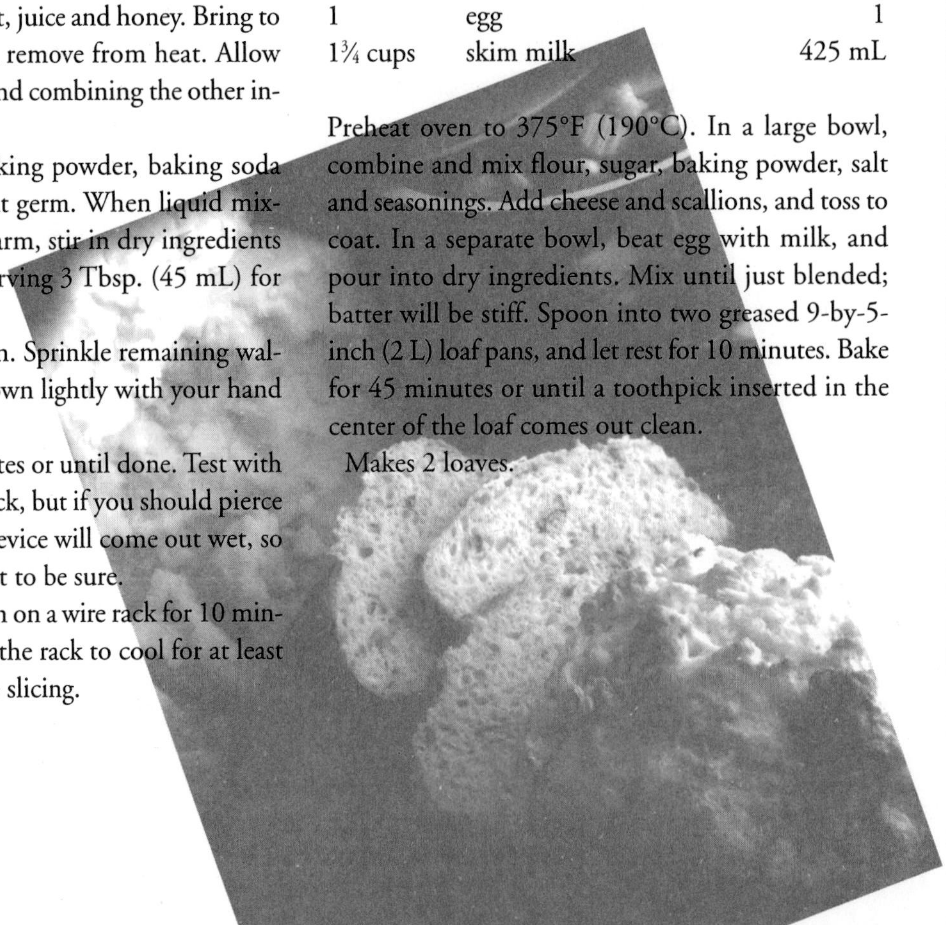

Baking-Powder Biscuits

Baking, page 162

Buttermilk Apple-Spice Bread

Baking, page 175

Biscuits, Muffins & Quick Breads

HONEY WHEAT-GERM BREAD

A quick substitute for yeast bread, this bread is good for sandwiches, for toasting and for French toast—if you can keep it around that long.

4 cups	unbleached white flour or 3 cups (750 mL) white & 1 cup (250 mL) whole wheat pastry flour	1 L
2 cups	toasted wheat germ	500 mL
2 Tbsp.	baking powder	25 mL
2 tsp.	baking soda	10 mL
1½ tsp.	salt	7 mL
2	eggs, lightly beaten	2
⅔ cup	dark honey	150 mL
4 Tbsp.	melted butter or oil	50 mL
2 cups	buttermilk	500 mL

Preheat oven to 350°F (180°C). In a large bowl, combine flour, wheat germ, baking powder, baking soda and salt. In a smaller bowl, mix together eggs, honey, butter and buttermilk. Pour liquid ingredients into dry, and mix until just blended. Spoon into two greased 9-by-5-inch (2 L) loaf pans, let rest for 10 minutes, and bake for 50 to 55 minutes or until a toothpick inserted in the center of the loaf comes out clean.

  Makes 2 loaves.

BUTTERMILK APPLE-SPICE BREAD

Similar to a spice cake but slightly less sweet, this loaf may be served, like gingerbread, with whipped cream. Pears can be substituted for apples; simply omit the allspice and replace the cinnamon with ¾ tsp. (4 mL) ginger.

4 cups	unbleached flour	1 L
2 cups	rolled oats	500 mL
1 cup	brown sugar	250 mL
2 Tbsp.	baking powder	25 mL
1 tsp.	salt	5 mL
1 tsp.	baking soda	5 mL
1 tsp.	cinnamon	5 mL
½ tsp.	nutmeg	2 mL
¼ tsp.	allspice	1 mL
4-5 cups	large, firm apples, pared & chopped	1-1.25 L
3	eggs	3
2¼ cups	buttermilk	550 mL
4 Tbsp.	melted butter or oil	50 mL
2 tsp.	vanilla extract	10 mL

Preheat oven to 375°F (190°C). In a large bowl, combine flour, oats, sugar, baking powder, salt, baking soda and spices. Add apples, and toss to coat. In a smaller bowl, beat eggs, and mix in buttermilk, butter and vanilla. Pour liquid ingredients into dry, and mix until just blended. Spoon into two greased 9-by-5-inch (2 L) loaf pans, and bake for 1 hour and 10 minutes or until a toothpick inserted in the center of the loaf comes out clean.

  Makes 2 loaves.

Flatbread

CORN TORTILLAS

The dough for these tortillas is easy to make, but the rolling and cooking can be frustrating. Roll the dough thin, but not paper-thin, or it will not hold together. Handle gently, and move as little as possible between rolling and cooking. If you work slowly, you should have no problem.

2 cups	masa harina	500 mL
1⅛ cups	water	275 mL
2 tsp.	salt	10 mL

Combine ingredients to make a soft dough. Divide into egg-sized balls, then flatten, one by one, on a piece of wax paper. Place a second sheet of wax paper on top of dough, and roll out thin with a rolling pin. Stack tortillas with wax paper between each one. Cook in a dry, heavy skillet over medium-high heat. Serve while still warm.

Makes about 2 dozen small tortillas.

WHEAT TORTILLAS

Traditionally northern Mexican fare, wheat tortillas are particularly good served as a wrapper for refried beans, lettuce, onions, tomatoes, grated cheese, hot peppers and sour cream.

2 cups	flour	500 mL
1 tsp.	salt	5 mL
1 tsp.	baking powder	5 mL
1 Tbsp.	lard	15 mL
¾ cup	water	175 mL

Combine dry ingredients, and mix well. Cut in lard, then add enough water to make a stiff dough. Divide into 6 balls, and roll out thin on a floured board. Cook in a dry skillet over medium-high heat until just browned, approximately 2 minutes per side. Serve warm or cold.

Makes 6 tortillas.

PITA BREAD

Perhaps one of the world's best-known flatbreads, pita originates in the Middle East. Its pocket allows it to be used for convenient sandwich making, particularly for messy fillings. There is no mystery to making a pita's pocket, and this recipe is guaranteed to result in puffy, light pitas. Just be sure not to roll the dough any thinner than ¼ inch (5 mm).

2¼ cups	lukewarm water	550 mL
2 Tbsp.	yeast	25 mL
1 Tbsp.	sugar	15 mL
8-9 cups	flour	2-2.25 L
1 tsp.	salt	5 mL
¼ cup	oil	50 mL
	Cornmeal	

Combine water, yeast and sugar, and set aside for 10 minutes to allow yeast to dissolve. Combine flour and salt in a large mixing bowl, and form a well in the center. Pour in yeast mixture and oil, and blend thoroughly.

Knead dough on a floured board until stiff and elastic, about 15 minutes. Shape into a ball, and let rise, covered, until doubled in bulk, about 45 minutes. Punch down, and divide into 8 equal-sized pieces. Shape into balls, cover, and let rest for 20 minutes. Roll each ball into a circle ¼ inch (5 mm) thick, and arrange on cookie sheets that have been sprinkled with cornmeal. Cover, and let rest for another 30 minutes.

In a gas oven, bake bread on floor of oven at 500°F (260°C) for 5 minutes, then transfer to middle shelf, and bake for 5 more minutes or until puffed and golden brown. In an electric oven, bake first on lowest rack and then in middle of oven. Place pitas in paper bags when removed from the oven to keep moist while cooling. The tops will fall, but the pockets will remain.

Flatbread

CHAPATI

Served with traditional curried dishes, this Indian bread helps cool the mouth.

2½ cups	whole wheat pastry flour	625 mL
1 tsp.	salt	5 mL
1 Tbsp.	oil or ghee (clarified liquid butter)	15 mL
1 cup	lukewarm water	250 mL

Put flour in a mixing bowl, add salt, then rub in oil. Add water all at once, and mix until firm but not stiff. Knead for 15 minutes or more (the longer you knead, the lighter the bread), then wrap in plastic, and let rest for at least 1 hour. Shape dough into 3-inch (8 cm) balls, and roll paper-thin on a lightly floured board.

Cook chapati in a dry, heavy, very hot skillet, beginning with the ones that were rolled out first, about 1 minute per side.

Makes approximately 24 chapati.

PURI

This is essentially the same recipe as chapati, but the dough is deep-fried instead of dry-cooked. The result is a delicious but admittedly rich, bread that makes a tasty curry companion.

3 cups	whole wheat pastry flour	750 mL
1 tsp.	salt	5 mL
1 Tbsp.	oil or ghee (clarified liquid butter)	15 mL
1 cup	lukewarm water	250 mL
	Oil	

Place flour in a mixing bowl, add salt, then rub in oil. Add water all at once, and mix until firm but not stiff. Knead for 15 minutes or more for a light bread, then wrap in plastic, and let rest for at least 1 hour. Shape dough into 3-inch (8 cm) balls, and roll out on a lightly floured board until paper-thin.

Heat 1 inch (2.5 cm) oil in a heavy skillet until a haze rises from the oil. Fry puri, one at a time, over medium heat, spooning oil over the dough constantly, until it puffs up. Turn bread, and continue to fry in the same way. When both sides are golden brown, remove from skillet, drain, and serve while still warm.

Makes about 24 puri.

Flatbread

BARBARI BREAD

This Iranian sesame-seed bread is best when served fresh from the oven. Adding garlic or other herbs to the melted butter increases the savory flavor.

1 Tbsp.	yeast	15 mL
1 cup	lukewarm water	250 mL
2 Tbsp.	oil	25 mL
3-3½ cups	flour	750-875 mL
4 Tbsp.	melted butter or 1 egg, beaten	50 mL
2 Tbsp.	sesame seeds	25 mL

Dissolve yeast in water, then add oil, and stir. Add flour gradually to make a workable dough. Stir well, but do not knead. Cover, and let rise for 1 hour. Knead briefly for 2 or 3 minutes, then divide dough in half.

Form into two oval loaves ¼ inch (5 mm) thick on two greased cookie sheets. Lightly score the top of the bread with a knife, then brush with butter, and sprinkle with sesame seeds. Cover, and let rise for 30 minutes. Bake at 375°F (190°C) for 15 to 20 minutes.

Makes 2 loaves.

HASHA

This North African bread recipe uses semolina, the purified middlings of hard wheat.

1 Tbsp.	yeast	15 mL
1 tsp.	sugar	5 mL
3 Tbsp.	warm water	45 mL
1½ cups	semolina, plus extra to roll dough in	375 mL
1 tsp.	salt	5 mL
	Water	

Place yeast and sugar in a small bowl, and add warm water. Stir, and set aside until yeast dissolves. Combine semolina and salt in a large bowl, make a well in the center, then pour in yeast mixture, and add enough water (approximately 1½ cups/375 mL) to make a firm dough. Knead for 10 to 15 minutes.

Divide dough into three pieces, roll into balls, roll in semolina to coat, cover, and let rise for 2 hours or until doubled.

Place dough on preheated baking sheets, and pat out ½ inch (1 cm) thick. Prick all over with fork. Bake in a 350°F (180°C) oven for 30 minutes.

Makes 3 loaves.

Flatbread

LEFSE

This is a Norwegian herbed flatbread. The fennel and anise combine with rye flour to produce a chewy, tasty bread.

1 Tbsp.	yeast	15 mL
½ cup	lukewarm water	125 mL
½ cup	lard	125 mL
1½ cups	milk	375 mL
⅓ cup	corn syrup	75 mL
1 Tbsp.	salt	15 mL
1 Tbsp.	anise seeds	15 mL
1 Tbsp.	fennel seeds	15 mL
3 cups	rye flour	750 mL
3 cups	white flour	750 mL

Dissolve yeast in water. Melt lard, add milk and corn syrup, and heat to lukewarm. Add yeast with salt, anise and fennel, then stir in flour. Knead dough until shiny and soft, but not sticky. Form into a ball, place in a bowl, cover, and let rise for 1 hour or until doubled.

Punch down dough, and divide into 4 pieces. Pat into ovals approximately 12 inches (30 cm) long, then prick all over with a fork. Bake at 400°F (200°C) for 20 minutes.

Makes 4 loaves.

FLADBRØD

Delicious with a hearty soup or stew, this Danish flatbread is perhaps at its best when served warm and topped with butter and jam or preserves.

1½ cups	buttermilk	375 mL
¼ cup	melted butter	50 mL
3 cups	ground oatmeal (see *Note* below)	750 mL
1 tsp.	baking soda	5 mL
1 tsp.	salt	5 mL
2½ cups	flour	625 mL
	Butter	

Note: Grind oat flakes or oatmeal in a food processor until of a flourlike texture.

Combine all ingredients except butter, and blend until stiff. Knead dough until elastic, about 5 minutes. Cover, and let rest for 30 minutes. Divide dough into 12 pieces, and form into balls. Roll each ball into a circle about 6 inches (15 cm) in diameter.

Melt 2 Tbsp. (25 mL) butter in a preheated skillet. Cook flatbread one at a time for 3 minutes per side, adding more butter as needed.

Makes 12 pieces of bread.

Yeast Bread

OAT BRAN BREAD

You can vary this bread to suit individual tastes. Try using half white flour and half whole wheat flour.

1 cup	boiling water	250 mL
1 cup	oat bran	250 mL
2	packages active dry yeast	2
1 tsp.	honey, plus ¼ cup (50 mL)	5 mL
½ cup	warm water	125 mL
1 cup	warm skim milk	250 mL
1 Tbsp.	salt	15 mL
4-5 cups	flour	1-1.25 L
	Oil	

Pour boiling water over oat bran, mix, and set aside. Combine yeast, 1 tsp. (5 mL) honey and water in a small bowl. Stir to dissolve yeast, and set aside until foamy.

Combine milk, salt and remaining honey in a bowl. Add oat-bran mixture, and stir, then add yeast. Stir in 2 cups (500 mL) flour (if using whole wheat, add it first). Beat well, about 200 strokes by hand or 2 minutes with an electric mixer. Add 2 cups (500 mL) flour, ½ cup (125 mL) at a time, beating well after each addition, until it is too stiff to beat.

Turn dough onto a lightly floured surface, and knead in remaining flour. After all the flour has been worked into the dough, knead the dough for 10 more minutes or until it is smooth, pliable and elastic. (The dough will be just a little stickier than regular bread dough.) Place in a mixing bowl, and smear lightly with oil. Cover with plastic wrap, and set aside in a warm place for 1 to 1½ hours, until doubled in bulk. Punch down dough, and knead for 1 or 2 minutes, then divide in half. Allow the loaves to rest for about 10 minutes.

Grease two 8-by-4-inch (1.5 L) loaf pans. Shape dough to fit, then place in pans, cover lightly with plastic wrap, and set aside until the hump of the bread has reached the top of the loaf pan.

Bake loaves at 375°F (190°C) for 45 to 50 minutes. Brush loaves with water once or twice while they're baking. When done, loaves should sound hollow when tapped on the bottom. Remove from pans, and cool on wire racks.

Makes 2 loaves.

Yeast Bread

THE EDIBLE ENVELOPE

Westerners may boast with pride that the ice-cream cone is the perfect edible food container, but long before the popularization of frozen treats, unleavened bread was playing that role in other parts of the world. In many Eastern cultures, eating with one's hands—traditionally a necessity—reflects the epitome of table etiquette. In India, for example, diners use their fingers with the utmost grace when eating; chapati flatbread is broken with the left hand and used as a dipping spoon with the right. In Latin America and Middle Eastern countries, unleavened breads such as tortillas and pitas are easily folded over, wrapped around or slipped under other foods, because they not only are flexible but maintain their integrity when broken.

BUCKWHEAT BREAD

This all-purpose bread has the characteristic flavor of buckwheat flour and is especially tasty when served with cheese. A long, slow rising makes the loaf light, but it can be sliced extremely thin, thanks to buckwheat's adhesive quality. Just before the second rising, you may also stir in 1 cup (250 mL) uncooked kasha that has been soaked in 2 cups (500 mL) boiling water and squeezed dry.

1 Tbsp.	active dry yeast	15 mL
$\frac{1}{3}$ cup	lukewarm water	75 mL
3 Tbsp.	buckwheat honey or other dark, full-flavored honey	45 mL
$2\frac{1}{2}$ cups	milk	625 mL
1 cup	buckwheat flour	250 mL
3 cups	whole wheat flour	750 mL
2	eggs	2
1 Tbsp.	(scant) salt	15 mL
$\frac{1}{4}$ cup	melted butter	50 mL
5-6 cups	white flour	1.25-1.5 L

Sprinkle yeast over water in a large bowl. When yeast dissolves and foams, beat in honey, milk, buckwheat flour and 2 cups (500 mL) whole wheat flour. Cover with a damp towel, set in a warm place, and let rise until very bubbly, about $2\frac{1}{2}$ hours if ingredients were cold from the refrigerator, less if they were at room temperature.

Stir down the batter, then beat in the remaining whole wheat flour, eggs, salt and butter. Add white flour, stirring, then kneading, first in the bowl and then on a board, until the dough is smooth but somewhat sticky. Cover with plastic wrap or a damp towel, and allow to rise until doubled, about $1\frac{1}{2}$ hours.

Butter two 9-by-5-inch (2 L) loaf pans. Knead dough on a floured surface about 20 times or until it is elastic and smooth. Shape dough into 2 loaves, and put them in the pans. Cover, and allow to rise until half as big again. Bake at 375°F (190°C) for about 45 minutes or until well browned and a tap on the bottom produces a hollow sound. Cool on wire racks.

Makes 2 loaves.

Yeast Bread

EGG BREAD

This makes a rich, light, golden bread that is very similar to French brioche but contains far less butter.

1 tsp.	sugar	5 mL
¼ cup	tepid water	50 mL
2½ tsp.	active dry yeast	12 mL
4½ cups	unbleached high-gluten (bread) flour, or more as needed	1.1 L
1 tsp.	salt	5 mL
10 Tbsp.	butter, cut into chunks	125 mL
6	eggs, beaten well with ½ cup (125 mL) heavy cream	6

Glaze
1	egg, beaten with 3 Tbsp. (45 mL) cream or milk	1

Combine sugar and water in a small bowl, sprinkle yeast on top, and set aside until yeast is dissolved and foamy. In a large bowl, combine 4 cups (1 L) flour with salt, stirring with a wire whisk until thoroughly blended. Using your fingertips, rub the butter into the flour until it is evenly distributed and the flour is the texture of coarse meal.

Add egg mixture, and beat well, then add yeast mixture, and beat again. The result is a very soft, sticky dough. Beat in remaining flour, and work the dough, stirring and beating, until it is shiny and smooth and no longer curdled-looking. Compared with ordinary bread dough, this dough will still be very soft and sticky; but it should pull away more or less cleanly from your palm if you knead for a moment, then lift your open hand away. If necessary, beat in a little more flour.

Cover tightly with plastic wrap, and allow to rise until doubled, about 2 hours in a warm room, longer in a cool one. Punch down, transfer dough to a clean bowl, cover tightly, and refrigerate at least overnight but not more than 36 hours.

Butter two loaf pans. Turn dough onto a lightly floured surface, and knead briefly. Divide in half, roll each half into a rough cylinder, and place in the pans. Cover loosely with plastic wrap, and allow to rise until doubled. Heat oven to 400°F (200°C).

Brush the risen loaves with glaze, place in oven, and lower heat to 375°F (190°C). Bake for 50 minutes or until bread is well risen and richly browned. Alternatively, divide dough after overnight rising, braid, and place on buttered baking sheets. Raise, glaze, and bake as above, heating oven to 425°F (220°C), turning it down to 400°F (200°C) and allowing about 40 minutes of baking time.

Makes 2 large loaves.

MY HEART'S BROWN STOLLEN

There are perhaps as many traditional recipes for stollen as there are bakers of stollen. Though less rich, this version is as good as the ones of old.

This recipe makes two large stollen or several small ones. It keeps well for over a week, but if you want to keep it longer, store in the freezer. It is truly special sliced thin and served for holiday tea.

A note on the baking: Try to use heavy cookie sheets, and keep the bread away from the bottom of the oven if yours tends to overheat there, as most do. It may help to place a second cookie sheet under the first one, especially on the bottom rack. Turn and reverse the loaves halfway through if they are not baking evenly.

Dough

4 Tbsp.	active dry yeast	50 mL
½ cup	lukewarm water	125 mL
7 cups	whole wheat flour	1.75 L
2 cups	whole wheat pastry flour	500 mL
2 tsp.	salt	10 mL
1 cup	small-curd cottage cheese	250 mL
2 cups	hot water	500 mL
¾ cup	honey	175 mL
¼ cup	rum (opt.)	50 mL
3	eggs	3
¾ cup	butter at room temperature	175 mL

Fruit Mixture

3 cups	dried fruit (include a good amount of apricots plus currants, peaches, pineapple & prunes)	750 mL
1 Tbsp.	almond extract	15 mL
1½ cups	toasted almonds, coarsely chopped	375 mL
3 cups	raisins	750 mL
2 Tbsp.	grated lemon zest	25 mL
2 Tbsp.	grated orange zest	25 mL
¼ cup	melted butter	50 mL
½ cup	confectioners' sugar	125 mL

Dissolve yeast in water. Set aside. Stir flour and salt together. Thoroughly mix cottage cheese with hot water, honey and rum, if desired, then blend in eggs and dissolved yeast. Add to flour mixture.

Mix dough, and knead for about 10 minutes, then work in butter. Stop kneading when butter is incorporated (you will be working the dough more when you add the fruit and nuts).

Put the dough in a buttered bowl, cover with a towel, and let rise in a warm place. Deflate it after 1½ to 2 hours, when your wet finger makes a hole in the center of the dough that does not fill in. Return dough to its warm place to rise again.

Meanwhile, prepare the fruit. Chop dried fruit into raisin-sized pieces. If the apricots or peaches are leathery, pour boiling water over them, and let stand until they are soft but not mushy. The fruit should be firm in texture so that it doesn't get lost in the dough as it is kneaded in. Sprinkle almond extract over the almonds.

Press the dough flat on a large floured surface, and gently roll it as large as it will tolerate without tearing.

Cover dough, and let rest for 10 minutes. Combine fruit, zest and almonds, and turn onto the dough. Roll or fold them together, and knead so that the dough incorporates them uniformly.

Divide dough, and form into balls—one ball for each loaf—and let it rest again, covered, for at least 15 minutes. You can make two large stollen or as many smaller ones as you like.

To shape, press or roll each ball into a long oval; then fold it lengthwise, not quite in half, and press closed.

Place the shaped stollen on greased cookie sheets, and let rise again in a warm, humid place until dough slowly returns a gently made fingerprint. Bake at 325°F (160°C) for about 1 hour for large stollen, proportionately less for the smaller. Allow plenty of time for baking, since the fruit holds moisture, but watch closely so that the stollen do not overbake.

Paint the loaves with butter as soon as they are removed from the oven. When cool, dust with confectioners' sugar.

Yeast Bread

ORANGE DOUGHNUTS

These doughnuts are quite light, and the orange adds an unexpected, but delicious flavor. A wok makes an excellent substitute for a deep fryer.

1	package yeast	1
¼ cup	warm water	50 mL
2 tsp.	grated orange zest	10 mL
¾ cup	warm orange juice	175 mL
¼ cup	butter, melted	50 mL
½ cup	sugar	125 mL
¾ tsp.	salt	4 mL
4-5 cups	flour	1-1.25 L
1	egg	1
	Oil	
	Confectioners' sugar	

Soften yeast in water. Combine orange zest, juice, butter, sugar and salt. Beat in 1 cup (250 mL) flour, then yeast, then egg. Add flour to make a soft dough. Knead on a floured board, adding more flour if necessary, until smooth, about 5 to 7 minutes. Place in a greased bowl, turning to grease surface of dough. Chill thoroughly for 1 to 2 hours.

Roll out on a floured board to ½-inch (1 cm) thickness. Cut with 2½-inch (6 cm) doughnut cutter. Let rise until puffy, about 1½ to 2 hours. Fry in hot oil until browned (doughnuts will float in the oil when done). Lift out with a slotted spoon, and drain on paper towels. Dust with confectioners' sugar.

Makes about 18 doughnuts.

BASIC CROISSANT DOUGH

1 Tbsp.	yeast	15 mL
¼ cup	warm water	50 mL
1 Tbsp.	sugar	15 mL
1 cup	milk	250 mL
1 tsp.	salt	5 mL
1 Tbsp.	butter, plus 1 cup (250 mL), cold	15 mL
2½-3 cups	flour	625-750 mL
Glaze		
1	egg yolk	1
2 Tbsp.	milk	25 mL

Dissolve yeast in water with sugar. Let stand until frothy. Scald milk, add salt and 1 Tbsp. (15 mL) butter, then cool to room temperature. Stir yeast and milk mixtures together in a bowl, and add flour, ½ cup (125 mL) at a time, until you have a smooth, slightly sticky dough. Turn dough into a buttered bowl, cover loosely, and refrigerate overnight.

The next day, remove dough and 1 cup (250 mL) butter from refrigerator. Slice butter into ⅛-inch (3 mm) slices. Roll dough on a lightly floured surface to a ½-inch-thick (1 cm) rectangle. Arrange butter slices on half of the dough. Fold the other half over it, and pinch the edges to seal. Roll out ½ inch (1 cm) thick, and fold into thirds. Rotate dough so that the edge of the final fold is nearest you. Roll out to give a ½-inch-thick (1 cm) rectangle.

Repeat folding, rotating and rolling process 3 times, folding exactly the same way each time. If the dough begins to blister, set in the refrigerator for about 20 minutes between rollings. On the final rolling, roll out ⅛ inch (3 mm) thick. Cut down the middle of the long side, and cut each half into triangles. Starting at the large end, roll each one up to a crescent shape, turning the ends together as you go. Place on a baking sheet, and let rise for 30 minutes.

To make glaze, lightly beat together egg yolk and milk. Brush croissants with glaze, then bake for 5 minutes in a 425°F (220°C) oven; reduce temperature to 350°F (180°C), and bake for 8 to 10 minutes.

Makes about 12 croissants.

Sourdough

TRADITIONAL SOURDOUGH STARTER

This surefire sourdough starter has a smooth but distinctly sour flavor and performs reliably, improving with age. Prepare 12 to 15 hours in advance.

2 cups	milk	500 mL
2 cups	unbleached flour	500 mL

Mix milk and flour together with a wooden spoon in a 20-quart (20 L) nonmetallic container sterilized with boiling water. Cover with a lid slightly ajar, and let stand overnight in a warm place (75°-80°F/24°-27°C) until the starter bubbles and has a sour smell.

If, for some reason, this recipe fails to spark a viable culture, start again. For better assurance of success, substitute buttermilk for whole milk and add 1 Tbsp. (15 mL) active dry yeast and 1 Tbsp. (15 mL) sugar. *Note: If the starter turns any color or if mold forms on it, throw it out and try again.*

WHOLE WHEAT SOURDOUGH BISCUITS

Quicker to make than sourdough breads, these biscuits are ready in less than two hours. Fluffy and moist, they have a delicate nutty taste and are best served hot from the oven.

$1\frac{2}{3}$ cups	unbleached flour	400 mL
1 cup	whole wheat flour	250 mL
$1\frac{1}{4}$ tsp.	salt	6 mL
$1\frac{1}{4}$ tsp.	baking powder	6 mL
$\frac{1}{2}$ tsp.	baking soda	2 mL
$\frac{1}{2}$ cup	chilled butter	125 mL
1 cup	sourdough starter	250 mL
$\frac{3}{4}$ cup	buttermilk	175 mL

Sift together flour, salt, baking powder and baking soda. Cut $\frac{1}{2}$-inch (1 cm) lumps of butter into dry ingredients, and work in with your fingers until they are pea-sized. In a separate bowl, combine starter and buttermilk. Stir gently into dry ingredients just until blended. Do not overmix, or biscuits will be tough. Turn out onto a well-floured board; dough will be very moist. Lightly flour, and roll 1 inch (2.5 cm) thick. Cut with a 2-inch (5 cm) biscuit cutter. Place on an ungreased baking sheet so that sides of biscuits touch slightly. Let rise in a warm place (80°-90°F/27°-32°C) for 45 minutes or until doubled in height. Bake in a preheated 400°F (200°C) oven for 15 to 20 minutes or until light brown.

Makes 1 dozen biscuits.

Sourdough

LIGHT-WHEAT COUNTRY SOURDOUGH BREAD

Chewy and resilient, with a porous interior, this French-style country bread owes its excellent texture to a three-day fermentation, in which the starter is made the first day. If you wish, a portion of the dough can be held aside for future bakings, producing a tangy sourdough loaf.

1 tsp.	active dry yeast	5 mL
1 cup	warm water	250 mL
1 Tbsp.	nonfat dry milk	15 mL
1 cup	whole wheat flour	250 mL
2 cups	warm water	500 mL
3 cups	unbleached flour	750 mL
1 Tbsp.	salt	15 mL
1 cup	wheat germ or 1 cup (250 mL) cracked wheat soaked in boiling water, cooled & drained, or $\frac{1}{4}$ cup (50 mL) raw sunflower seeds	250 mL
2½-6 cups	unbleached flour	675 mL-1.5 L
	Oil to grease bowl & pan	
	Cornmeal	

Day 1: Mix together yeast, 1 cup (250 mL) water, milk and whole wheat flour in a large nonmetallic bowl. Cover with plastic wrap, and let sit overnight.

Day 2: Stir, and add 2 cups (500 mL) water and unbleached flour. Cover with plastic wrap, and allow to rest overnight again.

Day 3: Stir in salt, wheat germ and at least 2 cups (500 mL) flour. (If using cracked wheat, more flour will be required.) Turn onto a board, and knead for 10 minutes, adding flour so that dough is pliable but not sticky. (The dough must be firm enough to rise on its own.)

Place in a greased bowl, and cover with plastic wrap. Allow to rise at room temperature (65°-70°F/18°-21°C) until doubled in size, about 1½ to 2 hours. Punch down dough, and cut off about 6 oz. (175 g) to use as the starter in future bakings, if you wish. (The reserved dough should be allowed to stand at room temperature overnight, covered with water. Treated in this fashion, it will keep for up to 10 days in the refrigerator, or it can be frozen. It can then be added to the next batch in place of the starter.)

Shape into two rounded loaves. Place on greased baking sheet sprinkled with cornmeal. Cover with a cloth, and allow to rise until almost tripled in size, about 2 hours.

Preheat oven to 425°F (220°C). Slash bread in a tick-tack-toe pattern with a sharp blade, spray with water, and place in oven. Bake 35 to 40 minutes or until bread sounds hollow when tapped. For a thicker crust, spray bread twice during the first 10 minutes of baking.

Makes 2 loaves.

Sourdough

HANDLING SOURDOUGH STARTER

Sourdough starter should be stored in a glass, ceramic or plastic refrigerator container. Keep the lid slightly ajar to allow the gas produced by the starter to dissipate. (Never store starter in a metal container or use a metal spoon to stir it, as metal will interfere with the yeast reactions and spoil the flavor.) Once the starter has fermented, keep it refrigerated, and before using it, thoroughly blend in any liquid that has collected on the surface. Feed the starter after each use with 1 cup (250 mL) flour and 1 cup (250 mL) milk or water.

If you don't use the starter for 10 days, if it fails to raise the dough properly or if the bread has an "off" taste, pour out half and replenish with 1 cup (250 mL) each water and flour. (You may also sterilize the starter container with boiling water.) Let the starter sit at room temperature, lightly covered, for 4 to 5 hours or overnight before refrigerating it again.

SOURDOUGH OATMEAL BREAD

The best part of this slightly tart bread is its chewy crust, which tastes of lightly toasted oats. The "sponge" must be prepared the day before.

1 cup	sourdough starter	250 mL
1 cup	warm water (110°F/43°C)	250 mL
4½ cups	unbleached flour	1.1 L
2 tsp.	salt	10 mL
3 cups	rolled oats (not quick-cooking)	750 mL
⅔-1 cup	water	150-250 mL
	Flour for kneading	
	Oil to grease bowl & pan	
	Yellow cornmeal	
1	egg white, beaten with 1 tsp. (5 mL) water	1
	Rolled oats for topping	

To make the sponge, stir together starter, warm water and 1½ cups (375 mL) flour in a nonmetallic bowl. Let stand, covered with plastic wrap, in a warm place overnight, until bubbly.

Stir in remaining flour, salt, oats and enough water to make a soft, pliable dough. Turn out onto a floured board, and knead until dough is smooth and elastic, working in additional flour as necessary. Place in a lightly oiled bowl, and turn to coat sides and top. Cover with plastic wrap, and let rise at room temperature until at least doubled, about 2 hours.

Punch down dough, and divide in half; roll each half into an oval by pushing it with the heels of your hands. Fold in half down the middle; flatten again, and fold down the middle once more. Pinch seam to seal. Place loaves, seam side down, on a greased baking sheet that has been sprinkled with cornmeal, cover with a cloth, and let rise until doubled, approximately 1 hour. Brush loaves with egg white, sprinkle oats on top, and slash diagonally with a sharp blade. Bake in a preheated 425°F (220°C) oven for 35 to 40 minutes or until loaves make a hollow sound when tapped lightly.

Makes 2 loaves.

SOURDOUGH
CINNAMON-APPLE SWIRLS

Sourdough can be used for sweet desserts. These substantial breakfast rolls are improved nutritionally by mixing whole wheat pastry flour with white flour.

Dough

1 cup	sourdough starter	250 mL
2 cups	whole wheat pastry flour	500 mL
2 cups	unbleached flour	500 mL
½ cup	warm milk	125 mL
½ tsp.	cinnamon	2 mL
½ tsp.	salt	2 mL
1 tsp.	baking powder	5 mL

Filling

1½ tsp.	cinnamon	7 mL
½ cup	brown sugar	125 mL
¾ cup	chopped walnuts	175 mL
3 cups	apples, thinly sliced	750 mL
2 Tbsp.	melted butter	25 mL
¼ cup	honey	50 mL

To make dough, combine starter, 1 cup (250 mL) whole wheat flour, 1 cup (250 mL) unbleached flour and milk in a nonmetallic container. Cover with plastic wrap, and let rise in a warm place until doubled in bulk. Stir in cinnamon, salt and baking powder. Gradually add remaining whole wheat flour, and turn out onto a well-floured board. Knead in remaining unbleached flour as needed to make a soft, pliable dough.

Roll out a 9-by-14-inch (23 x 35 cm) rectangle.

To make filling, mix cinnamon, sugar and walnuts until well blended. Add apples, and toss until coated. Gently pat apple mixture onto dough, leaving a 1½-inch (4 cm) margin at the top.

Roll up firmly from the bottom, jelly-roll style, keeping dough taut. (Unless dough is rolled tightly, rolls will fall apart when sliced.) Seal top edge of roll by pinching along seam. Using a serrated knife, slice dough into 1-inch (2.5 cm) rounds, and place on a greased 9-by-13-inch (23 x 33 cm) baking pan. Sides of rounds should barely touch. Let rise in a warm place, covered with plastic wrap, for 30 to 45 minutes or until doubled in bulk.

Heat butter and honey together in a small pan, and brush over rounds. Bake at 375°F (190°C) in top third of oven for 25 minutes or until brown and bubbling.

Makes 10 to 12 rolls.

Cookies & Squares

PEANUT BUTTER COOKIES

Honey gives these cookies a wonderful flavor. Some cooks use the bottom of a glass to press their cookies, but peanut butter cookies just aren't the same unless you use fork tines to flatten them.

1 cup	peanut butter	250 mL
½ cup	butter, softened	125 mL
½ cup	honey	125 mL
½ cup	brown sugar, firmly packed	125 mL
1	large egg, lightly beaten	1
1 tsp.	vanilla extract	5 mL
1¼ cups	white flour	300 mL
⅔ cup	whole wheat flour	150 mL
1 tsp.	baking soda	5 mL
½ tsp.	salt	2 mL
¾ cup	unsalted roasted peanuts, chopped (opt.)	175 mL

Preheat oven to 350°F (180°C), and place the baking rack in the center of the oven. In a mixing bowl, beat together peanut butter, butter and honey. Gradually beat in sugar, egg and vanilla. In a separate bowl, stir together flour, baking soda and salt. Stir into the peanut butter mixture.

With lightly floured hands, roll dough into 1-inch (2.5 cm) balls. Place the balls at least 2 inches (5 cm) apart on greased baking sheets. Press flat with the back of a fork, and sprinkle peanuts on top, if desired. Bake one sheet at a time for 10 to 12 minutes or until tops are golden.

Makes about 5 dozen cookies.

OAT BRAN RAISIN COOKIES

These cookies are chewy and delicious. Make sure the oil is fresh and mild. One cup (250 mL) semisweet chocolate chips may be substituted for the raisins. For spicy cookies, add 1 tsp. (5 mL) cinnamon, ½ tsp. (2 mL) cloves and ½ tsp. (2 mL) allspice to dry ingredients. For the fat-conscious, avoid adding coconut.

¾ cup	vegetable oil	175 mL
1 cup	brown sugar, firmly packed	250 mL
½ cup	sugar	125 mL
2	eggs	2
2 tsp.	vanilla extract	10 mL
1½ cups	rolled oats	375 mL
1½ cups	oat bran	375 mL
1 cup	flour	250 mL
½ tsp.	salt	2 mL
½ tsp.	baking soda	2 mL
1 cup	raisins	250 mL
½ cup	chopped walnuts or pecans	125 mL

Beat together oil, sugar, eggs and vanilla. Add oats, oat bran, flour, salt and baking soda. Stir to mix well. Add raisins and nuts, and blend evenly. Drop by tablespoonfuls onto an ungreased cookie sheet. Bake for 12 to 15 minutes at 350°F (180°C); the cookies should not brown very much. Remove to a wire rack to cool.

Makes 4 dozen cookies.

Cookies & Squares

SCRUMPTIOUS GRANOLA BARS

A wholesome, nutty treat for those who love the earnest taste of granola.

1 cup	butter	250 mL
1 cup	brown sugar	250 mL
2	eggs	2
¼ cup	unsulphured molasses	50 mL
1 tsp.	vanilla extract	5 mL
1¾ cups	flour	425 mL
½ tsp.	baking soda	2 mL
1½ cups	rolled oats	375 mL
¾ cup	wheat germ	175 mL
¾ cup	shredded coconut	175 mL
¾ cup	sunflower seeds	175 mL
¾ cup	dried apricots, chopped	175 mL
⅓ cup	toasted sesame seeds	75 mL

Cream together butter, sugar, eggs, molasses and vanilla. Sift together flour and baking soda, and add to creamed mixture, blending well. Add remaining ingredients, and mix well.

Place in a 9-by-13-inch (3.5 L) greased pan, and bake at 350°F (180°C) for 20 to 25 minutes. Cool for 10 minutes, and cut while still warm.

Makes 12 large bars.

LEMON-ZUCCHINI COOKIES

A lighthearted way to use the zucchini harvest when the appeal of ratatouille wears thin.

2 cups	flour	500 mL
1 tsp.	baking powder	5 mL
½ tsp.	salt	2 mL
¾ cup	butter	175 mL
¾ cup	sugar	175 mL
1	egg, beaten	1
1 tsp.	grated lemon zest	5 mL
1 cup	zucchini, shredded	250 mL
1 cup	chopped walnuts	250 mL
	Lemon Frost (recipe follows)	

Stir together flour, baking powder and salt. In a large bowl, blend butter and sugar, then add egg, and beat until fluffy. Stir in flour mixture until smooth. Add lemon zest, zucchini and walnuts, and mix well.

Drop by teaspoonfuls onto greased cookie sheet, and bake at 375°F (190°C) for 15 to 20 minutes. Remove from oven. While cookies are warm, drizzle with Lemon Frost.

Makes 6 to 7 dozen cookies.

LEMON FROST

1 cup	confectioners' sugar	250 mL
4 tsp.	lemon juice	20 mL

Mix together until well blended.

DECORATIVE ICING

When writing with icing, you will need to soften it slightly more than when simply spreading it.

2 Tbsp.	*butter or margarine, melted*	*25 mL*
2 cups	*confectioners' sugar, sifted*	*500 mL*
1 tsp.	*vanilla extract or lemon juice, strained*	*5 mL*
2-3 Tbsp.	*milk*	*25-45 mL*
	Vegetable food coloring or seedless raspberry jam for coloring	

Combine butter, sugar, vanilla and 2 Tbsp. (25 mL) milk. Beat until smooth. If icing is too stiff, add more milk, one drop at a time. Place 2 Tbsp. (25 mL) icing in each of several small bowls, and stir in food coloring. (Remember that soft tints are more appealing to eat than primary colors.) When cookies are cool, spread icing on them or write or draw designs by squeezing icing out of a small hole cut in one corner of a pint-sized (500 mL) plastic bag.

Makes about ¾ cup (175 mL) icing.

OLD-FASHIONED SUGAR COOKIES

The holiday season just wouldn't be the same without a tin of sugar cookies. Roll and cut, then ice in bright colors or decorate with colored sugar.

¾ cup	unsalted butter at room temperature	175 mL
1 cup	sugar	250 mL
2	large eggs, lightly beaten	2
1 tsp.	vanilla or almond extract	5 mL
2¾-3 cups	flour	675-750 mL
1 tsp.	baking powder	5 mL
1 tsp.	salt	5 mL
1	egg white (opt.)	1
	Colored sugar (opt.)	
	Decorative Icing (see box)	

Grease baking sheets, and set aside. Preheat oven to 350°F (180°C). In a large bowl, beat together butter and sugar with an electric mixer until well blended. Add eggs and vanilla, and beat well. Combine 2¾ cups (675 mL) flour, baking powder and salt, and sift over the butter mixture. Beat with a wooden spoon or an electric mixer set at the lowest speed until flour is incorporated and dough forms a ball. It should be pliable but not sticky; add more flour, 1 Tbsp. (15 mL) at a time, if needed. Divide dough into 4 portions, and chill until ready to roll.

Roll dough out ⅛ to ¼ inch (3-5 mm) thick on a lightly floured surface or between floured sheets of wax paper, pressing gently with a rolling pin. Dip 2-inch (5 cm) cutters into flour, and cut shapes. Use a spatula to transfer cookies onto baking sheets, placing them 1½ inches (4 cm) apart. If desired, brush with lightly beaten egg white and sprinkle with colored sugar instead of decorating with icing after baking.

Bake for 8 to 12 minutes or until cookies are golden around the edges. Let cool for a couple of minutes, then transfer with a spatula to wire racks to cool completely. Decorate with icing, and let stand until icing has set. Store, layered with wax paper, in an airtight container.

Makes 5 dozen cookies.

Cookies & Squares

HAZELNUT SHORTBREAD

In Scotland, shortbread is said to bring good luck and is often carried as a gift when one goes visiting. Appropriate for the Christmas basket, this utterly rich, buttery cookie is even more divine with toasted ground hazelnuts.

1 cup	hazelnuts	250 mL
1 cup	butter at room temperature	250 mL
½ cup	plus 2 Tbsp. (25 mL) confectioners' sugar	125 mL
2 cups	flour	500 mL
¼ tsp.	nutmeg	1 mL
5-6 oz.	bittersweet or semisweet chocolate, chopped	150-175 g

Preheat oven to 325°F (160°C). Spread hazelnuts in a roasting pan, and toast for 10 to 14 minutes, tossing occasionally, until golden in color and husks have loosened. Turn hazelnuts out into a textured towel, wrap for 3 to 4 minutes, then rub vigorously to remove the husks. Let cool, and chop finely in a food processor or in small batches in a blender. Set aside ¾ cup (175 mL) hazelnuts, and reserve the rest to sprinkle over cookies.

Increase oven temperature to 350°F (180°C). Place butter in a large mixing bowl, and sift sugar onto it. With a wooden spoon or an electric mixer, blend butter and sugar. Sift flour over the butter-sugar mixture. Add nutmeg and ¾ cup (175 mL) hazelnuts. Blend thoroughly; dough will form into a ball. Do not overwork the dough, or it will toughen.

To make cookie wedges, flour your finger lightly, divide dough in half and place each ball directly on an ungreased baking sheet. Pat balls into round disks about 7 inches (18 cm) in diameter and ½ inch (1 cm) thick. Divide the rounds into quarters with a sharp knife, then divide each quarter into thirds, making 12 equal wedges. (Do not separate wedges at this time.) Bake for 25 to 30 minutes.

Place chocolate in the top of a double boiler set over low heat, and stir until smooth. Dip one end of each cookie into the chocolate, sprinkle with reserved hazelnuts, and set on wax paper until chocolate is hardened. (If necessary, place cookies in the refrigerator for a few minutes to set chocolate.) Store, layered with wax paper, in an airtight container.

Makes 24 wedges.

Cookies & Squares

DANISH OAT COOKIES

In Denmark, tradition holds that all holiday visitors must taste your homemade cookies. If they do not, it is said, they will carry off the spirit of the holidays when they leave. To protect your home, make enough of these for everyone. Buttery, with the crunch of crisp toasted oats, they are irresistible.

1 cup	butter	250 mL
$\frac{3}{4}$ cup	sugar	175 mL
1	large egg, lightly beaten	1
1 tsp.	vanilla extract	5 mL
2 cups	rolled oats (not instant)	500 mL
$\frac{1}{2}$ cup	flour	125 mL
$\frac{1}{2}$ cup	toasted wheat germ	125 mL

Preheat oven to 350°F (180°C). (If using raw wheat germ, toast it in a roasting pan for 5 minutes until golden.) Place butter in a small saucepan, and set over low heat until melted. Set aside to cool slightly. Measure sugar into a large mixing bowl. Pour butter over sugar, and beat with a wooden spoon or an electric mixer. Add egg and vanilla, and beat again. Add oats, flour and wheat germ, and beat until thoroughly blended. The batter will feel quite soft.

Drop by teaspoonfuls about 1½ inches (4 cm) apart onto an ungreased baking sheet. Bake for 10 to 15 minutes or until a dark golden edge forms around the cookies; they will be golden brown on top.

Leave cookies on the sheet until set but still warm, about 4 minutes. Use a spatula to lift them to a wire rack to cool. (When fresh from the oven, these cookies are too fragile to lift, but when cold, they are too crisp and will break.) Store in an airtight container.

Makes about 5 dozen cookies.

ORANGE REFRIGERATOR COOKIES

A delicate and tasty treat for the holiday season.

	Zest of 1 orange	
2 cups	sugar	500 mL
$\frac{1}{2}$ cup	butter	125 mL
1	egg	1
3 oz.	cream cheese	75 g
2 Tbsp.	orange juice	25 mL
1 tsp.	vanilla extract	5 mL
2 cups	flour	500 mL
$\frac{1}{8}$ tsp.	baking soda	0.5 mL
$\frac{1}{8}$ tsp.	baking powder	0.5 mL
$\frac{1}{2}$ tsp.	salt	2 mL
	Butter, melted	

Chop orange zest in a food processor for 10 seconds. Mix with 1 cup (250 mL) sugar, and set aside. Then add butter, egg and remaining sugar to processor, and process for 1 minute. Add cream cheese, orange juice and vanilla, and pulse to mix.

Sift together flour, baking soda, baking powder and salt. Spoon into food processor, and pulse just to mix.

Line a small bowl with plastic wrap, place dough in bowl, cover, and refrigerate until firm, about 4 hours.

Divide dough in half, and shape into 2 rolls, each 1½ inches (4 cm) in diameter. Place in freezer for 1 hour.

Line 2 baking sheets with parchment paper, then brush paper lightly with melted butter. Cut rolls into ¼-inch (5 mm) slices, and place on cookie sheets, leaving 1½ inches (4 cm) around each cookie. Sprinkle cookies with a little of the orange-sugar mixture.

Bake at 375°F (190°C) for 8 minutes. Cool on paper, then remove.

Makes 40 cookies.

PFEFFERNÜSSE
(Peppernut Spice Cookies)

In German households, the scent of baking Pfeffernüsse signals the start of the Christmas holiday season. Although the list of ingredients is long, the procedure is simple and the flavor memorable. These cookies are sturdy enough to be sent through the mail without crumbling.

½ cup	dark brown sugar, firmly packed	125 mL
¼ cup	honey	50 mL
¾ cup	unsulphured molasses	175 mL
¼ cup	unsalted butter or margarine	50 mL
3½ cups	flour	875 mL
1½ tsp.	grated lemon zest	7 mL
1 tsp.	each salt, baking powder & baking soda	5 mL
1 tsp.	each nutmeg, cinnamon & cardamom	5 mL
¾ tsp.	allspice	4 mL
½ tsp.	freshly ground pepper	2 mL
¼ tsp.	ground cloves	1 mL
¼ tsp.	anise seeds, crushed (opt.)	1 mL
1	large egg, lightly beaten	1

Icing

1	egg white	1
1 tsp.	honey	5 mL
2 cups	sifted confectioners' sugar	500 mL
2 Tbsp.	fresh lemon juice, plus extra if needed	25 mL

In a 2½-quart (2.5 L) saucepan, combine sugar, honey, molasses and butter. Set pan over medium heat, and stir with a wooden spoon until sugar melts. Do not let mixture boil. Remove from heat, and let cool.

In a large mixing bowl, combine flour, lemon zest, salt, baking powder, baking soda and spices. When molasses mixture is cool, beat in egg. Gradually stir the flour mixture into the molasses mixture in the saucepan. When combined, stir hard with a wooden spoon. Chill dough in the refrigerator for 30 minutes.

To make the icing, use an electric mixer to beat together the egg white, honey, sugar and lemon juice. The icing should be the consistency of sour cream; add more lemon juice, if necessary. Cover with plastic wrap until needed.

Grease baking sheets, and set aside. Preheat oven to 350°F (180°C). To form cookies, dampen your hands and roll walnut-sized lumps of dough into balls between your palms. Set balls on baking sheets 1½ inches (4 cm) apart, and bake for 12 to 15 minutes until lightly golden. Transfer to a wire rack set over wax paper.

While the cookies are still warm, use your finger or the back of a spoon to "paint" them with icing. Set iced cookies back on the wire rack to dry completely. (Alternatively, the cookies can be rolled in confectioners' sugar while they are still warm, then cooled on the wire rack.) Store, layered with wax paper, in an airtight container.

Makes about 7 dozen cookies.

COOKIES DONE RIGHT

Although cookie baking requires little special equipment, a reliable oven thermometer is a must, since cookies bake for such a short time and can burn easily in an unevenly heated oven. Built-in oven thermometers tend to keep rather rough estimates of temperature, so for accuracy, buy an inexpensive oven thermometer to set on the oven rack. Check cookies initially at the minimum baking time suggested in the recipe, then watch them carefully.

For cutting decorative cookies, a fluted pastry wheel, in the absence of a cookie cutter, creates an elegantly scalloped edge on geometric shapes and reduces waste and the continuous rerolling of trimmed excess dough.

ANNA OLSON'S SPRITZ COOKIES

Spritsar are traditional Swedish Christmas cookies formed with a cylindrical cookie press, or *spritz-spruta*. The cookies are equally delicious molded by hand into balls, pretzels or rings.

1 cup	butter at room temperature	250 mL
$\frac{1}{2}$ cup	sugar	125 mL
1	large egg, separated	1
1 tsp.	almond extract	5 mL
$2\frac{1}{4}$-$2\frac{1}{2}$ cups	flour	550-625 mL
	Tinted or plain sugar, currants, raisins, finely chopped almonds or silver balls for decoration	

Preheat oven to 350°F (180°C). With an electric mixer, beat butter and sugar until well blended and creamy. Add egg yolk and almond extract, and beat well. Sift $2\frac{1}{4}$ cups (550 mL) flour over the butter mixture, and beat with a wooden spoon or with the mixer at low speed until flour is thoroughly incorporated. Form dough into a ball; if it is too sticky, add 2-4 Tbsp. (25-50 mL) flour. Chill dough before molding.

If using a cookie press, follow manufacturer's directions, and press out cookies $1\frac{1}{2}$ inches (4 cm) apart on ungreased baking sheets. Wait a few seconds for the dough to adhere to the baking sheet, then twist the press slightly as you lift it straight up. The cookie should stay flat. If the cookies do not press out easily, chill the baking sheet for a few minutes in the refrigerator. (If the dough is too stiff to press out, beat another egg yolk into it.) If molding the cookies by hand, you will need up to $2\frac{1}{2}$ cups (625 mL) flour. Lightly flour your hands when shaping them.

Brush cookies with lightly beaten egg white, and sprinkle with sugar or other decorations. Bake about 1 inch (2.5 cm) apart for 8 to 12 minutes or until slightly golden around the edges. Cool on a wire rack, and store, layered with wax paper, in an airtight container.

Makes about 5 dozen cookies.

Cookies & Squares

GINGERBREAD PLACE CARDS

From this gingerbread, you can make holiday place cards or large edible Christmas cards, writing the guests' names with icing. For a Chanukah party, cut dreidel shapes and decorate with Hebrew letters or names. If you are using cookie cutters, follow the procedure below, but bake cookies for a shorter time if they are small.

½ cup	margarine	125 mL
½ cup	sugar	125 mL
½ cup	unsulphured molasses	125 mL
2 cups	flour	500 mL
1½ tsp.	ginger	7 mL
½ tsp.	each baking soda, salt, nutmeg & cinnamon	2 mL

Icing

1 Tbsp.	fresh lemon juice	15 mL
1	large egg white	1
1¾ cups	confectioners' sugar, sifted	425 mL
	Pinch each cream of tartar & salt	

Preheat oven to 350°F (180°C). Melt margarine in a small saucepan over low heat. Transfer to a large mixing bowl. Add sugar and molasses, and beat well. Combine flour, ginger, baking soda, salt, nutmeg and cinnamon, and sift over the butter mixture. Beat until flour is thoroughly incorporated and dough forms a ball. If the dough feels too soft to hold together, add a little more flour. Knead dough several times on a lightly floured surface. Place in a plastic bag, and refrigerate.

Cut out a cardboard pattern: for place cards, it should be 2 by 3 inches (5 x 8 cm); for Christmas cards, 4 by 6 inches (10 x 15 cm). Rub both sides of the pattern with a little flour to prevent it from sticking to the dough. Remove a portion of the dough from the refrigerator, and place it on a sheet of wax paper. With a lightly floured rolling pin, roll it out ¼ inch (5 mm) thick. Set the pattern on the dough, and gently cut around the edges with a paring knife. Peel away the scraps, and using a spatula, transfer the card to an ungreased baking sheet. You can mold the scraps into small balls or long, thin rolls, moisten the undersides with a drop of water and press them onto the edges of the cards for trim. Roll dough out again, and repeat.

Bake gingerbread 1½ inches (4 cm) apart for 10 to 15 minutes or until cookies are firm and edges are slightly darker in color than the centers. With a spatula, transfer cookies to a wire rack to cool completely before icing them.

To make icing, combine all ingredients, and beat until mixture is smooth and has the consistency of softly whipped cream. Add more sugar if it is too thin. Cover the bowl with plastic wrap until needed; this icing hardens quickly. To make a decorating tube, cut a small hole in one corner of a heavy-duty pint-sized (500 mL) plastic bag and drop in a metal decorating tip with a small round hole. (You can omit the metal tip and simply use a tiny hole cut in the bag.) Add icing to the bag, seal, and roll down edges. Squeeze icing as desired. Store cookies, layered with wax paper, in an airtight container.

Makes 12 place cards, 6 Christmas cards or about 24 small gingerbread people.

Cookies & Squares

CHOCOLATE-CHIP OATMEAL COOKIES

This classic cookie recipe is a long-standing favorite with *Harrowsmith Country Life* staff. Make lots, because they won't last long.

1 cup	butter	250 mL
½ cup	white sugar	125 mL
1 cup	brown sugar	250 mL
1	egg	1
1 tsp.	vanilla extract	5 mL
1½ cups	flour	375 mL
1½ cups	rolled oats	375 mL
¾ cup	shredded coconut	175 mL
1 tsp.	baking soda	5 mL
1 tsp.	baking powder	5 mL
	Pinch salt	
1 cup	semisweet chocolate chips	250 mL

Cream butter, then add sugar, and mix thoroughly. Stir in egg and vanilla. Combine dry ingredients, and add to creamed ingredients. Mix thoroughly, then stir in chocolate chips.

Drop by spoonfuls onto greased cookie sheet, and bake at 375°F (190°C) for 10 to 12 minutes.

Makes 5 dozen cookies.

PUMPKIN COOKIES

Lovers of spicy hermit cookies will enjoy these autumn pumpkin treats.

2 cups	white flour	500 mL
½ cup	whole wheat flour	125 mL
4 tsp.	baking powder	20 mL
½ tsp.	salt	2 mL
½ tsp.	cinnamon	2 mL
½ tsp.	nutmeg	2 mL
½ cup	butter	125 mL
1¼ cups	brown sugar	300 mL
2	eggs	2
1 tsp.	vanilla extract	5 mL
1½ cups	pumpkin puree	375 mL
1 cup	nuts	250 mL
1 cup	raisins	250 mL

Preheat oven to 375°F (190°C). Grease cookie sheets. Sift together flour, baking powder, salt and spices. Cream butter, and blend in brown sugar. Beat in eggs and vanilla. Mix in pumpkin, and add nuts and raisins. Fold into flour mixture. Drop by teaspoonfuls onto cookie sheets. Bake for 15 minutes.

Makes 4 dozen cookies.

Cookies & Squares

CASHEW CARDAMOM BALLS

Sophisticated, sweet and sinfully rich-tasting, Cashew Cardamom Balls easily qualify as gourmet fare. They are, however, so simple to make, you can turn them out for lunchbox treats.

1 cup	lightly toasted cashew pieces	250 mL
2-4	cardamom seedpods	2-4
1 cup	dates, very finely chopped	250 mL
	Finely grated zest of 1 orange	
½ cup	dried coconut, toasted, then powdered in blender, or sugar	125 mL

Chop cashews very finely by hand (a blender chops them too finely). Remove cardamom seeds from pods, then grind with a mortar and pestle or between two spoons. Combine cashews and cardamom in a bowl with dates and orange zest. Knead mixture with fingertips until uniform, then form into balls and roll in coconut.

Makes 18 balls.

OAT BRAN BROWNIES

Even hard-core chocolate addicts will love these brownies. The bananas are essential for a moist texture; their flavor is not pronounced.

Brownies

½ cup	cocoa powder	125 mL
1 Tbsp.	instant coffee	15 mL
2	very ripe bananas	2
1 cup	brown sugar	250 mL
⅔ cup	sugar	150 mL
4	eggs	4
1 tsp.	vanilla extract	5 mL
1 cup	oat bran	250 mL
½ cup	flour	125 mL
¼ tsp.	salt	1 mL
1 cup	chopped nuts, raisins or sunflower seeds	250 mL

Frosting

⅓ cup	cocoa powder	75 mL
1 cup	confectioners' sugar	250 mL
1 tsp.	vanilla extract	5 mL
3 Tbsp.	milk or coffee	45 mL

To make brownies, combine cocoa, coffee, 1 Tbsp. (15 mL) water and bananas in a large bowl, and mix until smooth. Add sugar, eggs and vanilla, and mix well. Add oat bran, flour and salt, stir to blend, then add nuts. Spread brownie mixture in a greased and floured 9-by-13-inch (3 L) baking pan. Bake at 350°F (180°C) for 30 to 35 minutes. Cool in pan.

To make frosting, sift cocoa and sugar together, mixing well. Add vanilla and 1 Tbsp. (15 mL) milk. Stir to blend, then add enough liquid to make frosting of spreadable consistency. Spread over cooled brownies. Cut into squares.

Makes about 2 dozen brownies.

Cookies & Squares

MERINGUE KISSES

Crisp, sweet, light and innocent of fat, meringue kisses are unquestionably a cookie for our time. Be sure to make them on a dry day.

½ cup	egg whites (3 to 4 eggs, depending on size)	125 mL
	Pinch salt	
¼ tsp.	cream of tartar	1 mL
¾ cup	superfine granulated sugar	175 mL
1 tsp.	vanilla extract	5 mL
⅓ cup	sifted confectioners' sugar	75 mL

Combine egg whites with salt and cream of tartar, and beat with an electric mixer on medium speed until foamy and light.

Add 2 Tbsp. (25 mL) granulated sugar, and beat until mixture has thickened to the texture of very soft ice cream. Continue to beat, adding remaining granulated sugar in a thin, steady stream, until the meringue stands in stiff peaks when the beaters are lifted. Beat in vanilla, then confectioners' sugar.

Heat oven to 175°F (80°C). Line baking sheets with parchment paper or brown paper, anchoring the corners with dabs of meringue. Drop the mixture either from a pastry tube fitted with a star tip or from a spoon to make tablespoon-sized mounds, keeping them well separated so that air can circulate.

Bake for about 75 minutes. They should not brown at all; if coloring threatens, turn off heat and let them finish in the cooled-off oven.

Cool on baking sheets, then peel the paper from the meringues rather than peeling the meringues from the paper. They get sticky quickly in damp weather but will keep indefinitely if kept dry.

Makes about 3 dozen cookies.

HONEY PUMPKIN CHEWS

These easy-to-make drop cookies have the spice flavor of a pumpkin pie, with walnuts adding crunch.

½ cup	butter at room temperature	125 mL
¾ cup	honey	175 mL
2	eggs	2
1½ cups	pureed pumpkin or other winter squash	375 mL
2¼ cups	whole wheat pastry flour	550 mL
3 tsp.	baking powder	15 mL
1 tsp.	salt	5 mL
½ tsp.	ginger	2 mL
½ tsp.	nutmeg	2 mL
1 tsp.	cinnamon	5 mL
½ cup	toasted wheat germ	125 mL
1 cup	raisins or ½ cup (125 mL) candied ginger, finely chopped	250 mL
1 cup	chopped walnuts	250 mL

Preheat oven to 350°F (180°C). Cream together butter and honey. Add eggs and pumpkin. Set aside.

Sift together flour, baking powder, salt, ginger, nutmeg and cinnamon. Add wheat germ, raisins, walnuts and pumpkin mixture, and stir until well blended.

Drop by heaping spoonfuls onto a greased cookie sheet. Bake for 15 minutes or until bottoms are brown (that happens quickly with honey, so watch cookies carefully). Remove from pans to a cooling rack right away.

Makes about 3 dozen cookies.

LEMON CRISPS

These delightfully thin, tart lemon-glazed slices are old-fashioned icebox cookies. The dough is mixed, rolled into a cylinder and stored in the freezer before being sliced and baked. For the flavor to penetrate fully, the glaze must be painted on while the cookies are still hot.

½ cup	butter	125 mL
1 cup	sugar	250 mL
1	large egg, lightly beaten	1
2 tsp.	grated lemon zest	10 mL
2 Tbsp.	fresh lemon juice	25 mL
1 tsp.	lemon extract	5 mL
2 cups	cake flour	500 mL
3 Tbsp.	confectioners' sugar	45 mL
2 Tbsp.	cornstarch	25 mL
½ tsp.	baking soda	2 mL

Glaze
⅔ cup	confectioners' sugar, sifted	150 mL
1 tsp.	grated lemon zest	5 mL
4 tsp.	fresh lemon juice	20 mL

Lightly grease baking sheets, and set aside. Preheat oven to 350°F (180°C). In a large bowl, beat together butter and sugar with an electric mixer until well blended and creamy. Add egg, lemon zest, juice and lemon extract. Beat well. Combine flour, confectioners' sugar, cornstarch and baking soda, and sift over butter mixture. Beat with a wooden spoon or with the mixer set at lowest speed until dry ingredients are thoroughly incorporated.

Divide dough into 4 equal portions. Turn out each portion onto a piece of wax paper, shape into logs about 2 inches (5 cm) thick, and wrap well. Set in a plastic bag, and freeze for about 45 minutes or until needed. (If logs are too hard to slice, let them sit for about 1 minute.) Cut scant ¼-inch-thick (5 mm) slices, and set them 1½ inches (4 cm) apart on baking sheets.

Bake for 10 minutes or just until light golden brown around the edges. With a spatula, lift cookies onto a wire rack set over a sheet of wax paper.

To make glaze, stir together sugar, lemon zest and juice. While the cookies are hot, use a pastry brush to coat them with the glaze. As the cookies cool, the glaze will become shiny. Store, layered with wax paper, in an airtight container.

Makes about 4 dozen cookies.

Chapter 8

DESSERTS & SWEETS

"A refreshing, delicate dessert that yet does not taste too sensible is indeed a rarity," wrote M.F.K. Fisher in *How to Cook a Wolf*, published in 1942. In the face of the gluttonous excess of chocolate and cheesecake that has dominated the dessert menus of the past two decades, Fisher might reword this wartime wisdom: At the close of the century, a refreshing and delicate dessert that one can comfortably finish is indeed a rarity.

While dessert may stand as the gastronomical crowning glory to a fine meal, it shouldn't be too cumbersome a crown to wear. It takes a skillful touch for even experienced cooks to serve a dessert that, while giving the slightest suggestion of perpetual feast, is effortless for the palate. Increasingly, cooks are living by the principle that less is more, rather than depending on a repertoire of rich recipes.

We believe that if the main course itself has satisfied the guests' appetites, don't tamper with success. With this in mind, we have included desserts that represent a wide selection of traditional offerings. Fruit crisps and cobblers that make perfect use of the harvest from the orchard, traditional pound cakes and light homemade fruit sherbets and ices are all simple dessert classics that will enhance rather than compete with the lingering memories of a fine meal.

For occasions that demand satisfaction of more immediate sugar cravings, however, Tiger Butter, Chocolate Truffles and Meringue Kisses are a few slightly more obvious sweet endings. But, in deference to Shakespeare's poetic wisdom that "sweets grown common lose their dear delight," we remind you that a little sweetness in life goes a long way.

APPLE DUMPLINGS

These dumplings are not biscuits but elegant purse-like pastries that surround the baking apples. They can be made hours ahead and held in the refrigerator until baking time. Once baked, however, they do not keep well, so serve immediately.

2 cups	unbleached flour	500 mL
2 Tbsp.	sugar	25 mL
½ tsp.	salt	2 mL
¼ cup	solid vegetable shortening	50 mL
½ cup	butter	125 mL
	Ice water	
6	large baking apples	6
⅔ cup	raspberry or blackberry preserves	150 mL
⅓ cup	chopped almonds	75 mL
1 tsp.	grated orange zest	5 mL
1	egg white, lightly beaten	1

Combine flour, sugar and salt in a mixing bowl or a food processor fitted with a steel blade. Cut in shortening and butter until the mixture resembles coarse crumbs. Add approximately ¼ cup (50 mL) ice water, just enough to hold the mixture together. Divide dough into six balls, and flatten into disks. Wrap dough in plastic wrap, and chill.

Meanwhile, peel the apples, and core about three-quarters of the way down, working with a knife until halfway, then finishing with a small-tipped spoon, being careful not to puncture the bottom of the apple. Trim the bottoms, if necessary, to allow the apples to stand upright.

Mix together preserves, almonds and orange zest, then stuff apples with filling.

On a lightly floured board, roll out each ball of dough to a circle about 8 inches (20 cm) in diameter. Brush with egg white, and place an apple in the center of each circle. Bring the dough up over the apple, and press the edges together, using egg white to make them stick. For decoration, scraps of dough can be used to make apple leaves; stick to the top of the dumplings with a little egg white. Place in a lightly buttered, large, shallow baking dish.

Chill for several hours in the refrigerator or for 10 minutes in the freezer. Bake in a preheated 400°F (200°C) oven until tops are golden brown, about 45 minutes. Serve warm.

Makes 6 dumplings.

APPLE PANDOWDY

A pandowdy is a cross between a pie and a pudding. With a filling that includes butter and a little cream, it is richer than an ordinary pie. Cornmeal makes the topping light and crunchy.

$1\frac{1}{4}$ cups	unbleached flour	300 mL
$\frac{1}{3}$ cup	cornmeal	75 mL
2 Tbsp.	sugar	25 mL
$\frac{1}{4}$ tsp.	salt	1 mL
$\frac{1}{4}$ cup	solid vegetable shortening	50 mL
$\frac{1}{3}$ cup	butter	75 mL
	Ice water	

Filling
6 cups	apples, peeled & sliced	1.5 L
$1\frac{1}{2}$ tsp.	cinnamon	7 mL
$\frac{1}{2}$ tsp.	mace	2 mL
$\frac{1}{3}$ cup	pure maple syrup	75 mL
$\frac{1}{4}$ cup	melted butter	50 mL

Topping
2 Tbsp.	pure maple syrup	25 mL
$\frac{1}{4}$ cup	apple cider or juice	50 mL
$\frac{1}{4}$ cup	light cream	50 mL

Combine flour, cornmeal, sugar and salt in a mixing bowl or a food processor fitted with a steel blade. Cut in shortening and butter until the mixture resembles coarse crumbs. Add just enough ice water to allow the mixture to hold together, about $\frac{1}{4}$ cup (50 mL). Divide dough into two balls, and flatten into disks. Wrap dough in plastic wrap, and chill while you prepare the filling.

In a separate bowl, combine apples with cinnamon, mace, $\frac{1}{3}$ cup (75 mL) maple syrup and butter.

Roll out one ball of dough about $\frac{1}{8}$ inch (3 mm) thick to fit into a $1\frac{1}{2}$-quart (1.5 L) baking dish. Place dough in the dish, and arrange to cover sides as best you can. Trim uneven edges.

Spoon apple mixture on top of dough. Roll out the second ball of dough, and place it over the apples. Seal against the sides of the dish.

Bake in a preheated 400°F (200°C) oven for about 10 minutes. Remove from the oven, and reduce heat to 325°F (160°C). Using a sharp knife or a chopper, chop the crust until it almost disappears into the fruit. Combine maple syrup, apple cider and cream, and pour over crust. Return to the oven, and continue to bake for 45 to 50 minutes. Serve warm.

Serves 4 to 6.

BLACKBERRY-APPLE GRUNT

Similar to cobblers, in that they combine fruit with nubs of biscuit dough, grunts are simmered on top of the stove rather than baked in the oven.

3	apples, peeled & cut into thick slices	3
½ cup	sugar	125 mL
4 tsp.	fresh lemon juice	20 mL
¼ tsp.	cinnamon	1 mL
½ cup	water	125 mL
2 cups	fresh or unsweetened frozen blackberries	500 mL

Dumplings

3 Tbsp.	sugar	45 mL
½ tsp.	cinnamon	2 mL
1 cup	flour	250 mL
1 tsp.	baking powder	5 mL
	Pinch salt	
½ cup	buttermilk	125 mL
2 Tbsp.	unsalted butter, melted	25 mL
	Ice cream, frozen yogurt or whipped cream for topping (opt.)	

In an 8- or a 9-inch (20-23 cm) skillet or a shallow flameproof casserole, combine apples, sugar, lemon juice, cinnamon and water. Toss gently. Cover, and bring to a boil. Reduce heat to low, and simmer, covered, for 2 minutes or until apples begin to soften. Add blackberries, and cook for 1 minute longer. Cover, and set aside while making dumpling dough.

In a small bowl, combine 1 Tbsp. (15 mL) sugar and cinnamon, and set aside. In a mixing bowl, stir together flour, remaining sugar, baking powder and salt. In a small bowl, stir together buttermilk and butter. Make a well in the center of the dry ingredients, pour in the buttermilk mixture, and stir until just combined.

Bring the fruit mixture to a simmer. Drop the dumpling batter by spoonfuls evenly over the simmering fruit mixture. Sprinkle the dumplings with the reserved cinnamon-sugar mixture. Cover the pan tightly with a lid or aluminum foil, and cook for 15 to 17 minutes or until dumplings are firm to the touch. Serve hot with ice cream, frozen yogurt or whipped cream, if desired.

Serves 8.

Desserts & Sweets

BLUEBERRY GRUNT

Despite its gluey appearance, Blueberry Grunt has a wonderful flavor; the biscuits are delicious and absorb the juice nicely.

6 cups	fresh or unsweetened frozen blueberries	1.5 L
1 cup	water	250 mL
1 cup	sugar mixed with 1 tsp. (5 mL) cornstarch	250 mL
½ tsp.	(scant) cinnamon	2 mL
1¾ cups	unbleached flour	425 mL
½ tsp.	salt	2 mL
1 Tbsp.	baking powder	15 mL
6 Tbsp.	butter	75 mL
¾ cup	milk (approx.)	175 mL
	Heavy cream for topping	

In a 12-inch (30 cm) skillet or a saucepan, combine blueberries, water, sugar-cornstarch mixture and cinnamon. Bring to a boil, then simmer for 10 minutes. Remove from heat while you prepare biscuit dough.

Sift together flour, salt and baking powder. Cut in butter until the mixture resembles coarse crumbs. Make a well in the center, and pour in milk. Mix just enough to combine. Drop by spoonfuls over blueberries. Cover tightly, and steam for 15 to 20 minutes, keeping the heat just high enough to allow the blueberries to bubble.

Serve warm in bowls with unsweetened heavy cream, whipped if desired.

Serves 6 to 8.

PEAR CRISP

Ripened pears are a must for this recipe. Leave unripened pears at room temperature for four to seven days to soften and develop a good, strong flavor. The addition of pear nectar (available at health-food stores) intensifies the flavor and makes this crisp so moist that whipped cream is superfluous.

Topping

¾ cup	rolled oats (not instant)	175 mL
½ cup	slivered almonds	125 mL
¾ cup	unbleached flour	175 mL
⅓ cup	sugar	75 mL
1 tsp.	cinnamon	5 mL
5 Tbsp.	butter	65 mL

Filling

10	large, ripe pears, peeled, quartered, cored & sliced	10
½ cup	brown sugar	125 mL
½ tsp.	cinnamon	2 mL
½ cup	pear nectar or juice	125 mL

Lightly butter a 9-by-13-inch (3 L) baking pan.

To make topping, combine oats, almonds, flour, sugar and cinnamon in a large bowl. Cut in butter until the mixture resembles coarse crumbs. Set aside.

To make filling, combine pears, brown sugar, cinnamon and pear nectar in a bowl. Toss to mix. Spread pear mixture in bottom of pan. Crumble topping over pears. Bake in a preheated 375°F (190°C) oven for 40 to 50 minutes. Serve warm.

Serves 10 to 12.

PEAR UPSIDE-DOWN CAKE

Spirals of pear top this moist, delicately spiced cake, which is best served warm.

Topping

¼ cup	butter	50 mL
½ cup	brown sugar, firmly packed	125 mL
	Juice of 1 lemon	
3	ripe pears, peeled & sliced into eighths	3

Cake

1⅓ cups	sifted unbleached flour	325 mL
2 tsp.	baking powder	10 mL
½ tsp.	salt	2 mL
1 tsp.	cinnamon	5 mL
½ tsp.	mace	2 mL
¼ tsp.	ginger	1 mL
¼ tsp.	cloves	1 mL
¼ tsp.	nutmeg	1 mL
⅓ cup	sugar	75 mL
⅓ cup	brown sugar	75 mL
⅓ cup	milk	75 mL
⅓ cup	oil	75 mL
2	eggs	2
½ tsp.	vanilla extract	2 mL
	Grated zest of 1 lemon	

To make topping, melt butter in a 10-inch (25 cm) cast-iron skillet. Stir in sugar and lemon juice, and cook over low heat, stirring constantly, until sugar is melted. Do not allow mixture to burn. Remove from heat, and arrange pears in a circular pattern in the butter-sugar mixture. Set aside.

Combine all cake ingredients in a large mixing bowl, and beat for 3 minutes at medium speed, occasionally scraping the sides of the bowl. Pour or spoon the batter over the pears in the skillet, taking care not to disturb their pattern.

Bake in a preheated 400°F (200°C) oven until a toothpick inserted into the center comes out clean, about 35 minutes. Let cool in the skillet on a wire rack for 5 minutes. Loosen the cake from the sides of the skillet, place a platter on top, invert, and lift off the skillet. If any fruit sticks to the bottom of the skillet, remove with a spatula and carefully place on top of the cake.

Serves 6 to 8.

Lemon-Yogurt Cheesecake

Desserts & Sweets, page 214

Vanilla-Peach & Raspberry Sherbets

Desserts & Sweets, pages 224 & 225

LAUFABRAUD

This is a traditional Icelandic Christmas bread. The cinnamon gives it a hint of sweetness, and it is often served warm with melted butter, sugar and a little more cinnamon as a delicious dessert bread.

1 cup	milk	250 mL
2 Tbsp.	butter	25 mL
2 tsp.	cinnamon	10 mL
3 cups	flour	750 mL
½ tsp.	salt	2 mL
¼ tsp.	baking powder	1 mL
	Shortening	

Combine milk, butter and cinnamon in a heavy pot, and bring to a boil. Turn off heat, and let stand for 15 minutes or until lukewarm.

Meanwhile, combine flour, salt and baking powder. Make a well in the center, and pour in milk mixture. Stir to make a stiff dough, then knead for 5 minutes. Divide dough into 10 pieces, roll into balls, cover, and let rest for 15 minutes. Roll as thinly as possible into circles, then place on wax paper, and let dry for 30 minutes.

Melt 2 Tbsp. (25 mL) shortening in a heavy skillet, and fry the breads, one at a time, adding more shortening as needed. Cook until golden brown and small bubbles form over the surface of the bread, approximately 2 minutes on each side. Drain, and serve warm or cold.

Makes 10 loaves.

CLASSIC POUND CAKE

Although this recipe has been adapted to modern ingredients, it is as close to traditional pound cake as you can get, with a strong buttery flavor and a dense velvety texture.

2 cups	sifted cake flour	500 mL
¼ tsp.	salt	1 mL
1 cup	butter at room temperature	250 mL
1¾ cups	sugar	425 mL
5	large eggs at room temperature	5
2 tsp.	vanilla extract or 1 Tbsp. (15 mL) grated lemon zest & 1 Tbsp. (15 mL) fresh lemon juice	10 mL

Preheat oven to 325°F (160°C). Grease and flour a 9-by-5-inch (2 L) loaf pan.

In a small bowl, sift together flour and salt. Set aside. In a mixing bowl, beat butter with an electric mixer until light and creamy. Add sugar gradually, and continue beating for 5 minutes or until fluffy. Beat in eggs, one at a time, beating well after each addition. Add vanilla. Fold in flour, mixing until batter is smooth and blended. Spoon into pan. Shake the pan to level the batter.

Bake for about 1¼ hours or until a cake tester inserted in the center comes out clean. Let the cake cool on a wire rack for 10 minutes. Remove the cake from the pan, and let cool completely.

Serves 12.

'LIGHT' POUND CAKE

Based on a traditional Swedish recipe, this cake is much lower in fat than a classic pound cake yet is surprisingly rich and buttery-tasting. It is wonderful served with fresh fruit salad.

	Vegetable oil	
2 Tbsp.	fine dry breadcrumbs	25 mL
¼ cup	butter	50 mL
1½ cups	sifted cake flour	375 mL
2 tsp.	baking powder	10 mL
	Pinch salt	
2	large eggs at room temperature	2
¾ cup	sugar	175 mL
1 tsp.	vanilla extract or 2 tsp. (10 mL) grated lemon zest	5 mL
⅓ cup	buttermilk	75 mL

Preheat oven to 350°F (180°C). Lightly coat the inside of a 9-by-5-inch (2 L) loaf pan with vegetable oil. Sprinkle breadcrumbs evenly over the pan, and tap out excess.

In a heavy saucepan, melt butter over low heat (do not let it boil). Set aside. In a small bowl, stir together flour, baking powder and salt. In a mixing bowl, combine eggs and sugar; beat with an electric mixer for 5 to 7 minutes or until the mixture leaves a ribbon trail when the beaters are lifted. Blend in vanilla.

Sift half of the flour mixture over the egg mixture. Using a rubber spatula, fold until blended. Stir butter into buttermilk, and pour half over the flour-egg mixture. Fold until blended. Repeat with the remaining flour and buttermilk mixtures.

Pour batter into prepared pan, and bake for 30 to 35 minutes or until a cake tester inserted in the center comes out clean. Let the cake cool in the pan on a wire rack for 10 minutes. Remove the cake from the pan, and let cool completely.

Serves 12.

LEMON POPPY-SEED POUND CAKE

Poppy seeds come from the opium poppy (*Papaver somniferum*) but lack the narcotic properties of the plant's other parts. While it is illegal to cultivate opium poppies without a permit, using poppy seeds is perfectly legal.

2 cups	flour	500 mL
½ tsp.	baking soda	2 mL
¼ tsp.	salt	1 mL
¾ cup	butter at room temperature	175 mL
1½ cups	sugar	375 mL
3	large eggs at room temperature	3
3 Tbsp.	poppy seeds	45 mL
1 Tbsp.	grated lemon zest	15 mL
1 tsp.	vanilla extract	5 mL
1 cup	light sour cream or plain yogurt	250 mL

Preheat oven to 325°F (160°C). Grease and flour a 9-by-5-inch (2 L) loaf pan.

Sift together flour, baking soda and salt. Set aside. In a mixing bowl, combine butter and sugar; beat with an electric mixer until light and fluffy. Add eggs, one at a time, beating well after each addition. Add poppy seeds, lemon zest and vanilla, and beat well. Add the flour mixture alternately with the sour cream, making three additions of flour and two of sour cream. Beat at low speed until smooth.

Spoon batter into prepared pan. Shake the pan to level the batter. Bake for 1¼ to 1½ hours or until the top is springy and a cake tester inserted in the center comes out clean. Let the cake cool in the pan on a rack for 10 minutes. Remove the cake from the pan, and let cool completely.

Serves 12.

Desserts & Sweets

CHOCOLATE HAZELNUT POUND CAKE

A "company" pound cake, if ever there was one, topped with a rich chocolate glaze.

1 cup	hazelnuts	250 mL
4 oz.	semisweet or bittersweet chocolate, chopped	115 g
2 cups	flour	500 mL
½ tsp.	baking soda	2 mL
¼ tsp.	salt	1 mL
1 cup	butter at room temperature	250 mL
1½ cups	sugar	375 mL
3	large eggs at room temperature	3
2 Tbsp.	Frangelico (hazelnut liqueur) or brandy	25 mL
⅔ cup	buttermilk	150 mL

Glaze

6 oz.	semisweet or bittersweet chocolate, chopped, or 1 cup (250 mL) chocolate chips	175 g
¼ cup	butter	50 mL
1 Tbsp.	light corn syrup	15 mL

Preheat oven to 350°F (180°C). Spread hazelnuts in a single layer on a baking sheet, and toast for about 10 minutes or until hazelnuts are lightly browned and skins are papery. Allow hazelnuts to cool, then rub off skins and chop hazelnuts. Set aside.

Reduce oven temperature to 325°F (160°C). Grease and flour a 10-inch (4 L) Bundt pan. In a double boiler over very hot, not simmering, water, melt chocolate. Set aside. Sift together flour, baking soda and salt. Set aside. In a mixing bowl, combine butter and sugar, and beat with an electric mixer until light and fluffy. Add eggs, one at a time, beating well after each addition. Add chocolate and liqueur, and beat well. Add flour mixture alternately with buttermilk, making three additions of flour and two of buttermilk. Beat at low speed until smooth. Fold in hazelnuts.

Spoon batter into prepared pan. Shake the pan to level the batter. Bake for 50 to 60 minutes or until the top is springy and a cake tester inserted in the center comes out clean. Let the cake cool in the pan on a wire rack for 10 minutes. Then invert the cake onto the rack, remove the pan, and let cool completely before glazing.

To make glaze, combine chocolate, butter and corn syrup in a small heavy-bottomed saucepan. Heat over low heat, stirring, until mixture is smooth. Spoon the glaze over the cooled cake, letting it dribble down the sides.

Serves 18 to 20.

BUTTERMILK POUND CAKE

Rich yet light, this spicy pound cake is tantalizingly aromatic. Serve it plain—using glazes or fruit sauces would obscure its fragrance.

3 cups	flour	750 mL
½ tsp.	baking soda	2 mL
¼ tsp.	salt	1 mL
1 tsp.	nutmeg	5 mL
½ tsp.	cinnamon	2 mL
¼ tsp.	allspice	1 mL
¼ tsp.	mace	1 mL
	Pinch cloves	
1 cup	butter at room temperature	250 mL
2 cups	sugar	500 mL
3	large eggs at room temperature	3
1 tsp.	vanilla extract	5 mL
1⅓ cups	buttermilk	325 mL

Preheat oven to 325°F (160°C). Grease and flour a 9-inch (3 L) tube pan or a 10-inch (4 L) Bundt pan.

In a small bowl, sift together flour, baking soda, salt, nutmeg, cinnamon, allspice, mace and cloves. Set aside. In a mixing bowl, combine butter and sugar; beat with an electric mixer until light and fluffy. Add eggs, one at a time, beating well after each addition. Add vanilla, and beat well. Add flour mixture alternately with buttermilk, making three additions of flour and two of buttermilk. Beat at low speed until smooth.

Spoon batter into prepared pan. Shake the pan to level the batter. Bake for 1¼ to 1½ hours or until the top is springy and a cake tester inserted in the center comes out clean. Let the cake cool on a wire rack for 10 minutes. Then invert the cake onto the rack, remove the pan, and let cool completely before serving.

Serves 16.

A POUND OF CURE

Size rather than shape is crucial to success when selecting a pound-cake baking pan. Drier, less tender cakes come out of an oversize pan, which slows the baking process; yet if the pan is too small, the batter overflows. A fluted tube, or Bundt, pan (which directs the heat to the center of the cake, thus speeding up the cooking time) is the pan of choice for many pound-cake bakers, who complete the festive presentation with a dusting of confectioners' sugar or a drizzled glaze of melted chocolate.

CHRISTMAS FRUITCAKE

Well worth every bit of effort, moist and delicious fruitcakes are an unparalleled holiday treat. We suggest you make this fruitcake about a month in advance to allow the flavors to marry.

¾ cup	unsulphured dried apricots	175 mL
¾ cup	orange juice	175 mL
1 cup	chopped dried figs	250 mL
1 cup	chopped dried apples	250 mL
1 cup	apple juice	250 mL
2 cups	currants	500 mL
2 cups	chopped walnuts or filberts	500 mL
2 cups	whole wheat flour	500 mL
1 tsp.	each cinnamon, nutmeg & allspice	5 mL
½ tsp.	ground cloves	2 mL
1 tsp.	baking powder	5 mL
½ tsp.	baking soda	2 mL
1 tsp.	salt	5 mL
3	large eggs	3
⅓ cup	safflower or corn oil	75 mL
	Grated zest of 2 lemons & 1 orange	
1 tsp.	vanilla extract	5 mL
½ cup	brown sugar, firmly packed	125 mL
	Red wine	
	Brandy for soaking cakes	

Grease two 8-by-4-inch (1.5 L) loaf pans, and line completely with greased parchment or brown paper.

Place apricots and orange juice in a small saucepan, bring to a boil, cover, and turn off heat. Let sit for 5 minutes to rehydrate. Drain, reserving juice.

Repeat procedure in the same saucepan with figs and apples in apple juice. Drain, reserving juice.

Chop apricots, and combine with figs, apples, currants and nuts in a large mixing bowl. Set aside.

Preheat oven to 300°F (150°C). Sift flour with spices, baking powder, baking soda and salt. Combine eggs, oil, lemon and orange zest, vanilla and sugar. Add wine to reserved juices to make 1 cup (250 mL), and stir into egg mixture.

To make batter, stir flour mixture into egg mixture, then combine with fruits and nuts. Pour batter into loaf pans, and bake for 1¾ hours on lowest rack of oven. Test by inserting a table knife into center of cake. It will come out clean when fruitcake is done.

Let the cakes cool in pans on wire racks until they reach room temperature, then remove from pans. Carefully pour brandy on all surfaces, then wrap cakes in brandy-soaked cloth and aluminum foil. Store in a cool, dark place. Once a week during storage, moisten cloth with more brandy.

Makes 2 fruitcakes.

LEMON-YOGURT CHEESECAKE

Guiltless indulgence is the legacy of this lemony and dense cheesecake.

Crust

1 cup	graham cracker crumbs	250 mL
½ cup	gingersnap crumbs	125 mL
⅓ cup	crushed walnuts	75 mL
⅓ cup	vegetable oil or melted butter	75 mL
½ tsp.	cinnamon	2 mL
½ tsp.	ginger	2 mL
1 Tbsp.	honey	15 mL

Cheesecake

8 oz.	low-fat cream cheese	250 g
8 oz.	yogurt	250 g
2 cups	Yogurt Cheese (recipe follows)	500 mL
1 cup	sugar	250 mL
1 Tbsp.	grated lemon zest	15 mL
2 Tbsp.	lemon juice	25 mL
4	eggs at room temperature, beaten until thick	4

Topping

1 pint	fresh strawberries, hulled & sliced in half	500 mL
½ cup	sugar	125 mL

To make crust, butter and chill an 8-inch (2 L) springform pan. Mix all ingredients together. Press into the bottom and partway up the side of the pan. Chill at least 15 minutes.

To make cheesecake, beat together cream cheese, yogurt, Yogurt Cheese, sugar, lemon zest and juice with an electric mixer. Stir in eggs. Spoon mixture carefully into the crust-lined pan.

Bake at 300°F (150°C) for 1 hour and 10 minutes or until the center sets. Cool in the oven, with the door ajar, for 1 hour. Refrigerate for 3 hours or more, then remove sides from pan.

To make topping, mix strawberries and sugar; let stand for 1 to 2 hours, then spoon over cheesecake.
Serves 8.

YOGURT CHEESE

Line a colander with a large cotton tea towel or a double thickness of cheesecloth, and place the colander in the sink. Pour in 48 oz. (1.5 kg) yogurt. After 15 minutes, transfer colander to a bowl. Cover with plastic wrap, and refrigerate overnight. Gathering the edges of the towel together, gently squeeze out any remaining liquid. Transfer cheese to a separate container. Refrigerate until ready to use. Keeps for up to 1 week.

Makes 2 cups (500 mL).

ORANGE-ALMOND TART

Orange and almond flavors blend together beautifully in this tart. A quick but very attractive finale to a full-course dinner.

½ cup	butter, softened	125 mL
½ cup	sugar, plus 2 Tbsp. (25 mL)	125 mL
1	egg yolk	1
1 tsp.	almond extract	5 mL
2 tsp.	vanilla extract	10 mL
1½ cups	flour	375 mL
¾ cup	sliced toasted almonds	175 mL
8 oz.	cream cheese, softened	250 g
2 Tbsp.	almond liqueur	25 mL
	Mandarin oranges to cover tart	
¼ cup	apricot jam	50 mL

Cream butter and ½ cup (125 mL) sugar. Beat in egg yolk, almond extract and 1 tsp. (5 mL) vanilla. Mix in flour and ½ cup (125 mL) almonds. Press dough into 10-inch (25 cm) tart pan. Prick shell. Bake at 375°F (190°C) until golden, about 10 minutes. Set aside to cool.

Beat cream cheese and remaining sugar until smooth. Beat in liqueur and remaining vanilla. Spread in tart shell, then chill until firm. Top with orange segments.

Whisk jam and 1 Tbsp. (15 mL) water over medium heat until jam is melted, then boil for 30 seconds. Cool slightly, then brush over oranges. Sprinkle with remaining almonds.

HOT-FUDGE PUDDING CAKE

This pudding cake is so sweet and gooey, you would never guess that it is nearly fatless—and neither will your company.

⅔ cup	flour	150 mL
⅓ cup	oat bran	75 mL
2 tsp.	baking powder	10 mL
⅔ cup	sugar	150 mL
⅓ cup	cocoa powder	75 mL
½ cup	skim milk	125 mL
1 Tbsp.	oil	15 mL
1 tsp.	vanilla extract	5 mL
¼ cup	chopped walnuts	50 mL

Topping

⅓ cup	cocoa powder	75 mL
1 cup	brown sugar	250 mL
1¾ cups	hot coffee or 2 tsp. (10 mL) instant coffee dissolved in 1¾ cups (425 mL) boiling water	425 mL

Combine flour, oat bran, baking powder, sugar and cocoa in a 9-inch (2.5 L) baking dish or a 1½-quart (1.5 L) soufflé dish. Add milk, oil and vanilla, and stir to blend. Fold in walnuts.

To make topping, combine cocoa and brown sugar so that the cocoa is evenly dispersed. Sprinkle over batter. Pour hot coffee over all.

Bake for 45 minutes at 350°F (180°C). During baking, the cake will rise, leaving a thick pool of hot-fudge sauce beneath. To serve, spoon out pieces of cake and heap on the sauce.

Serves 6.

Desserts & Sweets

MEREDITH'S HARVEST PIE

Though pumpkin is *de rigueur* for harvest-season pies, other squashes, like butternut and Hubbard, make a smoother, sweeter and more subtly flavored filling.

1	10-inch (25 cm) pie shell	1
2	large eggs	2
3 cups	cooked, mashed squash	750 mL
1 cup	low-fat milk, scalded	250 mL
3 Tbsp.	molasses, or more to taste	45 mL
½ cup	brown sugar	125 mL
	Pinch salt	
2 tsp.	cinnamon	10 mL
½ tsp.	nutmeg	2 mL
½ tsp.	allspice	2 mL
	Pinch cloves	

Bake the pie shell, covered with foil and weighted down, at 425°F (220°C) for about 8 minutes. Remove foil, and bake for 3 minutes longer. Cool.

Beat eggs lightly, then blend into squash until mixture is smooth. Stir in remaining ingredients.

Preheat oven to 450°F (230°C). Spoon filling into pie shell, and bake for 10 minutes. Reduce heat to 350°F (180°C), and bake for 30 to 40 minutes longer or until filling is puffed and set in the middle.

Makes one 10-inch (25 cm) pie.

THE WORLD'S BEST BUTTER TART

This butter tart is superior to anything you will ever buy in a supermarket. Its combination of puff pastry and Grandpa Barber's butter tart filling—a family recipe handed down for at least three generations— makes for a delicious dessert. Butter is the key ingredient here. Pastry and filling together use most of a heart-stopping pound.

1 cup	brown sugar, firmly packed	250 mL
½ cup	butter	125 mL
1	egg, lightly beaten	1
2 tsp.	vanilla extract	10 mL
1 tsp.	vinegar	5 mL
	Pinch freshly grated nutmeg	
¾ cup	raisins	175 mL
	Puff Pastry (facing page)	

In a mixing bowl, cream together sugar and butter. Beat in egg, vanilla, vinegar and nutmeg. Stir in raisins.

On a lightly floured surface, roll out puff pastry as instructed. Cut out rounds to fit ungreased tart tins. Fill shells one-half to two-thirds full. Bake in a 375°F (190°C) oven for about 30 minutes or until pastry is golden and filling is set.

Makes up to 24 tarts.

Desserts & Sweets

PUFF PASTRY

Adapted from Mrs. Nourse's Modern Practical Cookery, published in 1845, this surprisingly easy recipe calls for 3 cups (750 mL) flour, 1 cup (250 mL) butter and ¾ cup (175 mL) cold water.

Keep butter refrigerated until you need it, and cool your hands in cold water (then dry thoroughly) before you start. Place flour in a bowl. Cut (or "rub," as Mrs. Nourse would have it) ¼ cup (50 mL) butter into flour, using your fingers or a pastry fork. By the time you finish, the mixture will have clumped together a bit and will have the texture of confectioners' sugar, but it should not feel greasy if you are keeping everything cool.

Make a well in the center of the flour mixture, and pour in cold water, ¼ cup (50 mL) at a time, mixing lightly with your hands as you do. Never overmix pastry. When dough clumps together, press into a ball and flatten a bit. Lightly flour a board, and roll out dough until it is about 12 inches (30 cm) square. It will be a bit crumbly. Flip over whenever dough begins to stick; reflour the board, and also lightly dust the surface of the dough to keep the rolling pin from sticking.

Next, slice the remaining butter about ⅛ inch (3 mm) thick, and place the pieces in a single layer on half of the rolled-out dough. Fold dough in half, and roll it out to roughly 18 inches (45 cm) square, then fold it in half and in half again. Wrap in plastic wrap, refrigerate for 20 minutes, and roll out to about the same dimensions. Repeat this procedure two more times.

Roll out dough about ⅛ inch (3 mm) thick. Cut into 3½-inch (9 cm) rounds; makes approximately 24 tart shells. If everything works out the way you want it to, you will need a scant tablespoon (15 mL) filling for each tart, because the air incorporated into the folding and rolling expands during baking and makes the pastry puff up—thus its name!

THE HARROWSMITH BUTTER TART

This delicious recipe maximizes the nutritional benefits of the butter tart without sacrificing flavor. The tasty pastry is too delicate to hold a runny filling securely, so the maple-flavored filling is somewhat thick.

¼ cup	pecans, finely chopped	50 mL
¾ cup	flour	175 mL
½ cup	whole wheat pastry flour	125 mL
¼ tsp.	salt	1 mL
⅓ cup	vegetable shortening	75 mL
⅓ cup	ice water (approx.)	75 mL

Filling

½ cup	brown sugar, firmly packed	125 mL
¼ cup	maple syrup	50 mL
¼ cup	melted butter or margarine	50 mL
1	egg, lightly beaten	1
1 tsp.	vanilla extract	5 mL
	Pinch salt	
	Raisins (opt.)	

In a bowl, mix pecans with flour and salt. Cut in shortening until it is pea-sized. Lightly stir in enough water so that the mixture will hold together. Press into a ball, and refrigerate for several hours for easiest rolling, or prepare right away, if desired. On a lightly floured board, roll out about ⅛ inch (3 mm) thick, turning over as necessary and reflouring to prevent sticking. Cut into twelve 3½-inch (9 cm) circles, and press into 3-inch (8 cm) tart tins.

To make filling, mix together all ingredients except raisins. Place several raisins, if using, in each tart shell, then fill about half full with mixture. Bake in a 375°F (190°C) oven for 20 minutes or until pastry is lightly browned. Loosen edges with a knife, and let cool for 5 minutes. Remove from tins, and let cool completely.

Makes about 12 tarts.

PISTACHIO & SESAME PHYLLO ROLLS

A delicacy in Middle Eastern households, these nutty rolls have a light and crunchy phyllo shell and are drenched in sweet lemony syrup.

4 cups	pistachios, coarsely ground	1 L
1 cup	sesame seeds, lightly toasted	250 mL
2 tsp.	cinnamon	10 mL
1 tsp.	cloves	5 mL
1 lb.	thin phyllo sheets	500 g
$\frac{3}{4}$ cup	butter, clarified	175 mL

Syrup

3 cups	sugar	750 mL
$2\frac{1}{2}$ cups	water	625 mL
2 tsp.	fresh lemon juice, strained	10 mL

Lightly grease a 12-inch (3 L) round baking pan. Preheat oven to 375°F (190°C).

Combine pistachios, sesame seeds, cinnamon and cloves in a bowl, and set aside.

Unroll the phyllo, and cover with a damp cloth to keep it from drying out. Layer 3 sheets of phyllo, one at a time, brushing each layer with butter. Spoon about $\frac{2}{3}$ cup (150 mL) pistachio mixture over the phyllo, leaving approximately $1\frac{1}{2}$ inches (4 cm) on the near edge and sides.

Fold the near edge over the filling, then fold in the sides, and gently roll to form a fairly tight cylinder about $1\frac{1}{2}$ inches (4 cm) in diameter. Brush with butter as you roll, and be careful not to tear the phyllo. Gently lift the cylinder into the prepared pan, and start a spiral from the center out. Place the phyllo cylinders end to end in the baking pan to complete the spiral. Make cuts in the coils about $1\frac{1}{2}$ inches (4 cm) apart. Bake for about 30 minutes or until the phyllo is golden and crisp.

While phyllo is baking, make syrup. Combine sugar, water and lemon juice in a medium saucepan. Bring to a boil, reduce heat, and simmer for 5 to 7 minutes. Cover to keep warm.

As soon as the phyllo rolls are ready, remove from the oven and pour hot syrup over the pastry. Let cool, and serve.

Makes 36 to 40 pieces.

Desserts & Sweets

GALAKTOBOUREKO
(Custard-Filled Phyllo Squares)

A rich but surprisingly soothing conclusion to an exotic Greek meal.

Syrup

2 cups	sugar	500 mL
1 cup	water	250 mL
1	cinnamon stick	1
5-6	whole cloves	5-6
2 tsp.	fresh lemon juice, strained	10 mL
1 Tbsp.	orange liqueur (opt.)	15 mL

Filling

1 cup	sugar	250 mL
¾ cup	fine semolina	175 mL
6 cups	milk	1.5 L
1 Tbsp.	orange liqueur	15 mL
3	whole eggs at room temperature	3
½ tsp.	grated orange zest	2 mL
12-16	thin phyllo sheets	12-16
½ cup	unsalted butter, clarified Cinnamon (opt.)	125 mL

To make syrup, combine sugar and water in a medium saucepan, and bring to a boil over medium heat. Reduce heat, and add cinnamon stick, cloves and lemon juice. Simmer for 10 minutes. Stir in liqueur, remove from heat, and let cool.

To make filling, combine sugar, semolina and milk in a large saucepan. Stir constantly with a wooden spoon over medium heat for about 20 minutes or until mixture is thick and creamy. Stir in liqueur, and remove from heat. Beat eggs until pale and frothy, then pour quickly into the semolina mixture together with orange zest, stirring vigorously. Let cool slightly.

Lightly grease a 9-by-12-by-3-inch (3 L) baking pan, and preheat oven to 350°F (180°C). Layer 10 sheets of phyllo on bottom of prepared pan, brushing each with butter. Spread filling evenly over phyllo, and top with 6 to 8 more sheets of phyllo, brushing each with butter. Score the phyllo either by making three rows down the length and four across the width to form 12 large pieces or by cutting first down the length of the pan, then diagonally into diamonds.

Bake for about 45 minutes or until the phyllo is golden and the filling is set but creamy. Pour the cooled syrup over the pastry immediately. Sprinkle with cinnamon, if desired, and serve warm or cold.

Serves 10 to 12.

Desserts & Sweets

PLUM PUDDING

The "figgy" pudding is a must-have holiday classic that rounds out any traditional Dickensian dinner.

2 Tbsp.	butter at room temperature	25 mL
2 Tbsp.	vegetable oil	25 mL
½ cup	honey	125 mL
3	eggs	3
1 cup	dried figs, chopped, or pitted prunes, packed	250 mL
1	apple, peeled, quartered & sliced	1
1 cup	apple juice	250 mL
	Grated zest of 1 lemon	
1 tsp.	vanilla extract or brandy	5 mL
1 cup	raisins	250 mL
1 cup	walnuts, finely chopped	250 mL
2 cups	soft whole wheat breadcrumbs	500 mL
1 cup	whole wheat flour	250 mL
1 tsp.	baking powder	5 mL
½ tsp.	salt	2 mL
¼ tsp.	baking soda	1 mL
1 tsp.	cinnamon	5 mL
½ tsp.	nutmeg	2 mL
¼ tsp.	ground cloves	1 mL
	Brandy	

Cream butter, oil and honey together. Separate eggs, and set whites aside. Beat yolks until creamy, then add to the honey mixture. Put figs and apple slices in a blender or a food processor with apple juice, and process into a jamlike consistency. Combine with lemon zest, vanilla, raisins, walnuts and breadcrumbs with honey mixture.

Sift flour with baking powder, salt, baking soda, cinnamon, nutmeg and cloves. Combine with honey mixture. Beat egg whites until they form stiff peaks, then fold gently into batter. Turn batter into a greased 2-quart (2 L) pudding mold or a casserole with a lid. Cover tightly.

Place the pudding mold on a rack inside a pot large enough to provide 2 inches (5 cm) of space all around for steam to circulate. Pour enough boiling water into the pot to come halfway up the sides of the mold.

Cover the pot, and let water boil briskly for a few minutes, then reduce heat to low. Steam pudding for 2½ hours or until the top springs back when touched. Replenish water if needed; check after the first hour.

To unmold, slide a knife around the sides of the pudding and turn it out onto a plate. Splash with brandy, ignite, and serve with a scoop of ice cream.

Makes 12 servings.

PERSIMMON PUDDING

Many cooks recommend using small Virginia persimmons rather than the large Japanese varieties to give this pudding a superior texture.

1 cup	whole wheat flour	250 mL
½ tsp.	baking soda	2 mL
¼ tsp.	salt	1 mL
1 tsp.	cinnamon	5 mL
¼ cup	honey	50 mL
3 Tbsp.	vegetable oil	45 mL
2	eggs	2
1 tsp.	vanilla extract	5 mL
1 cup	persimmon pulp	250 mL
½ cup	raisins	125 mL

Sift flour, baking soda, salt and cinnamon together.

Beat together honey, oil, eggs, vanilla, persimmon pulp and raisins. Mix liquid and dry ingredients just until smooth, and pour into a greased 1½-quart (1.5 L) pudding mold or baking dish. Cover mold tightly. Follow steaming instructions for Plum Pudding (facing page). Steam for 2½ hours.

Serve warm with unsweetened whipped cream or vanilla ice cream.

Makes 6 servings.

LITE TOPPING

To top cakes, pandowdies, cobblers, crisps and grunts, try a low-calorie skim-milk substitute instead of heavy cream. Half an hour before serving dessert, measure ½ cup (125 mL) chilled evaporated skim milk into a mixing bowl, and place in the freezer along with the beaters. Once ice crystals form around the edge, beat the milk at high speed for several minutes until soft peaks form. Then beat in 1 Tbsp. (15 mL) confectioners' sugar and ½ tsp. (2 mL) vanilla extract, and continue to beat until the mixture is light and fluffy. Experiment with flavored toppings by substituting a fruit liqueur for the sugar and vanilla. There is little fat in this mixture, so the whipped texture will hold for only a few minutes. Serve immediately.

Desserts & Sweets

LEMON BREAD PUDDING

Made with beaten egg whites, this lemony bread pudding is lighter than traditional versions and is best served warm.

3½ cups	stale white bread, cut into small cubes & toasted	875 mL
2 cups	milk	500 mL
1 cup	orange juice	250 mL
¼ tsp.	salt	1 mL
3	eggs, separated	3
⅓ cup	brown sugar	75 mL
1 tsp.	vanilla extract	5 mL
½ tsp.	cinnamon	2 mL
3 Tbsp.	lemon juice	45 mL
½ cup	currants	125 mL

In a large bowl, soak bread cubes in milk, orange juice and salt for 15 minutes. Beat together egg yolks, sugar, vanilla, cinnamon and lemon juice. Stir in currants. Pour over soaked bread. Stir lightly until well blended. Beat egg whites until stiff, then fold into pudding mixture. Pour into a greased 8-inch (2 L) square baking dish, and place dish in a pan of hot water. Bake at 350°F (180°C) for 45 minutes or until set.

   Serves 4.

BLUEBERRY-ORANGE SORBET

The distinctive flavor of blueberries is enhanced by a generous splash of fresh orange juice in this sorbet. Do not cut corners in this simple recipe— sieving the berries to remove their skins is essential to the dessert's silky texture.

¾ cup	sugar	175 mL
½ cup	water	125 mL
4 cups	fresh blueberries	1 L
½ cup	fresh orange juice	125 mL

In a small saucepan, combine sugar and water. Bring to a boil. Reduce heat, and simmer for 5 minutes. Chill syrup for 1 hour.

   In a food processor or a blender, puree blueberries and orange juice until smooth. Pass through a sieve, and chill, covered, for 30 minutes.

   Combine sugar syrup and blueberry puree. Freeze in an ice-cream maker, following manufacturer's directions. Alternatively, pour the mixture into a metal cake pan and freeze until almost solid, about 6 hours. Crack into chunks, and process in a food processor until smooth.

   Store and serve as for Strawberry & Watermelon Sorbet (facing page).

   Serves 6.

STRAWBERRY & WATERMELON SORBET

Since these fruits don't ripen in the same month, combine frozen strawberries and fresh-from-the-patch watermelon to make this cooling sorbet. Perfect for summer's dog days, it is the culinary answer to central air conditioning.

$\frac{1}{4}$ cup	sugar	50 mL
1	sprig mint	1
$\frac{1}{2}$ cup	water	125 mL
2 cups	watermelon chunks, seeds removed	500 mL
2 cups	unsweetened strawberries, hulled (fresh or frozen & thawed)	500 mL
2 Tbsp.	fresh lemon juice	25 mL

In a small saucepan, combine sugar, mint and water. Bring to a boil. Reduce heat, and simmer for 5 minutes. Discard mint, and chill syrup for 1 hour.

In a food processor or a blender, puree watermelon. Strain watermelon through a fine-meshed sieve into a bowl. Puree strawberries, and strain into the watermelon puree. Stir in lemon juice. Chill, covered, for 30 minutes.

Combine fruit puree and sugar syrup. Freeze in an ice-cream maker, following manufacturer's directions. Alternatively, pour the mixture into a metal cake pan and freeze until almost solid, about 6 hours. Crack into chunks, and process in a food processor until smooth.

Although sorbet is best if eaten the day it is made, it can be stored in a covered container in the freezer for up to a week. If frozen solid, transfer to the refrigerator for 30 minutes before serving.

Serves 6.

NUT CRISPS

Reminiscent of holiday shortbread, these cookies are thinner and more delicate, perfect companions to dessert ices.

1 cup	*butter, softened*	*250 mL*
1 cup	*sugar*	*250 mL*
1	*large egg yolk*	*1*
1 tsp.	*vanilla extract*	*5 mL*
1½ cups	*flour*	*375 mL*
1 cup	*nuts, finely chopped (pecans, walnuts or almonds)*	*250 mL*

Preheat oven to 375°F (190°C). Lightly oil a 17-by-11-inch (43 x 28 cm) rimmed baking sheet, or spray with nonstick cooking spray.

With an electric mixer, beat butter and sugar until light and fluffy. Beat in egg yolk and vanilla. Add flour, and beat at low speed just until incorporated. Stir in nuts with a wooden spoon.

Place dough on prepared baking sheet. Cover with plastic wrap, and pat so that dough covers the baking sheet. Smooth with a rolling pin to make an even thickness. Remove plastic wrap, and prick surface with a fork.

Bake until golden brown, 18 to 20 minutes. Place the pan on a wire rack, and let cool for 10 minutes. With a sharp knife, cut into rectangles, about 1 by 2¾ inches (2.5 x 7 cm). Cool cookies completely before removing from pan.

Store in an airtight container up to 4 days.

Makes 6 dozen cookies.

VANILLA-PEACH SHERBET

Although a sherbet, this dessert is every bit as satisfying as any premium ice cream. If you have lots of fresh peaches, peel and freeze them—then enjoy this dessert again in January.

1½ cups	peaches, peeled & sliced	375 mL
1 Tbsp.	fresh lemon juice	15 mL
½ cup	milk	125 mL
1 tsp.	vanilla extract	5 mL
2	large egg whites	2
¾ cup	sugar	175 mL
½ cup	water	125 mL

Puree peaches and lemon juice in a food processor or a blender. Transfer to a bowl, and stir in milk and vanilla. Chill, covered, for 30 minutes.

Place egg whites in a large mixing bowl. Set over a larger bowl of hot water, and stir for a few minutes until warmed slightly. Set aside.

In a small saucepan, combine sugar and water. Bring to a boil, stirring occasionally. Cook over medium-high heat, without stirring, until the syrup registers 240°F (115°C) and is at the soft-ball stage—when a bit of syrup dropped into ice water forms a pliable ball; this will take from 3 to 5 minutes. Remove syrup from heat. Set aside.

Beat egg whites with an electric mixer just until soft peaks form. Return the syrup to the heat until it boils. Gradually pour the hot syrup into the egg whites, but not directly onto the beaters, beating constantly. Continue beating until egg whites are cool and very stiff, about 5 minutes.

Combine the egg-white mixture and the peach puree with a whisk, using a gentle folding motion. Freeze in an ice-cream maker, following manufacturer's directions. Alternatively, pour the mixture into a metal cake pan, and freeze until almost solid, about 6 hours. Crack into chunks, and process in a food processor until smooth.

Although sherbet is best if eaten the day it is made, it can be stored in a covered container in the freezer for up to 10 days. If frozen solid, transfer to the refrigerator for 30 minutes before serving.

Serves 4 to 6.

Desserts & Sweets

RASPBERRY SHERBET

As in the Vanilla-Peach Sherbet, Italian meringue, which is cooked, is used in this intensely flavored, dark pink sherbet to give it a creamy, rich consistency and to eliminate any health concerns about using raw eggs.

2 cups	unsweetened raspberries (fresh or frozen & thawed)	500 mL
2 Tbsp.	fresh lemon juice	25 mL
2	large egg whites	2
½ cup	sugar	125 mL
¾ cup	water	175 mL

In a food processor or a blender, puree raspberries and lemon juice. Strain through a fine-meshed sieve into a bowl. Chill, covered, for 30 minutes.

Place egg whites in a large mixing bowl. Set over a larger bowl of hot water, and stir for a few minutes until warmed slightly. Set aside.

In a small saucepan, combine sugar and water. Bring to a boil, stirring occasionally. Cook over medium-high heat, without stirring, until the syrup registers 240°F (115°C) and is at the soft-ball stage— when a bit of syrup dropped into ice water forms a pliable ball; this will take from 3 to 5 minutes. Remove syrup from heat. Set aside.

Beat egg whites with an electric mixer just until soft peaks form. Return the syrup to the heat until it boils. Gradually pour the hot syrup into the egg whites, but not directly onto the beaters, beating constantly. Continue beating until egg whites are cool and very stiff, about 5 minutes.

Combine the egg-white mixture and the raspberry puree with a whisk, using a gentle folding motion. Freeze in an ice-cream maker, following manufacturer's directions. Alternatively, pour the mixture into a metal cake pan and freeze until almost solid, about 6 hours. Crack into chunks, and process in a food processor until smooth. Store and serve as for Vanilla-Peach Sherbet (facing page).

Serves 6 to 8.

CHOCOLATE TRUFFLES

This recipe calls for the truffles to be rolled in grated coconut. Two other tasty possibilities are cocoa powder or ground almonds.

12 oz.	semisweet chocolate	375 g
¾ cup	condensed milk	175 mL
1 tsp.	rum	5 mL
¾ cup	nonfat dry milk (opt.)	175 mL

Melt chocolate in a double boiler over hot but not boiling water. Remove from heat, and stir in milk and rum until well blended. Refrigerate for 1 hour or until stiff.

With buttered hands, shape mixture into 1-inch (2.5 cm) balls. Roll in coconut to coat, then store in the refrigerator.

Makes 2 dozen truffles.

Desserts & Sweets

CANDIED ORANGE PEEL

Delicious on its own as an after-dinner treat, incorporated into other dishes or used as a garnish, candied citrus peel is a simple and sweet treat.

6	navel oranges	6
1 cup	sugar	250 mL

With a small, sharp knife, remove peel from oranges, and scrape pith from peel. Save oranges for another use. Cut peel into julienne strips, then mince strips.

Place peel in a heavy saucepan, cover with cold water, and bring to a boil. Drain, and repeat this two more times. Return peel to saucepan after the third draining, cover with cold water, bring to a boil, boil for 1 minute, then drain.

Return peel to saucepan with sugar and 2 Tbsp. (25 mL) water. Bring to a boil over medium heat, stirring, then cook, stirring, for 20 minutes or until peel is dry. Spread on a baking sheet, let cool, then store in an airtight container.

Makes about 2 cups (500 mL).

TIGER BUTTER

Utterly addictive, Tiger Butter is a simple homemade candy for all fans of commercial chocolate-and-peanut-butter delights.

½ lb.	white chocolate, chopped	250 g
½ cup	smooth peanut butter	125 mL
½ lb.	semisweet chocolate, chopped	250 g

Line the bottom of a 9-inch (1.5 L) round or a 10-inch (3 L) square cake pan with wax paper. In a double boiler over hot but not boiling water, melt white chocolate. Scrape into a bowl, and stir in peanut butter. Clean and thoroughly dry the top of the double boiler, then melt semisweet chocolate over hot water. Pour the white chocolate mixture into the prepared pan, and spread evenly. Pour semisweet chocolate over top, and spread evenly. Draw a table knife through the chocolate to create a marbled effect. Place in the freezer for 30 minutes or until solid. Cut into wedges or squares, and serve straight from the pan.

Makes 16 candies.

Chapter 9

BEVERAGES

hiling away the hours on the front-porch swing, sipping long, cool drinks and letting our imaginations lazily roam is a time-honored North American pastime. Regrettably, it is a summer idyll that too few of us have a chance to indulge anymore. In fact, this particular form of escape from the sweltering summer heat at times seems better documented in literature and film than in actual experience. Visions of Huck Finn lounging by the Mississippi or of a sultry character from a Tennessee Williams play come easily to mind. But the truth is, both our spirits and our bodies would greatly benefit from just such a ritual.

We don't make much ceremony of the fact that our bodies desperately rely on liquids as well as food to stay healthy, although medical science reminds us that we should be downing multiple quarts of water each day. That route to good health may seem a little tedious to some, and so in this final chapter, we ask you to consider a few tastier ways to replenish your body's lost fluids. Consider, too, the immeasurable benefits, both emotional and physical, that will follow from a few minutes spent quietly savoring a glass of homemade lemonade, iced tea or one of the heartier beverages offered here.

Anyone in possession of a blender, a food processor or a juice extractor can create high-protein meals in a glass. Deliciously versatile, they range from glistening pure-fruit nectars to thick and frothy milk-shake-style concoctions, which are popular with kids and adults alike. These wholesome and nutritious drinks are intended to encourage the thirsty to forsake their gallons of nutrient-challenged soda pop and rediscover some traditional and delightfully inspired ways to wet their whistles.

Beverages

HOMEMADE LEMONADE

Jazz up this recipe for a simple, classic lemonade with novelty ice cubes made from brewed tea or diluted strawberry syrup.

5-6	lemons	5-6
4½ cups	water	1.1 L
1 cup	sugar	250 mL
1	lemon, sliced, for garnish	1

Juice enough lemons to make 1 cup (250 mL) juice, reserving lemon rinds. In a clear glass pitcher, combine juice, rinds and 3½ cups (875 mL) water. Cover, and set on a sunny porch or leave on the kitchen counter for about 4 hours.

Meanwhile, combine sugar and remaining water in a small saucepan. Place over medium heat, stirring constantly until sugar has dissolved and washing down any sugar crystals from the sides of the pan with a pastry brush dipped in water. Bring mixture to a boil. Boil for about 1 minute or until syrup is clear. (Sugar syrup can be stored in an airtight container in the refrigerator for up to 1 week.)

Remove lemon rinds from pitcher. Add about 1 cup (250 mL) sugar syrup, taste, and add more as necessary. Chill.

Just before serving, add lemon slices to pitcher. Serve over ice.

Makes about four 1-cup (250 mL) servings.

LEMON-LIME SPRITZERS

This lively, full-bodied version of traditional lemonade is zipped up with fresh lime wedges and mint. Experiment with different proportions of juice base and syrup to make it as tart or as sweet as you wish. The same simple syrup and sparkling-water combination can be mixed with a variety of juices, such as apricot, peach or pear juice blended with a base of orange, lemon or lime juice.

1 cup	sugar	250 mL
½ cup	water	125 mL
½ cup	fresh lemon juice	125 mL
½ cup	fresh lime juice	125 mL
9 cups	seltzer or sparkling water	2.25 L
	Crushed ice	
1	lime, cut into wedges	1
	Sprigs of mint	

In a small saucepan, combine sugar and water. Bring to a boil while stirring. Boil over medium heat, without stirring, for 2 minutes, then let cool. Refrigerate until chilled, at least 30 minutes.

Just before serving, combine sugar syrup and lemon and lime juice in a pitcher. Pour in seltzer, add crushed ice, and garnish with lime wedges and mint.

Serves 6.

Beverages

RORY'S STRAWBERRY NECTAR

This is a wonderfully tasty way to put slightly over-ripe strawberries to good use.

4 cups	strawberries, rinsed & hulled	1 L
4 cups	white grape juice	1 L
2-3 Tbsp.	fresh lime juice	25-45 mL
¼ cup	superfine sugar (see *Note* below)	50 mL
1	lime, sliced, for garnish	1

Note: You can make superfine sugar by whirling granulated sugar in a blender for about 1 minute or until finely ground.

In a blender or a food processor, puree strawberries with 2 cups (500 mL) grape juice (if using a blender, you will have to do this in two batches).

Strain mixture through a fine-meshed sieve into a large bowl, discarding seeds. Add remaining grape juice, lime juice and sugar. Mix well, and serve over ice, garnishing each glass with a lime slice.

Makes about six 1-cup (250 mL) servings.

RASPBERRY-LIME RICKEY

The ultimate thirst quencher, this refreshingly tart beverage suits adult tastes. Make plenty, though, because your children will probably like it too.

1 cup	raspberries, fresh or frozen	250 mL
¾ cup	sugar	175 mL
¼ cup	water	50 mL
3 cups	soda water	750 mL
¾ cup	fresh lime juice	175 mL
1	lime, sliced, for garnish	1

In a small saucepan, combine raspberries, sugar and water. Bring just to a simmer over medium heat, stirring constantly. Remove from heat, and strain mixture through a fine-meshed sieve into a bowl, pressing on the raspberries to extract all the pulp. Discard seeds. Let raspberry syrup cool. (Syrup can be stored, covered, in the refrigerator for up to 1 week.)

In a pitcher, stir together raspberry syrup, soda water and lime juice. Serve over ice, garnishing each glass with a slice of lime.

Makes about four 1-cup (250 mL) servings.

Beverages

CITRUS ICED TEA

A zesty citrus version of a cool summer classic.

⅔ cup	sugar	150 mL
⅔ cup	water	150 mL
2 Tbsp.	lemon zest	25 mL
2 Tbsp.	orange zest	25 mL
4 cups	brewed orange pekoe tea, cooled	1 L
⅔ cup	lemon juice	150 mL
½ cup	orange juice	125 mL
	Fresh mint sprigs for garnish	
1	orange, sliced, for garnish	1

In a small saucepan, combine sugar, water, lemon zest and orange zest. Simmer over medium heat, stirring constantly, until sugar has dissolved. Simmer for 10 minutes. Remove from heat, and let cool. Drain through a fine-meshed sieve into a bowl, pressing hard on the zests to extract all the flavor, then discard zests.

In a large pitcher, combine sugar syrup, tea and fruit juices. Serve over ice, garnishing each glass with a sprig of mint and an orange slice.

Makes about five 1-cup (250 mL) servings.

SPICY ORANGE TEA

This is a quick and simple way to dress up a pot of tea. It is best made with regular tea—if herbal teas are used, the flavors tend to compete with each other.

2 cups	water	500 mL
10	whole cloves	10
1	cinnamon stick	1
⅓ cup	honey	75 mL
1 cup	orange juice	250 mL
4	tea bags	4
	Angostura bitters	

Combine 1 cup (250 mL) water, cloves and cinnamon, and simmer, covered, for 10 minutes. Add honey, remaining water and orange juice, and bring to a boil. Remove from heat, add tea bags, and let steep, covered, for 5 minutes. Remove tea bags and spices. Add bitters to taste.

Serves 4.

Beverages

VIENNESE ICED COFFEE

This cooling drink is so rich and good that you might serve it for dessert. For the best results, use high-quality ice cream and strong coffee so that the flavor will not be diluted by the ice cubes.

3	cinnamon sticks	3
4 cups	freshly brewed, double-strength, dark-roast coffee	1 L
1 pint	vanilla ice cream	500 mL
	Ground cinnamon for garnish	

Add cinnamon sticks to hot coffee, and let cool. Remove cinnamon, and chill coffee. In a food processor or a blender, combine coffee and ice cream (if using a blender, you will have to do this in two batches). Process until smooth, and serve over ice, spooning the froth onto the top and dusting lightly with cinnamon.

Makes about five 1-cup (250 mL) servings.

ENERGY FRUIT DRINK

This beverage will fool people who hate yeast—especially children, who seem to have an uncanny ability to spot yeast no matter how well it is disguised. For those who like the taste of yeast, there needn't be so many flavor enhancers. Filling, tasty and rich in protein and vitamins, Energy Fruit Drink is a fast and complete breakfast or lunch.

1 cup	yogurt	250 mL
2	eggs	2
2 Tbsp.	maple syrup	25 mL
2	bananas	2
1 cup	apple cider or other unsweetened fruit juice	250 mL
1 tsp.	vanilla extract	5 mL
$\frac{1}{2}$ tsp.	cinnamon	2 mL
$\frac{1}{2}$ cup	strawberries	125 mL
3 Tbsp.	brewer's yeast	45 mL

Combine all ingredients in a blender, and blend well. Chill. Stir just before serving.

Makes about three 1-cup (250 mL) servings.

QUICK-ENERGY YEAST DRINK

Nutritional yeast (sometimes called delicious nutritious yeast) is available at most health-food stores.

1 cup	yogurt	250 mL
$\frac{3}{4}$ cup	fruit juice	175 mL
2 tsp.	nutritional yeast	10 mL
1 tsp.	wheat germ	5 mL
1 tsp.	bran	5 mL
1	banana, sliced	1
2 tsp.	honey	10 mL

Combine all ingredients in a blender, and blend until well mixed. Chill thoroughly.

Makes about two 1-cup (250 mL) servings.

Beverages

ORANGE-PEACH BUTTERMILK SMOOTHIE

If you do not have buttermilk on hand, substitute plain or vanilla-flavored yogurt. Buttermilk does, however, have a milder flavor and a creamier texture. As a variation, make this smoothie with a peeled mango or 2 cups (500 mL) hulled whole strawberries.

3	ripe peaches, peeled, pitted & quartered	3
6	ice cubes	6
¾ cup	buttermilk	175 mL
¼ cup	superfine sugar (see *Note* below)	50 mL
2 Tbsp.	frozen orange juice concentrate	25 mL
	Freshly grated nutmeg for garnish (opt.)	

Note: You can make superfine sugar by whirling granulated sugar in a blender for about 1 minute or until finely ground.

In a blender, combine peaches, ice cubes, buttermilk, sugar and orange juice concentrate. Process until smooth, about 2 minutes. Pour into chilled glasses, and garnish with nutmeg, if desired.

Makes about three 1-cup (250 mL) servings.

INSTANT VEGETABLE DRINK

For anyone watching calories, this beverage can serve as a lunch in itself. It is nutritious, tasty and filling.

1	tomato, chopped	1
½	cucumber, chopped	½
2	celery stalks, chopped	2
¼	green pepper, chopped	¼
2	carrots, chopped	2
2	green onions, chopped	2
1 tsp.	fresh parsley, chopped	5 mL
1 tsp.	fresh dill, chopped	5 mL
	Tomato juice	
	Salt & freshly ground pepper	

Blend all vegetables and herbs until liquefied. Add tomato juice, if needed, to make drink of desired consistency and salt and pepper to taste. Chill.

Makes 2 to 3 cups (500-750 mL).

Contributors

JENNIFER BENNETT
The Harrowsmith Butter Tart; Puff Pastry; The World's Best Butter Tart

INGRID BIRKER
Honey-Mustard Chicken

TERRY JOYCE BLONDER
All-Season Black Bean Salad; Almost Sour Cream; Cracked Wheat Salad; Creamy Baked Fish; Ethiopian Vegetables; Gingery Almond-Carrot Soup; Indonesian Rice Salad; Indonesian Sauce; Lemon-Rosemary Chicken; Spanish Rice Salad; Squash With Wild-Rice Stuffing; Sunburst Salad; Toasted Quinoa Salad; Two-Mustard Dressing

JOANNE CATS-BARIL
Andalusian Gazpacho; Avgolemono Soup; Avocado-Coriander Soup; Basil Jelly; Betty's Mexican Spoonbread; Blueberry Muffins; Broccoli, Cherry Tomato, Parsley Pesto & White Cheddar Pizza; Carrot-Coconut Muffins; Cauliflower, Béchamel & Gouda Pizza; Cheddar & Honey-Mustard Muffins; Chicken Potpie; Chicken Stock 1; Chilled Borscht; Consommé Madrilène; Corn Muffins; Cranberry-Citrus Chutney; Cranberry-Sage Stuffing; Curried Vegetables With Cream Biscuits; Ginger, Lemon & Walnut Muffins; Greek Rice & Beef Stuffing; Green Onion Spoonbread; Green Peppers Stuffed With Bacon & Basil; Green Vichyssoise; Herbed Cottage-Cheese Muffins; Lemon-Lime Jelly With Rosemary; Lemon-Parsley Stuffed Trout; Maple Walnut Muffins; Oatmeal-Apple Muffins; Orange & Chocolate Muffins; Orange & Green-Peppercorn Jelly; Oyster Stuffing; Peach Chutney; Plum Coulis; Plum Tomato, Scallion & Parmesan Pizza; Pollack Meunière; Potpie Pastry; Pumpkin Pecan Muffins; Ratatouille Pizza With Red Peppers, Parmesan & Mozzarella; Red Pepper, Tomato & Basil Stuffing; Ricotta, Zucchini & Tomato Pizza; Sautéed Shrimp With Rosemary, Thyme & Mushrooms; Sautéed Sole With Romaine Lettuce, Peas & Grapefruit Juice; Sea Scallop, Sweet Corn & Snap Pea Sauté; Semolina Pizza Crust; Smoked Ham, Asparagus Tips & White Cheddar Pizza; Sour Cherry Compote; Spiced Plum Jelly; Sunprint Bran Muffins; Tourtière; Tuna Sauté With Tomato Sauce; White Pizza Crust; Whole Wheat Pizza Crust; Wild Mushroom Tatin; Zucchini Spoonbread

ANDREA CHESMAN
Apple Dumplings; Apple Pandowdy; Blueberry Grunt; Buttermilk Pound Cake; Chicken Barley Soup; Chicken Soup With Matzo Balls; Chicken Tortilla Soup With Lime; Chocolate Hazelnut Pound Cake; Citrus Iced Tea; Classic Pound Cake; Freezer Bread & Butter Pickles; Freezer Dills; Freezer Oriental Lime Pickles; Gardener's Salsa; Half-Sour Dill Pickles; Homemade Lemonade; Hot & Sour Soup; Lemon Poppy-Seed Pound Cake; 'Light' Pound Cake; Low-Sugar Strawberry Jam With Apples; Microwave Low-Sugar Strawberry Jam; Old-Fashioned Low-Sugar Strawberry Jam; Orange-Peach Buttermilk Smoothie; Oriental Chicken Soup With Noodles; Pear Crisp; Pear Upside-Down Cake; Pomona's Universal Pectin Freezer Jam; Quick Crock Pickles; Raspberry-Lime Rickey; Roasted Garlic Soup With Herbed Croutons; Rory's Strawberry Nectar; Sunshine Strawberry Jam; Sure-Jell Light Freezer Jam; Tomato Chicken Soup Provençal; Traditional Giblet Gravy for Turkey; Traditional Herbed Bread Stuffing for Turkey; Turkey & Greens With Cranberry Vinaigrette; Turkey Muffalettas; Turkey Stock; Viennese Iced Coffee; Wild-Rice Dressing

HELEN CHESNUT
Chilled Borscht With Tomato Juice; Creamed Beets; Hot Potato & Beet Salad; Pickled Beets; Sautéed Beet Greens; Traditional Borscht

WINSTON COLLINS
Chicken With Cucumber & Cashews; Cream of Mustard Soup; Dijon Mustard; Eggplant With Black Beans; Fish With Yams & Ginger; Hot & Spicy Bean Curd; Lemon Bread Pudding; Mustard Dressing; Mustard Pickle; Mustard Sauce; Noodles With Peanut Sauce; Orange Crumb-Coated French Toast; Panzanella; Pappa al Pomodoro; Pasta con Mollica di Pane; Pommery Mustard; Pork With Chilies Soup; Pork With Sweet Peppers; Shrimp With Black Mustard Seeds & Cumin; Sole Florentine; Stir-Fried Beef; Three-Bread Stuffing for Turkey

PAMELA CROSS
Baking-Powder Biscuits; Barbari Bread; Barbecue Marinade; Barbecued Spareribs; Barbecued Stuffed Salmon; Basil Pesto; Beef Stock; Candied Orange Peel; Chapati; Chicken Stock 2; Chicken Wings With Barbecue Sauce; Chocolate Truffles; Corn Tortillas; Cream of Mushroom Soup; Curry Powder; Deviled Tofu Sandwich Filling; Dundee Marmalade; Energy Fruit Drink; Fish Curry; Fladbrød; Fruited Yogurt; Garam Masala; Garlic Mayonnaise; Greek Salad; Green Curry Paste; Grilled Vegetables With Pesto; Hasha; Herbed Yogurt Dip; Instant Vegetable Drink; Lamb Kabobs; Lamb-Spinach Curry; Laufabraud; Lefse; Madras-Style Curry Paste; Mayonnaise; Orange-Almond Tart; Orange-Currant Scones; Orange Doughnuts; Orange Napa Salad; Orange Refrigerator Cookies; Orange-Walnut Chicken Salad; Pasta Salad With Olives & Blue Cheese; Pita Bread; Popcorn Plus; Pretzels; Protein Muffins; Puri; Quick-Energy Yeast Drink; Rosemary Potatoes; Seasoned Crackers; Scrumptious Granola Bars; Spicy Orange Tea; Spinach & Artichoke-Heart Salad; Stuffed Potatoes; Sunshine Muffins; Vegetable Stock; Wheat Tortillas

ADELE DUECK
Roast Mustard Lamb

CAROL FERGUSON
Grill-Roasted Loin of Pork; Grilled Seafood Salad; Summer Garden Grill

CAROL FLINDERS
Apricot Sauce; Cashew Cardamom Balls; Cherokee Squash Drop Biscuits; Christmas Fruitcake; Holiday Squash; Honey Pumpkin Chews; Meredith's Harvest Pie; My Heart's Brown Stollen; Orange-Cranberry Bread; Persimmon Pudding; Plum Pudding; Sandy's Gingered Squash

SARAH FRITSCHNER
Apple-Carrot-Raisin Muffins; Hot-Fudge Pudding Cake; Oat Bran Bread; Oat Bran Brownies; Oat Bran Raisin Cookies

DAVID HARROP
Rhubarb Chutney; Rhubarb & Fig Jam

DIANE KOCHILAS
Galaktoboureko; Homemade Phyllo Dough; Pistachio & Sesame Phyllo Rolls; Savory Lamb Pie; Spanakopitta; Tyropittakia

LESLIE LAND
Berry Crème Brûlée; Buckwheat Blini; Buckwheat Bread; Buckwheat Crêpes; Buckwheat, Sesame & Corn Muffins; Egg Bread; Kasha With Sour Cream, Mushrooms, Onions & Herbs; Kulbiaka; Meringue Kisses; Tea-Leaf Eggs; Tortilla Española

LAURA LANGSTON
Blackberry-Apple Grunt; Chicken Stew With Corn Dumplings; Gado Gado; Groundnut Stew; Mushroom Filling for Perogies; Peanut Butter; Peanut Butter Cookies; Perogies With Potato Cheese Filling; Spaetzle; Spicy Asian Chicken; Tiger Butter; Vietnamese Noodle Salad; Won Ton Soup; Won Tons

ANN LOVEJOY
Curried Chicken Salad; Grilled Chicken & Red-Pepper Sandwiches; Herbed Yogurt Sauce; Iced Cherries; Lemon-Lime Spritzers

INGRID MAGNUSON
Salmon Seviche

RUX MARTIN
Beef Stew With Leeks & Mushrooms; Cheese-Herb Dumplings; Chicken Curry With Yogurt; Chicken Fricassee With Dumplings; Corncakes With Maple-Yogurt Topping; Lemon-Yogurt

Contributors

Cheesecake; Light-Wheat Country Sourdough Bread; Manhattan-Style Fish Stock; Marinated Yogurt Cheese; North American Bouillabaisse; Sourdough Cinnamon-Apple Swirls; Sourdough Oatmeal Bread; Traditional Sourdough Starter; Whole Wheat Sourdough Biscuits; Yogurt-Dill Salad Dressing

ANNE MENDELSON
'Fighting-Mad' Sauce for Penne; Fresh Tomato Soup; Quick-Cooking Tomato Sauce; Sugo Finto; Uncooked Tomato Sauce

MARTHA WATSON MURPHY
Blueberry-Orange Sorbet; Nut Crisps; Raspberry Sherbet; Strawberry & Watermelon Sorbet; Vanilla-Peach Sherbet

SUSAN G. PURDY
Anna Olson's Spritz Cookies; Danish Oat Cookies; Decorative Icing; Gingerbread Place Cards; Hazelnut Shortbread; Lemon Crisps; Old-Fashioned Sugar Cookies; Pfeffernüsse

IRIS RAVEN
Fruit Compote; Fruit-Filled Crêpes; Multigrain Muffins; Smoked Salmon & Goat Cheese Strata

From *Recipes in a Nut Shell*, 1988. Courtesy the Eastern Chapter of the Ontario Nut Growers, Ottawa, Canada
Warm Watercress & Pine Nut Salad

MEREDITH PAUL RUBENS
Buttermilk Apple-Spice Bread; Cheddar Herb Bread; Honey Wheat-Germ Bread

REGINA SCHRAMBLING
Bulgur-Chickpea Pilaf; Bulgur With Celery & Sage; Couscous Niçoise; Fast & Hot Couscous; Garlicky Couscous With Roasted Peppers; Leek, Shiitake & Kasha Pilaf; Orzo Primavera; Quinoa With Sun-Dried Tomatoes

MARIE SIMMONS
Chowder Stock; Codfish Chowder; Curried Mussel Chowder; Italian-Style Seafood Chowder; Mrs. Hussey's Chowder; New England Potato & Clam Chowder; Salmon Corn Chowder; Scallop Chowder

BONNIE STERN
Black Bean & Rice Salad; Grilled Vegetable Salad With Chèvre Dip & Garlic Toast; Provençal Tabouli Salad; Shrimp Quesadilla Salad; Spaghetti Salad With Tuna; Tuscany Chicken & Bread Salad

CYNTHIA R. TOPLISS
Spiced Cauliflower & Potatoes

Camden House Publishing has attempted to contact each of the authors of the recipes that were selected to appear in *The Best of Pantry*; however, due to the length of time that has passed since some of the original recipes were published, we have, unfortunately, lost contact with some of our contributors. We encourage any food writers we were unable to locate to write to The Editor, Harrowsmith Country Life, 25 Sheppard Avenue West, Suite 100, North York, Ontario M2N 6S7 to receive their complimentary copies of *The Best of Pantry*.

Index

Index

Index

Index

Index

Photo Credits

COLOR PHOTOGRAPHS

Page 33: Photograph by Becky Luigart-Stayner. Styling by Susan Herr.

Page 34: Photograph by Ernie Sparks. Concept and styling by Linda Menyes and Laurel Aziz.

Page 67: Photograph by Ernie Sparks. Concept and styling by Linda Menyes and Laurel Aziz.

Page 68: Photograph by Maria Robledo. Styling by Betty Alfenito (props) and Ann Disrude (food).

Page 101: Photograph by Ernie Sparks. Concept and styling by Linda Menyes and Clare Still.

Page 102: Photograph by Ernie Sparks. Concept and styling by Linda Menyes and Mariella Morrin.

Page 119: Photograph by Ernie Sparks. Concept and styling by Linda Menyes and Laurel Aziz.

Page 120: Photograph by Ernie Sparks. Concept and styling by Linda Menyes and Mariella Morrin.

Page 137: Photograph by Ernie Sparks.

Page 138: Photograph by Ernie Sparks. Concept and styling by Janice McLean and Mariella Morrin.

Page 155: Photograph by Ernie Sparks. Concept and styling by Linda Menyes and Laurel Aziz.

Page 156: Photograph by Ernie Sparks. Concept and styling by Linda Menyes and Laurel Aziz.

Page 173: Photograph by Ernie Sparks. Concept and styling by Linda Menyes and Laurel Aziz.

Page 174: Photograph by Ernie Sparks. Concept and styling by Linda Menyes and Laurel Aziz.

Page 207: Photograph by Ernie Sparks. Concept and styling by Linda Menyes and Mariella Morrin.

Page 208: Photograph by Ernie Sparks. Concept and styling by Linda Menyes.

BACKGROUND PHOTOGRAPHS

All background photographs by Ernie Sparks, with the exception of the photograph on page 44, by Becky Luigart-Stayner.